IMAGES
of America

COLQUITT COUNTY

I0792649

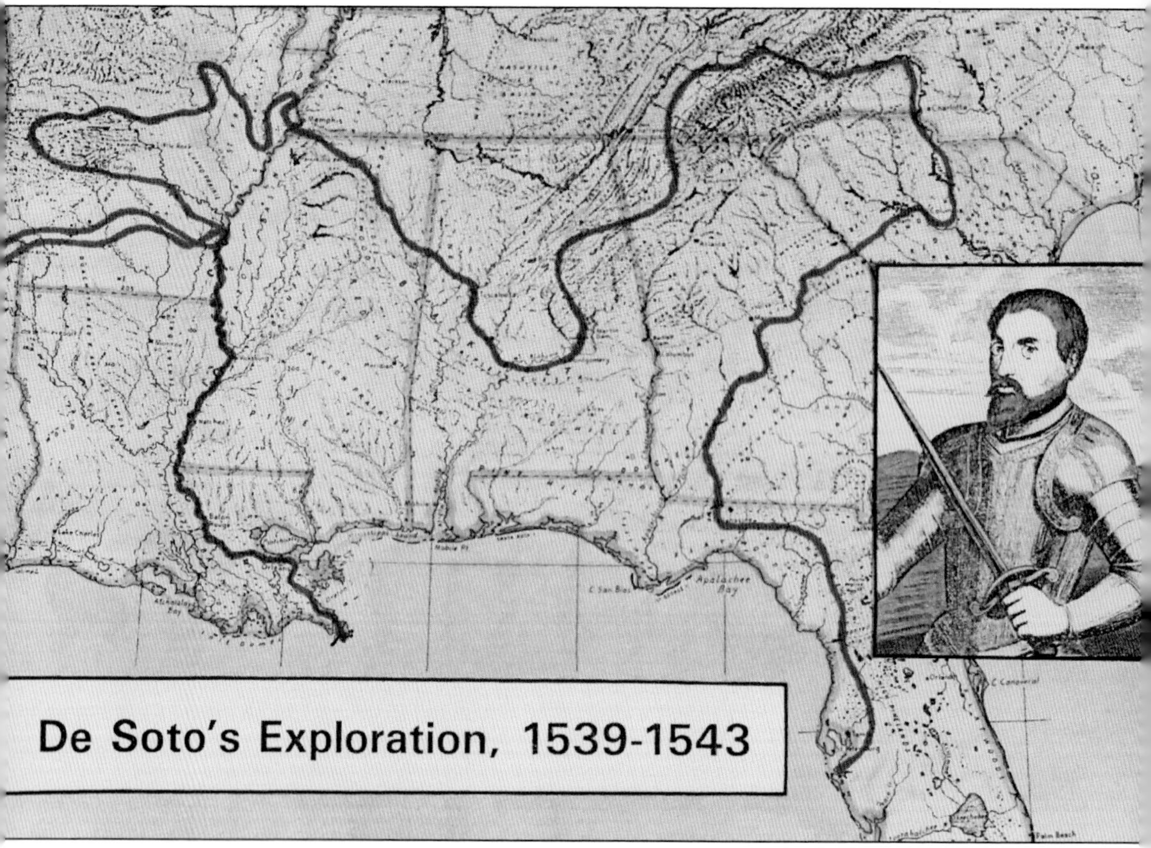

This early map shows Fernando de Soto's exploration of the southeastern United States from 1539 through 1543. Records from the expedition indicate that the party of explorers spent the night of March 21, 1540, on the banks of the Oclockney River (note the old spelling of the name) near a spot where a bridge currently spans the river on the western edge of Moultrie's city limits. (Archway Partnership Project of the University of Georgia.)

On the Cover: In the 1940s, the library staff realized that children and adults in the rural areas wanted library services. Because money was in short supply and building libraries in communities around the county was too costly, a bookmobile service was started. These small vans would carry the library to citizens in the county so that they could enjoy the same services as the city residents. In this photograph, taken December 10, 1948, bookmobile driver Catherine M. Bryant is shown with a group of children at Okapilco School. The children standing in line are, from left to right, Joe Ellis, Othelle Hall, Wayman Walker, Charlie Prince, Betty Fay Jones, Peggy Alderman, Elizabeth Rossman, Iris Bell, and Marie Jones. (Moultrie-Colquitt County Library.)

IMAGES
of America

COLQUITT COUNTY

Melody S. Jenkins

ARCADIA
PUBLISHING

ISBN 978-0-7385-6756-3

Published by Arcadia Publishing
Charleston SC, Chicago IL, Portsmouth NH, San Francisco CA

Printed in the United States of America

Library of Congress Control Number: 2008943884

For all general information contact Arcadia Publishing at:
Telephone 843-853-2070
Fax 843-853-0044
E-mail sales@arcadiapublishing.com
For customer service and orders:
Toll-Free 1-888-313-2665

Visit us on the Internet at www.arcadiapublishing.com

To Vera Jones Stinson, my mother, who taught me to love the past and appreciate my ancestors, and to Stephen Jack Jenkins, my late husband, who introduced me to this wonderful community and taught me to love its rich history.

Contents

Acknowledgments

This book is being released to mark the sesquicentennial of Moultrie, Georgia, and is a result of the Archway Partnership Project—a collaborative effort between Moultrie, Colquitt County, and the University of Georgia. When acknowledging those who contribute to any project, one always has the fear that someone will be overlooked. Such is the case with this project. Therefore, I will acknowledge groups and committees, rather than individuals, with the exception of one outstanding individual.

This book is by no means a definitive history of Colquitt County. I have attempted to add to other written histories of the county by providing photographs that will give the reader insight into the lives of the early residents of the area instead of merely historical facts. Without the encouragement and resources of Edwin L. Jackson, senior public service associate for the Carl Vinson Institute of Government of the University System of Georgia, this book would have never been written. Ed, as he is known to everyone, knows more about Georgia's history than anyone I have ever met. More importantly, his love of that history is contagious. You cannot engage in a conversation with Ed without wanting to know more about this great state. His knowledge runs much deeper than just facts about the state as a whole. He has delved into the past of many of the communities around the state and relates his knowledge in a most fascinating way. The Tourism Committee of the Moultrie–Colquitt County Chamber of Commerce endorsed the idea of publishing this book and provided much support to me. The staff of the Moultrie–Colquitt County Library provided encouragement and immeasurable knowledge in the completion of this book. Clint Chafin, a font of knowledge about the sports program in this county, fired my enthusiasm and sparked my curiosity when I was about to burn out. Geneva Leverett came to my rescue with information about the Vereen family. Jimmy Jeter and his wonderful staff aided with pictures and referrals to others in the community who might have information.

Key to Courtesy Line Abbreviations:

APP Archway Partnership Project of the University of Georgia
CTC Clint T. Chafin
FPCM First Presbyterian Church of Moultrie, Georgia
JMJ James M. Jeter
MCCH Museum of Colquitt County History
MCCL Moultrie-Colquitt County Library
MO *Moultrie Observer*
MSP Main Street Program of the City of Moultrie
OCC O. C. Causey
TPH Thomas P. Holman
WG Wayne Grandy

INTRODUCTION

On December 13, 1859, the handful of families living in the vicinity of the Ocklockney post office got an early Christmas present. Georgia governor Joseph E. Brown signed legislation incorporating the small village that served as the seat of government for Colquitt County, which itself had been created just three years earlier. The justices of the new county's inferior court had selected a central location in the county where a small wooden courthouse was built in 1857 or 1858. Named in honor of Revolutionary War hero William Moultrie, the new town would consist of the 50 acres surrounding the courthouse.

In the 1860 census, Colquitt County was the least-populated county in Georgia. This was largely due to the fact that the county was covered with extensive forests of virgin longleaf pine trees. The pines stood as a barrier to plantation agriculture, meaning that residents survived by subsistence farming and raising cattle and sheep. As a result, Colquitt County had few slaves and even fewer free blacks.

With the coming of the Civil War, five units were raised in Colquitt County to serve in the Confederate cause, but the county was so far removed from Sherman's March to the Sea that it saw no military action. In the decades after the war, little changed in the county, and its county seat remained little more than a village. For example, in 1881, the entire town of Moultrie consisted of a courthouse and jail, one small hotel, two stores, two stockades, one school, and 10 houses. As late as 1890, Moultrie's entire population consisted of 65 residents, and no railroad served the county.

Colquitt County's development was hindered by the fact that it lay in the center of Georgia's Pine Barrens (so called because the land was essentially barren of anything but pine trees). Those pine forests, however, would prove to be the magic that dramatically changed Colquitt County in just a few years.

The county was covered with virgin longleaf yellow pine forests that had never been cut. The trees were huge—as wide as 42 inches in diameter and over 60 feet in height. The abundance of tall trees would form the basis of two new industries. Timber and naval stores businessmen and works began migrating from the Carolinas to South Georgia in the late 1880s. Timber especially needed rail trams to transport cut logs to sawmills. As a result, Moultrie finally achieved rail access in 1893—an achievement that dramatically changed the town.

Railroads proved to be more than just transportation for naval stores and lumber from the forests to the market. They provided transportation for cotton and other goods as well as settlers and visitors. By 1910, the timber was virtually cut over, and people were looking for other ways to make a living. Fortunately a group of farsighted businessmen led by William Coachman Vereen had seen the need to diversify the economy of the county during the late 1800s. A committee of these businessmen began to study other communities and worked out a five-year plan for Colquitt County, which included plans to expand agriculture, manufacturing, and business for the betterment of the county. Crops were diversified, and livestock production increased.

Following World War I, Moultrie continued to grow because of the careful planning of these businessmen. Moultrie's population grew to more than 10,000 residents, banking resources exceeded $4.5 million, and the county received national recognition for its progressive agricultural program.

Tobacco was introduced as a major crop, and warehouses opened to sell the tobacco crop for the farmers. Improvements to the municipal infrastructure included a complete water system, electric lights, a storm and sanitary sewage system, a motorized fire department, and 2 miles of paved streets. By 1935, the Colquitt County Commissioners began working on rural electrification, and the first line was energized in 1937. Vereen Hospital was built in 1939 with funds provided as a gift by W. C. Vereen and matched with donations from the community.

World War II brought the opening of Spence Field as a training base for single-engine advanced pilot training. The opening of this army air base added greatly to the population of the county. Over 6,000 pilots were trained at the facility before it was closed in 1944. It would prove to be an asset for Moultrie and Colquitt County for many years to come. In 1951, Hawthorne School of Aeronautics received a contract to train U.S. Air Force pilots at the Spence Field base and operated there for 10 years. In 1968, Belford D. Maule moved his aircraft manufacturing company to the site, where it remains in operation today. Many of the instructors who came to Moultrie because of Spence Air Base and Hawthorne remained in the community to become active citizens and community leaders. Many of the trainees who attended the schools would return in later years to Colquitt County.

By the 1950s, Colquitt County had 51 manufacturing businesses with an annual payroll of more than $6 million. A $125,000 bond was passed by voters to build a new football stadium. Sunset Airport opened as a commercial airport just south of Moultrie. A convalescent wing was added to Vereen Memorial Hospital at a cost of $200,000. The Colquitt County Courthouse underwent major renovations to add a third floor, expanding county governmental offices.

The 1960s brought the disappointing news that the Spence Air Base would be closed. The loss of its $3-million annual payroll would have been economically devastating to most communities of its size, but Moultrie relied on its history of long-range planning and hard work to overcome this setback. Moultrie gained "Model Town" status and was included in a $100,000 program that promoted industrial research. Many new businesses were solicited as part of this program, and in 1964, a mobile home manufacturing plant was opened. A new post office and a National Guard armory were constructed. Swift and Company announced a $1-million expansion for the Moultrie plant. The voters passed a local bond issue to raise $125,000 in matching funds for a federal grant to build a new public library. The Moultrie–Colquitt County Library was opened in 1965, and services were greatly expanded. The crop that had been introduced into the county in the 1920s began to pay high dividends. Colquitt County farmers were now listed as the number-one producers of tobacco in the state of Georgia. The production of cotton rebounded, and Colquitt County was ranked second in the state in its production. All of these advances lead to an annual agricultural income in 1967 of close to $25 million.

Advances have continued in Colquitt to the present day. The ingenious pioneer spirit of its early settlers is evident today in Colquitt County's leaders and citizens, who are never afraid of hard work and are forward-thinking enough to overcome circumstances that would defeat other communities. This pictorial history is a testament to the dedication of these early citizens who found a home in the Pine Barrens and proved the members of the Georgia Assembly wrong in their assessment of Colquitt County as "an area that is practically useless."

One

Early Scenes of Moultrie

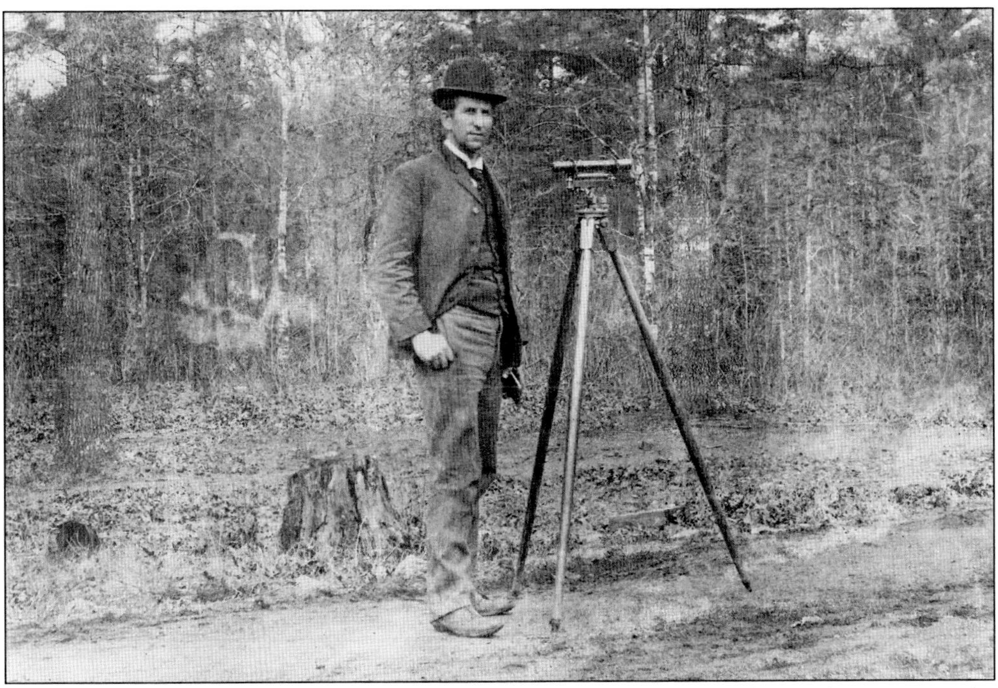

When Colquitt County was formed in 1856 from portions of Thomas and Lowndes Counties, the area was known as the Pine Barrens. The Thigpen Trail, running from Apalachicola, Florida, to the Carolinas, was the only road in the county, and the population listed in the first census after incorporation was 1,360. The first settlers were probably lured by the price of land; $5 per acre, with stories indicating that some land sold for 50¢ per acre. Surveyors, such as the one pictured here in the late 1800s, were in great demand. (APP.)

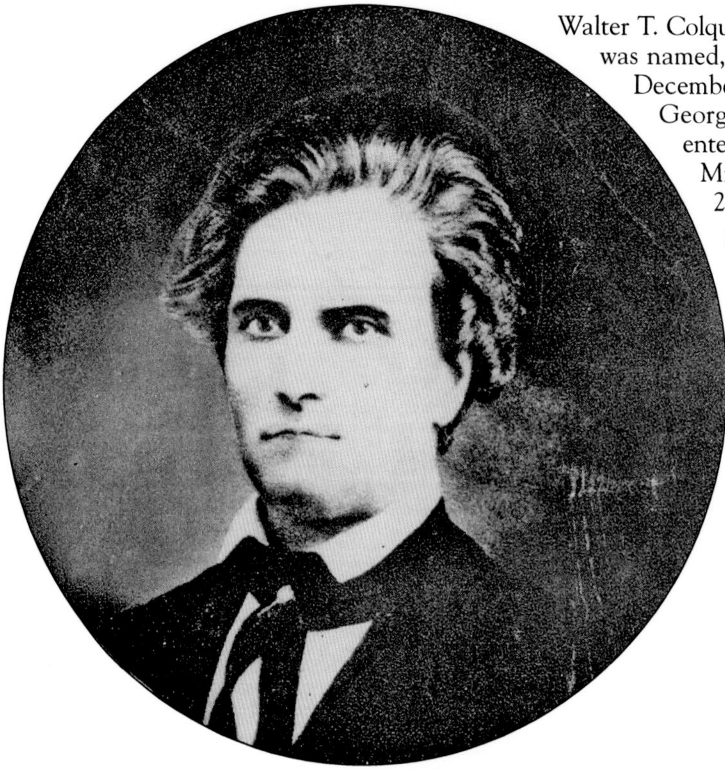

Walter T. Colquitt, for whom the county was named, was born in Virginia on December 27, 1799. He moved to Georgia with his parents and entered the legal profession in Milledgeville. At the age of 21, he was made a brigadier general of the state militia. He later served as a judge in the Chattahoochee Circuit, a state senator, and as both a federal representative and senator. He died in Macon, Georgia, on May 7, 1855. (MO.)

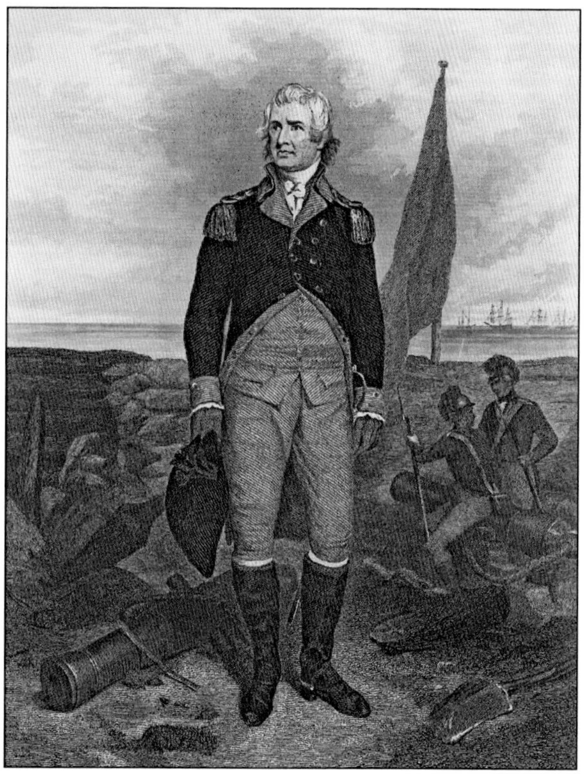

William Moultrie, for whom the city was named, was born in Charleston, South Carolina, on November 23, 1730. He served as a militia captain during the Cherokee expedition of 1761. After successfully defending Fort Sullivan against British attack during the Revolutionary War, Moultrie was commissioned a brigadier general in the Continental Army. Following the war, Moultrie served in the South Carolina House of Representatives, as lieutenant governor, and as governor. He died on September 27, 1805. (APP.)

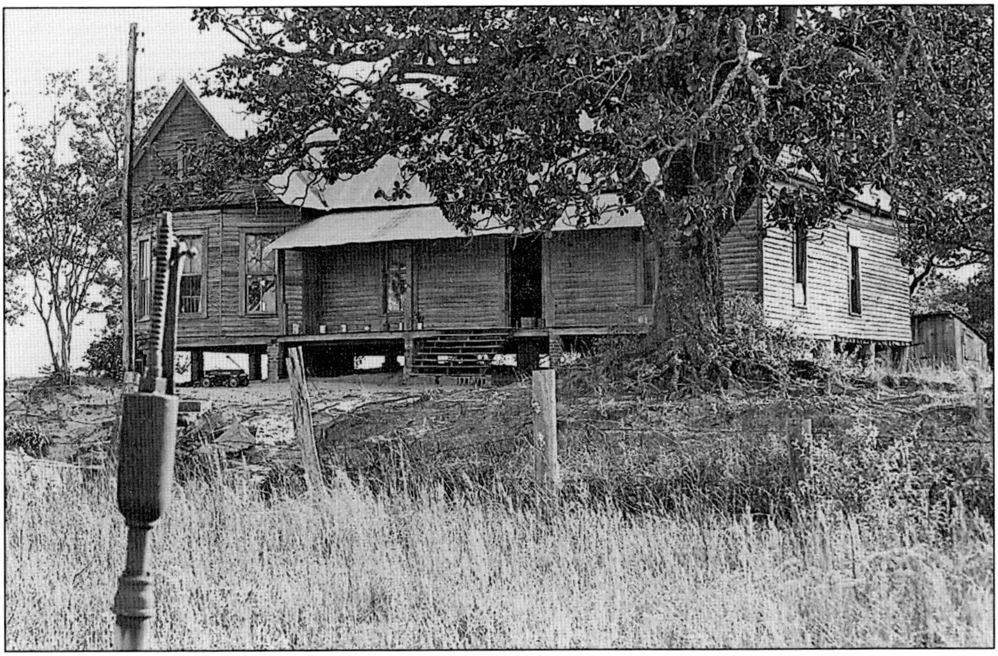

During the first two years of the county's existence, the Mims House, pictured here, served as a temporary courthouse. The house is located 4 miles northwest of Moultrie on the Old Albany Road. (MO.)

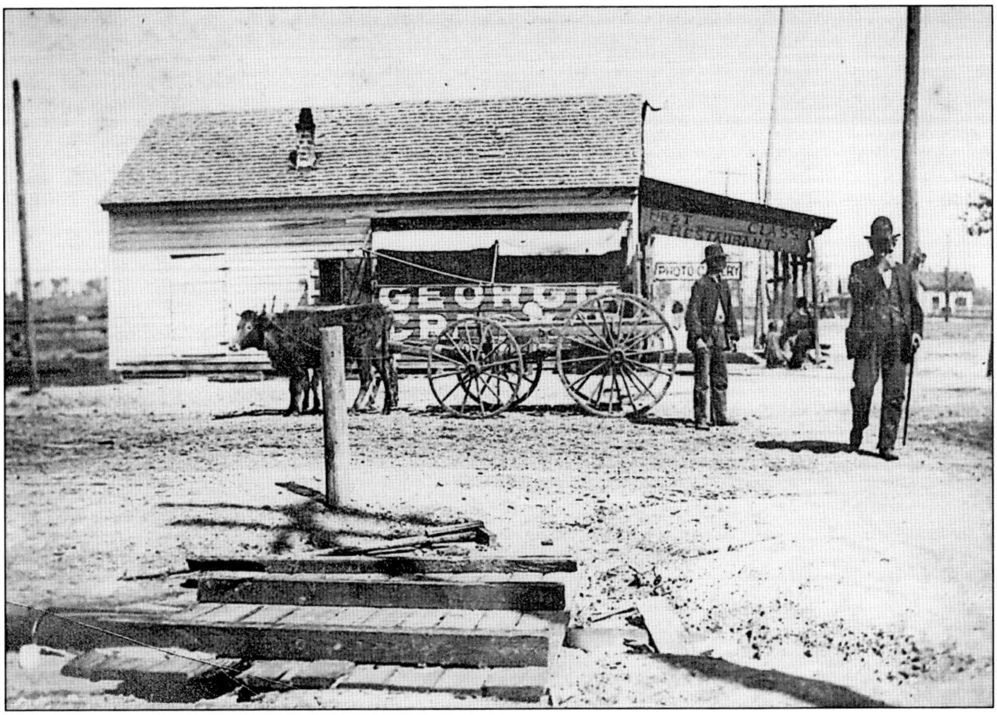

This scene from the early 1900s shows the area of Moultrie located one block north of the courthouse square where the Carnegie Library would be built in 1906–1907. The oxen and cart show the mode of transporting heavy supplies. (MO.)

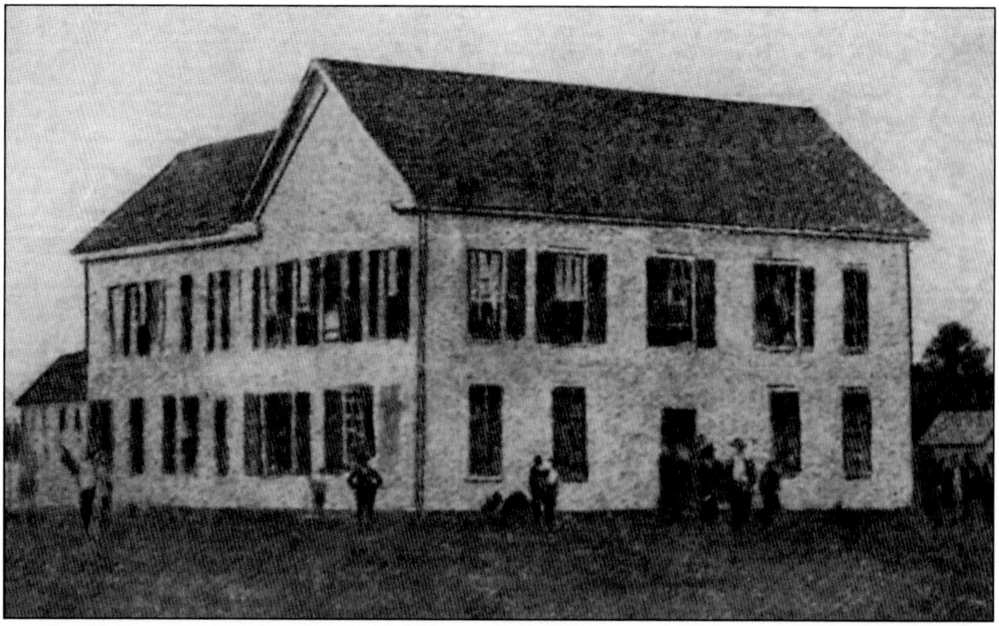

Two buildings preceded the early courthouse pictured above. One was destroyed by fire in 1881, and another one-story building was used temporarily. This structure, pictured in the late 1800s, was used from 1881 until 1902. It was originally rectangular, but an "L" was added to provide more space. A fence surrounded the square to prevent free-roaming livestock from grazing on the lawn. In 1900, the Colquitt County Commissioners called for a bond referendum to pay for the construction of a new brick courthouse. Construction began in April 1901. Andrew J. Bryan was the architect, and J. H. Harris and G. W. Milligan were the builders. The total cost of the construction was $29,500. County officials moved into their new offices, shown below, on September 1, 1902. (Above, MO; below, APP.)

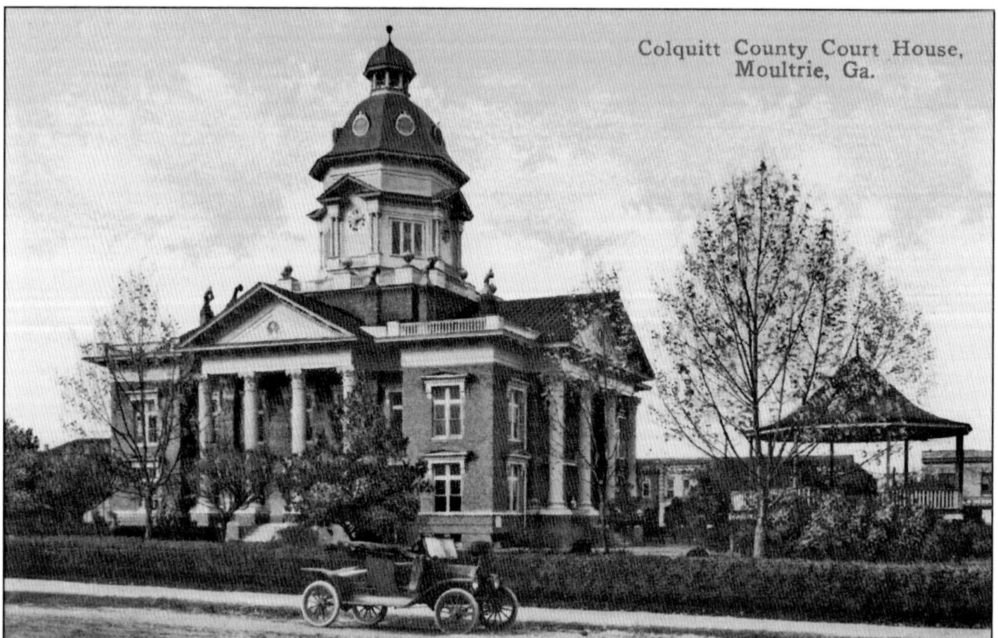

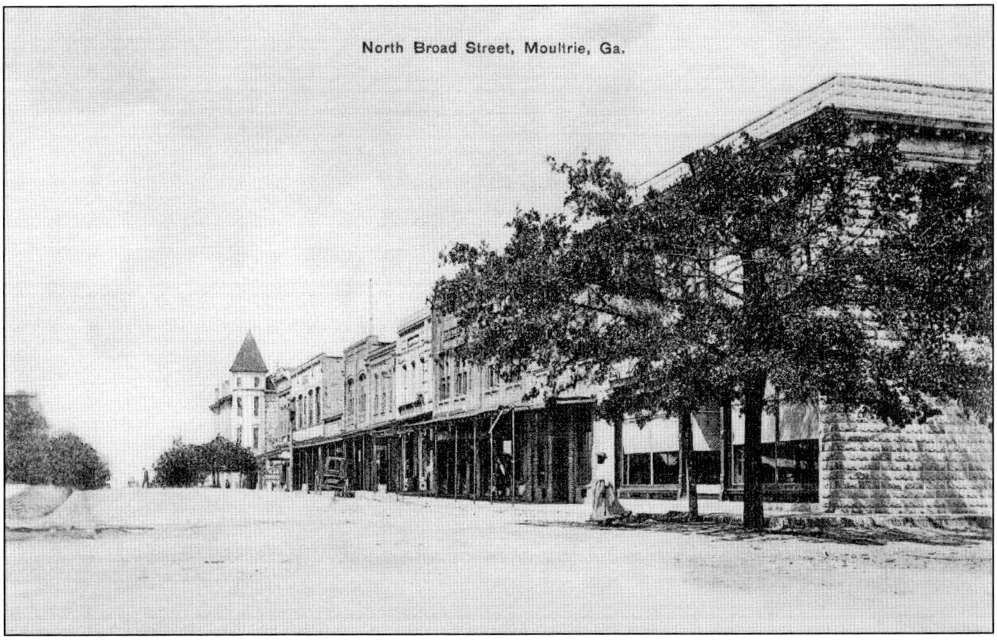

This scene of North Broad Street in the early 1900s shows the storefronts that faced the north side of the courthouse. The original Hotel Colquitt can be seen at the end of the block. This street is currently named Central Avenue, and many of these buildings still stand. The corner building in the foreground presently houses Abraham Baldwin Agricultural College's satellite campus. (APP.)

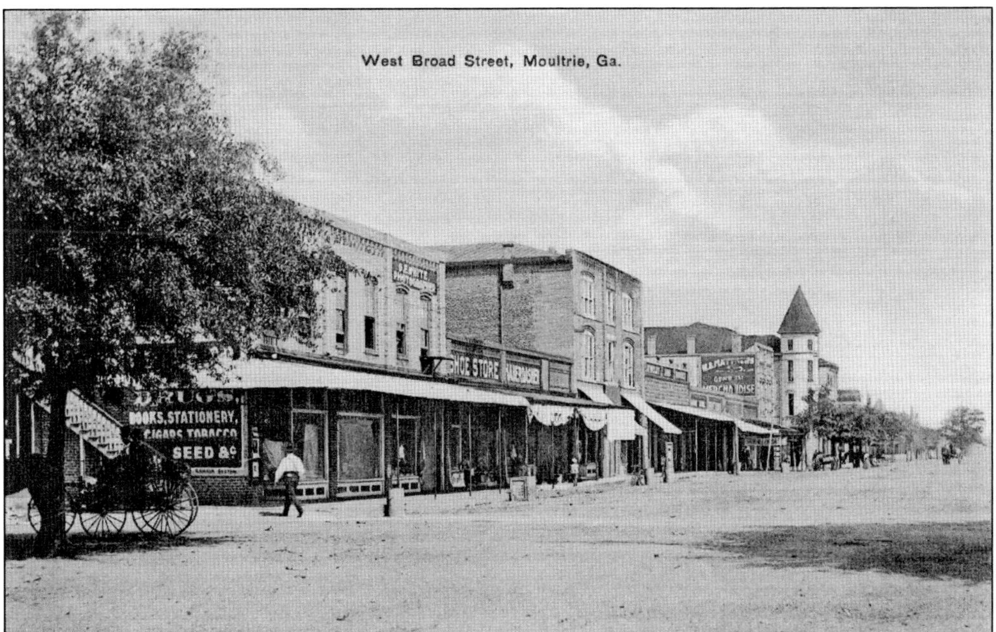

This scene of West Broad Street in the early 1900s shows the storefronts on the west side of the courthouse square. The Hotel Colquitt can be seen in the background. (APP.)

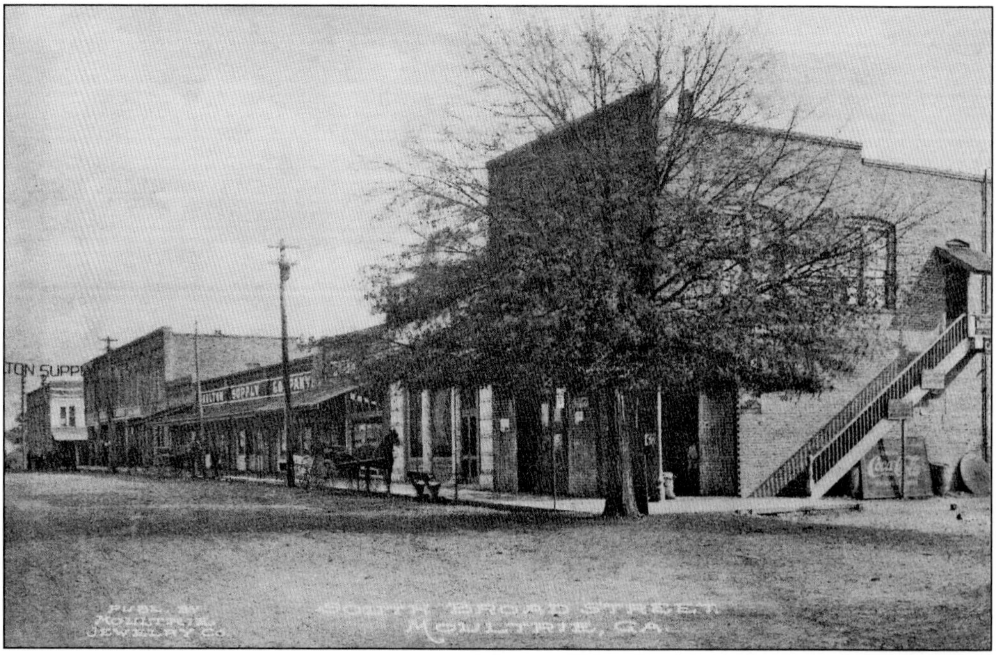

This scene of South Broad Street in the early 1900s shows the storefronts facing the courthouse on the south side of the square. The street is presently named First Avenue. Carlton Supply Company can be seen in the middle of the block. The corner building in the foreground was Guy's Drug Store. It still stands today and houses the Army-Navy Surplus Store. (APP.)

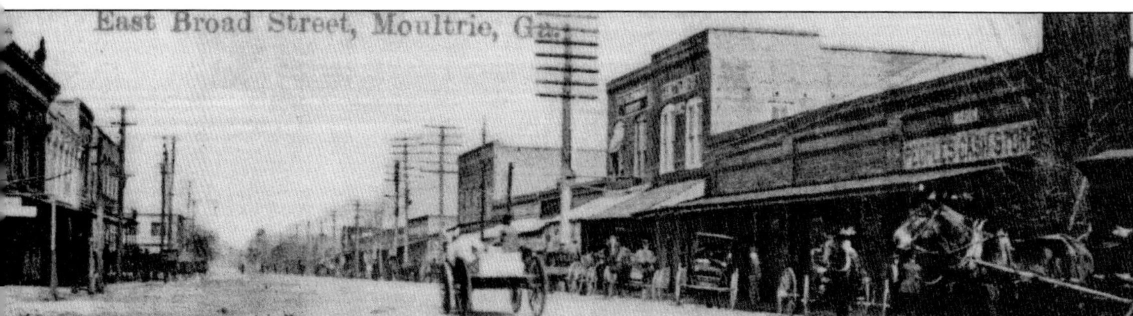

This scene of East Broad Street in the early 1900s shows the storefronts located one block south of the courthouse square. Horses and buggies were the common mode of transportation for the citizens, as seen here. The wagon loaded with supplies in the center of the street would have been pulled by a horse or, more probably, a mule. (MO.)

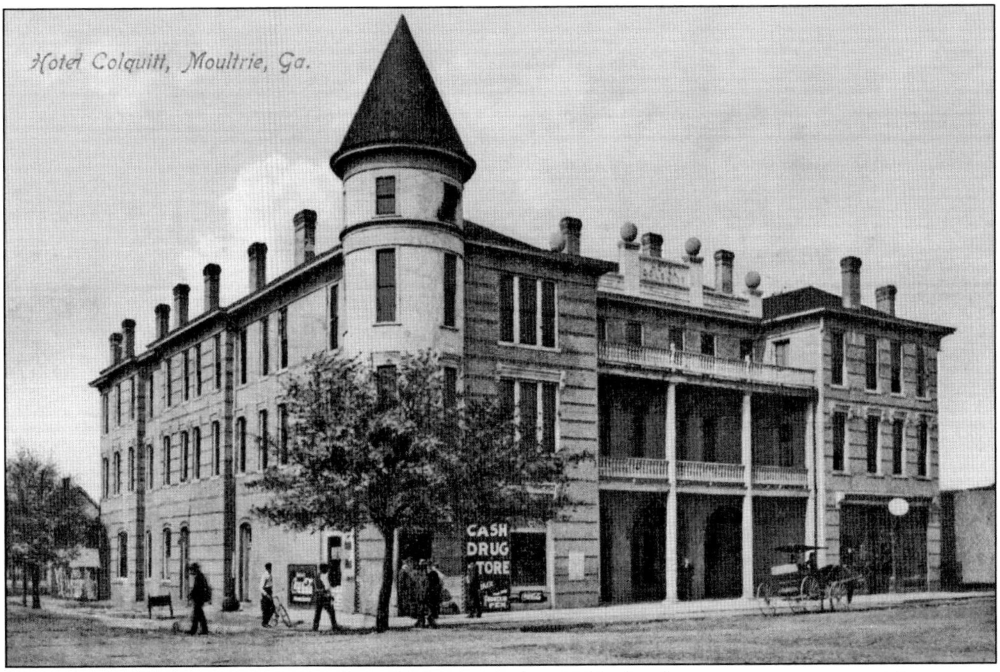

The Hotel Colquitt was completed in 1902. Pictured in 1910, the three-story structure with a corner tower was Moultrie's first and largest brick hotel. The first floor housed a drugstore, a restaurant, a barbershop, and a sample room for traveling salesmen to display their wares. A 75-car garage was located behind the hotel. (APP.)

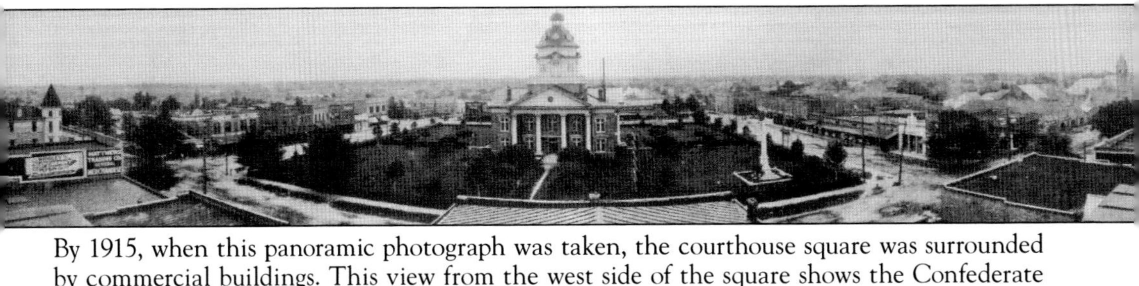

By 1915, when this panoramic photograph was taken, the courthouse square was surrounded by commercial buildings. This view from the west side of the square shows the Confederate Monument, which was erected in 1909 by the Moultrie United Daughters of the Confederacy, on the southwest corner. (JMJ.)

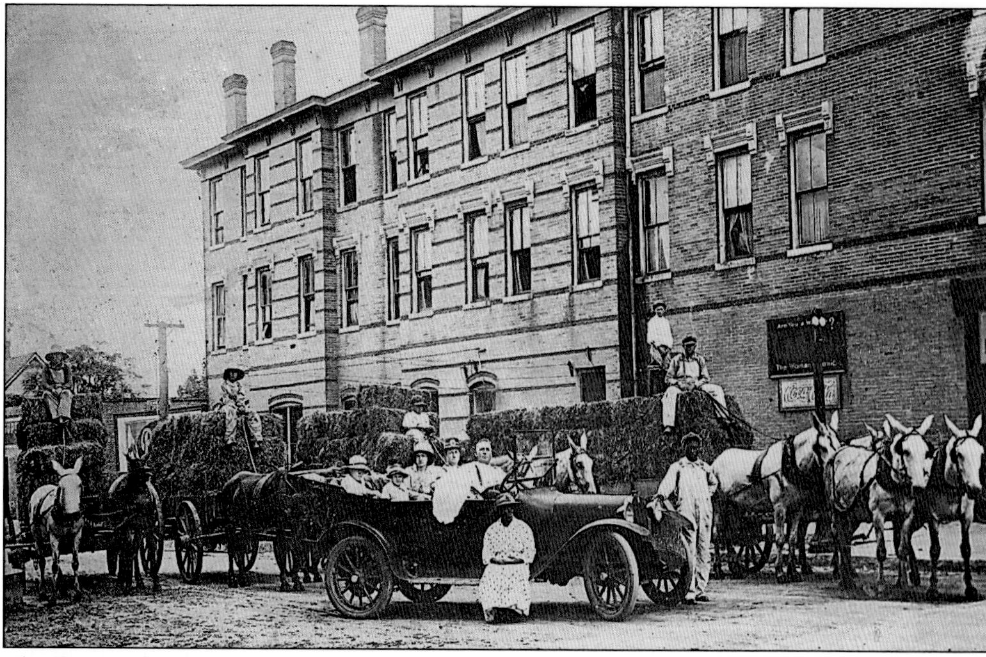

The Demott family sits in a parked car driven by George Demott on the south side of the Hotel Colquitt in 1916. Hay wagons pulled by teams of mules can be seen in the background. George Demott's son, Frank, is standing atop the hay wagon at right. (MO.)

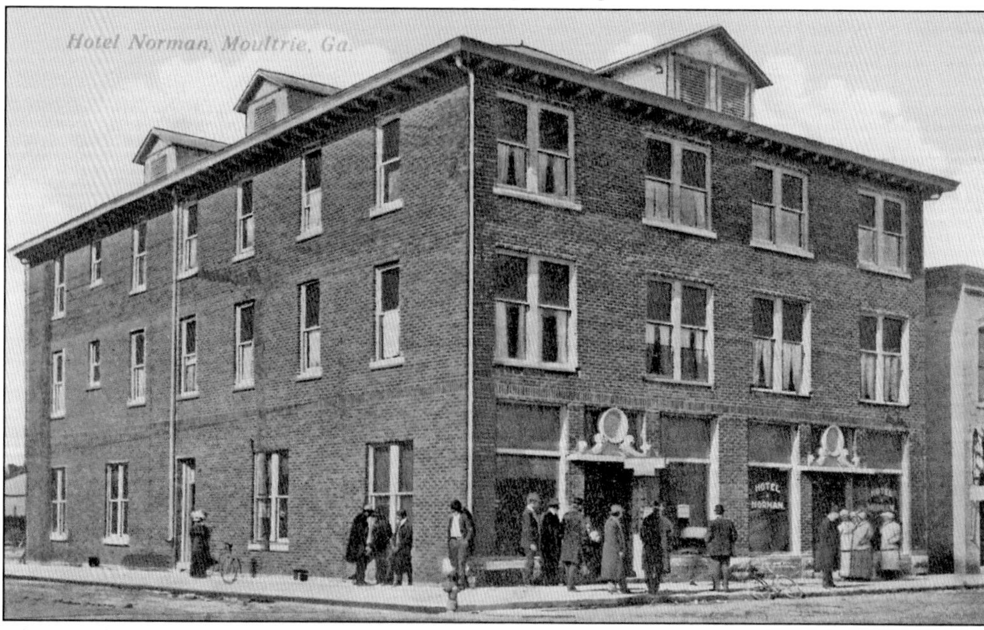

The Hotel Norman, a three-story brick building at the corner of Second Avenue and First Street SE, was once Moultrie's second largest hotel. It was built in 1909 by Jeremiah B. Norman after the Southern Hotel, a wooden structure on the site, burned. The Hotel Norman featured steam heat, electric lights, a barbershop, and a sample room for traveling salesmen. From 1915 until 1919, a portion of the first floor served as the post office. The hotel's popularity was heightened by the fact that it was located only a few blocks from the train depot. (APP.)

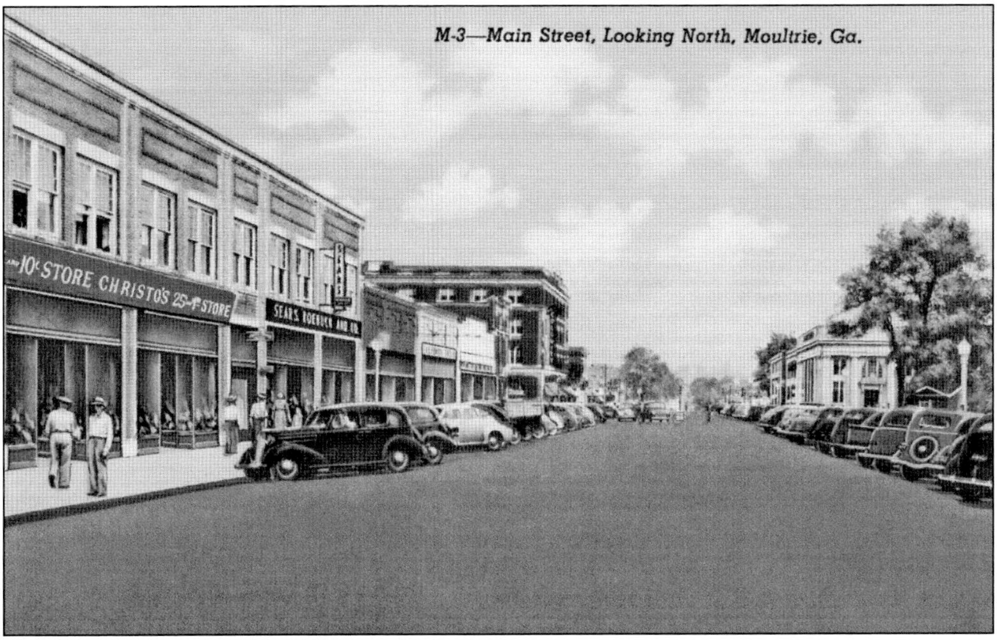

This postcard, printed in the 1930s, shows the portion of Main Street on the west side of the courthouse square. The recently built Hotel Colquitt can be seen in the background. City streets had been paved, and two-way traffic with angled parking was a citywide feature. (APP.)

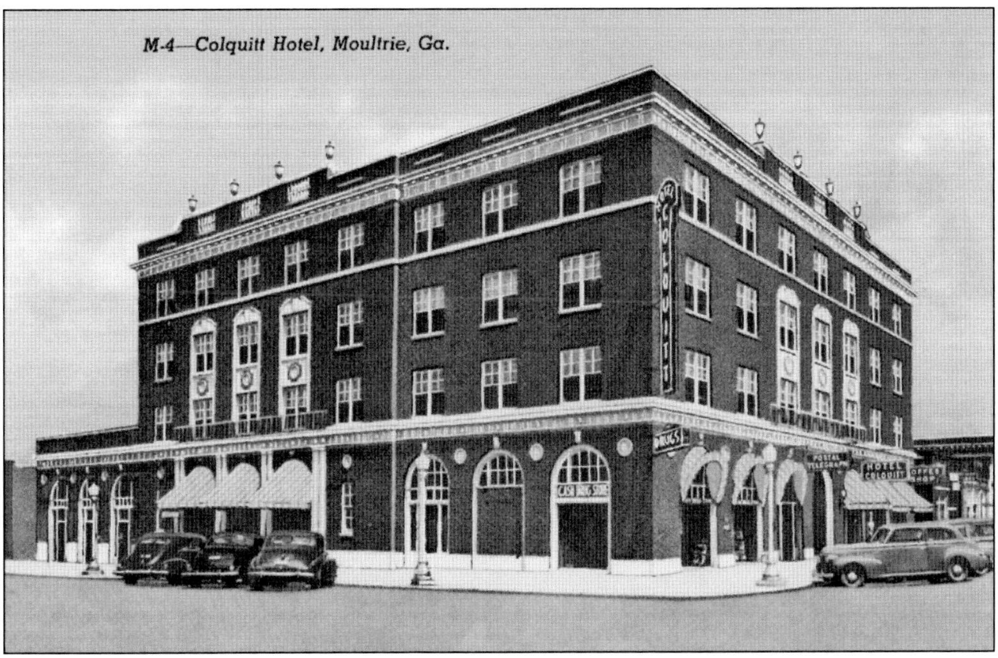

In 1928, the original Hotel Colquitt was razed and replaced by a four-story, red brick building. A drugstore occupied the corner of the first floor. The telegraph office and a coffee shop were also located on the first floor. This postcard shows the hotel in the 1940s. The entrance leading to the lobby and registration desk can be seen at the left under the striped awnings. (APP.)

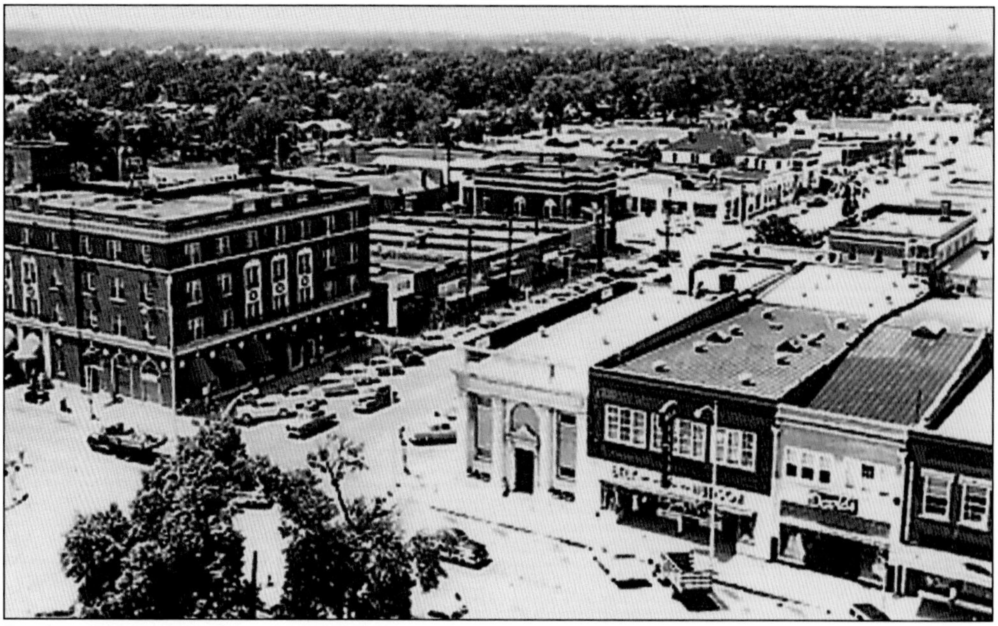

By the 1950s, when this photograph was taken, the Hotel Colquitt advertised that all 75 rooms had baths and boasted that 50 rooms featured air-conditioning. It was proclaimed "the best hotel of its size in the South." The Plantation Restaurant, located on the Main Street side of the first floor, was known far and wide for good food and friendly service. (MO.)

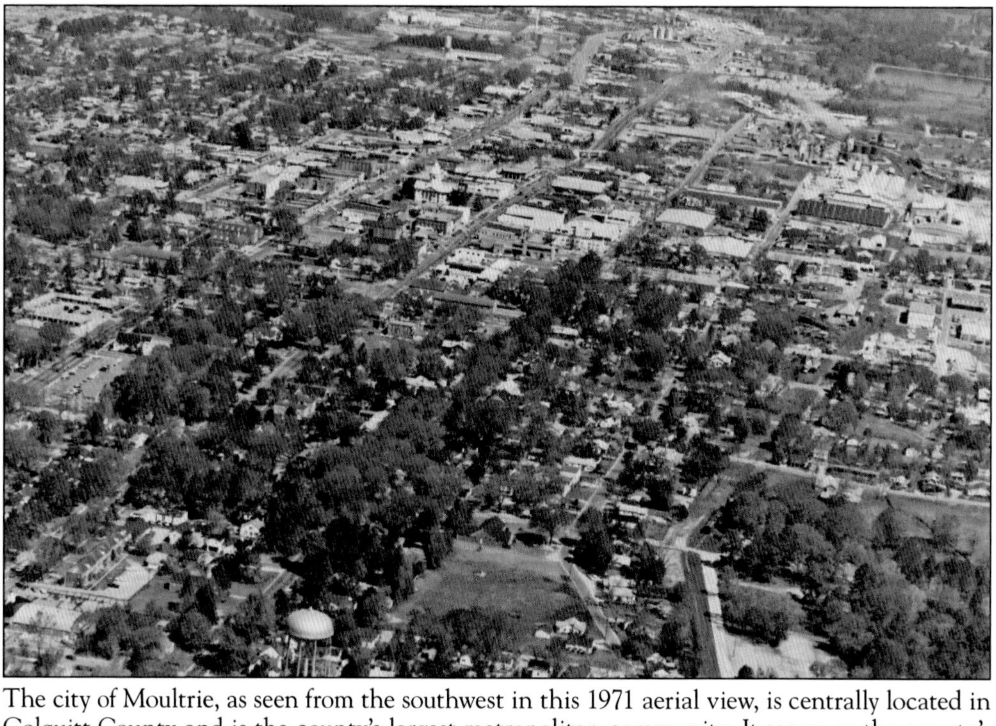

The city of Moultrie, as seen from the southwest in this 1971 aerial view, is centrally located in Colquitt County and is the county's largest metropolitan community. It serves as the county's seat of government. In the center of this photograph, the Colquitt County Courthouse can be seen as a dominant and distinctive landmark. (MCCL.)

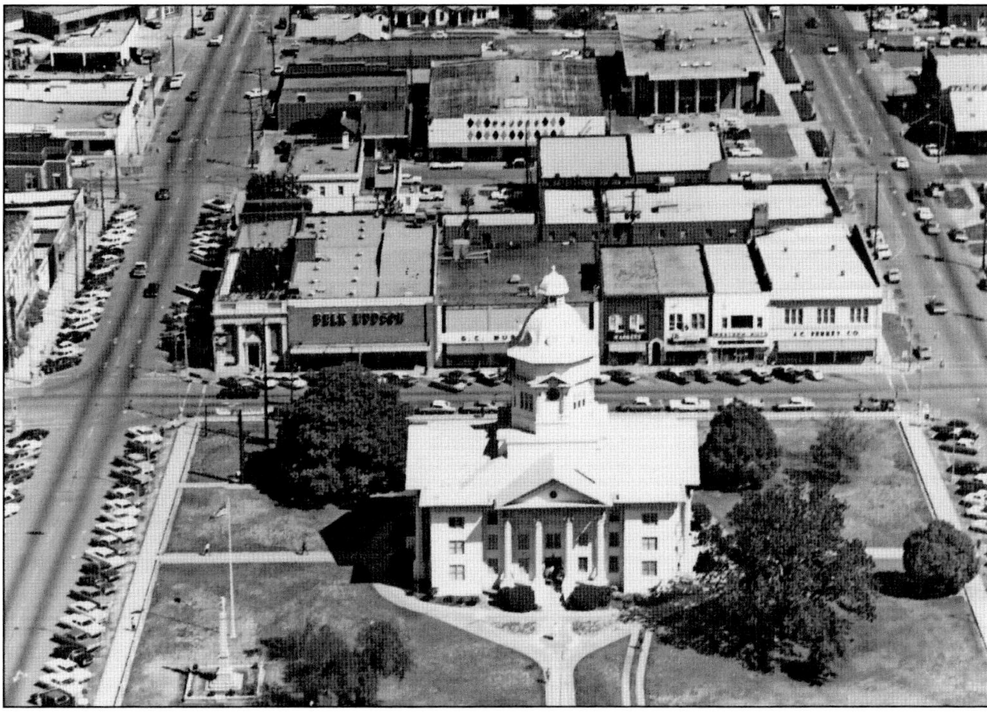

The Colquitt County Courthouse sits in the center of this 1971 aerial photograph of downtown Moultrie. Still a thriving commercial area, nationally known stores and locally owned businesses filled the buildings. Businesses on the north side of the square were, from left to right, C&S Bank, Belk-Hudson, G. C. Murphy, Warner's, Causey's Shoes, Western Auto, and J. C. Penney. (MCCL.)

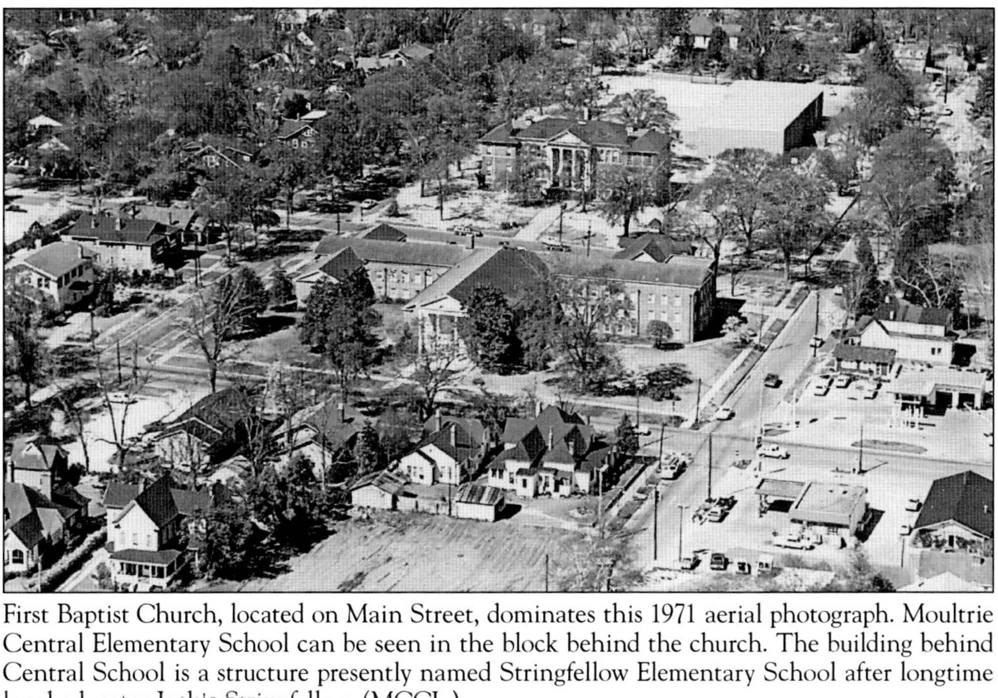

First Baptist Church, located on Main Street, dominates this 1971 aerial photograph. Moultrie Central Elementary School can be seen in the block behind the church. The building behind Central School is a structure presently named Stringfellow Elementary School after longtime local educator Jackie Stringfellow. (MCCL.)

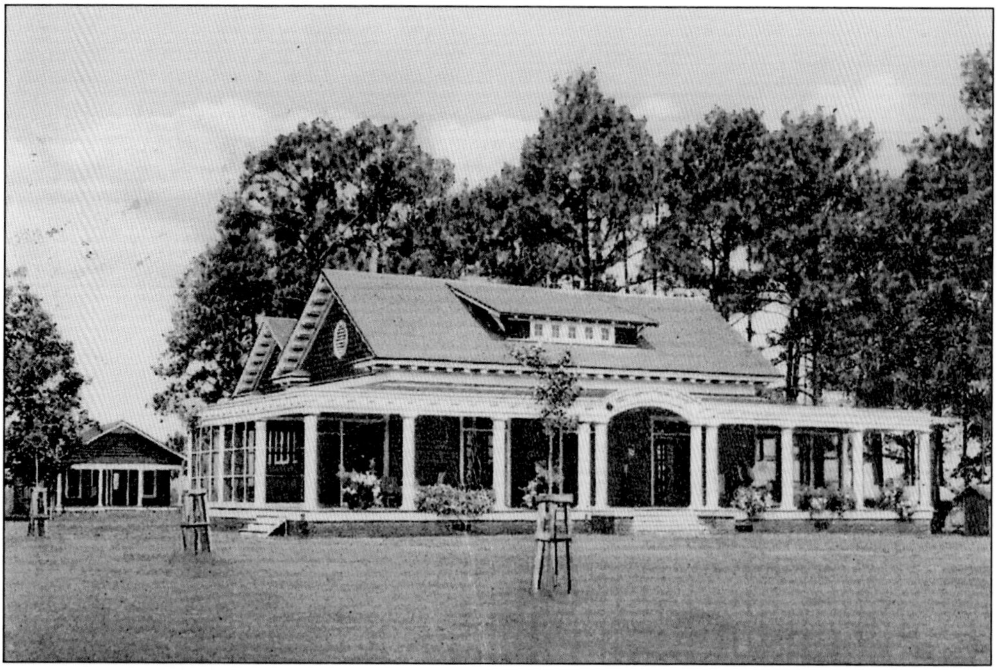

The Country Club on Magnificent Golf Links, which was the precursor to the present-day Sunset County Club, included a nine-hole golf course and this clubhouse. The country club was later moved farther south on Main Street. This building was purchased by the Moultrie Elks Club and was used by the membership for meetings and celebrations until 1986. (MO.)

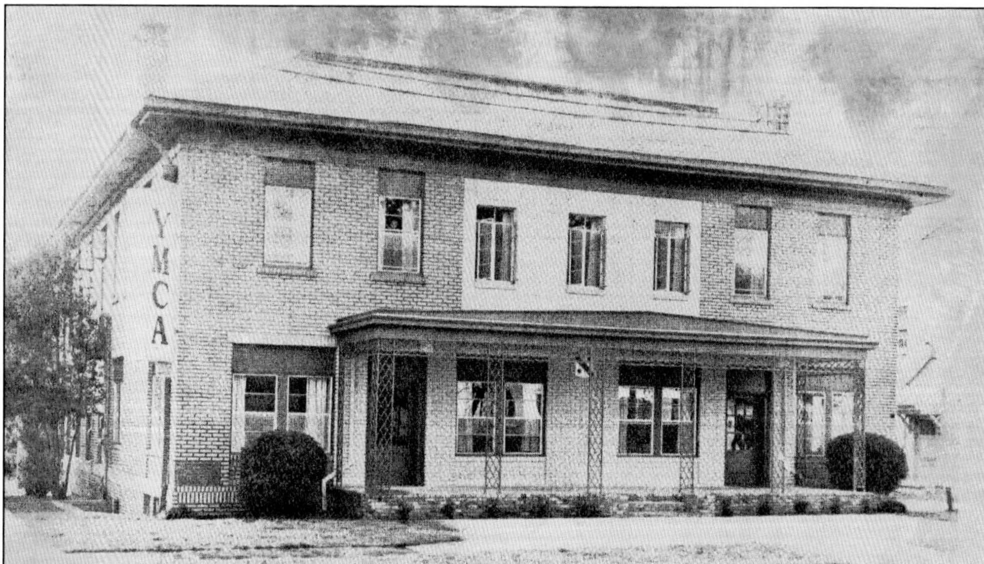

The first building that housed the Moultrie YMCA was completed in 1917 at a cost of $30,000. It was located at the corner of First Street and First Avenue SW. By the early 1970s, more space was needed for the rapidly increasing membership, and new programs demanded a more modern building. In 1974, a new building was constructed for the YMCA, and use of this building was abandoned. This structure still stands today and is used for commercial offices. (MSP.)

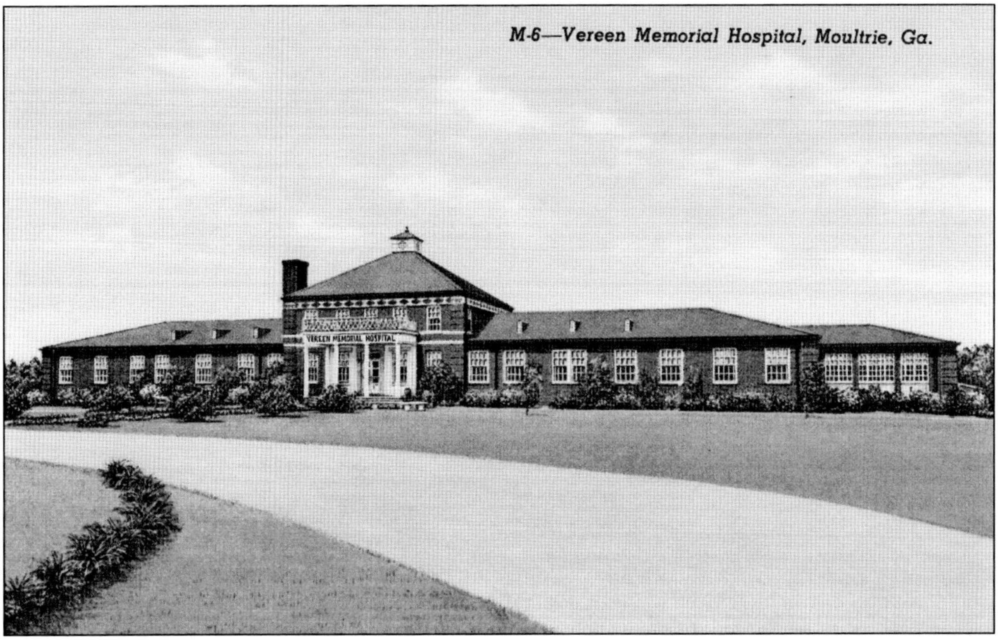

W. C. Vereen pledged $27,000 toward the construction of a hospital building in 1937, provided that Public Works Administration funds could be secured for the remainder of the costs. When it was found that the cost to build the hospital would be much higher than expected, Vereen increased his pledge to $50,000 and challenged the citizens to raise an additional $50,000. The challenge was met, and the 44-bed Vereen Memorial Hospital was dedicated on October 17, 1939. The photograph above shows the hospital as it was originally constructed. The photograph below shows the hospital after its expansion in 1954, which increased the bed capacity to 83 and added three operating rooms, a clinical laboratory, a new kitchen, and an obstetric and pediatric department and upgraded x-ray equipment. (Both, APP.)

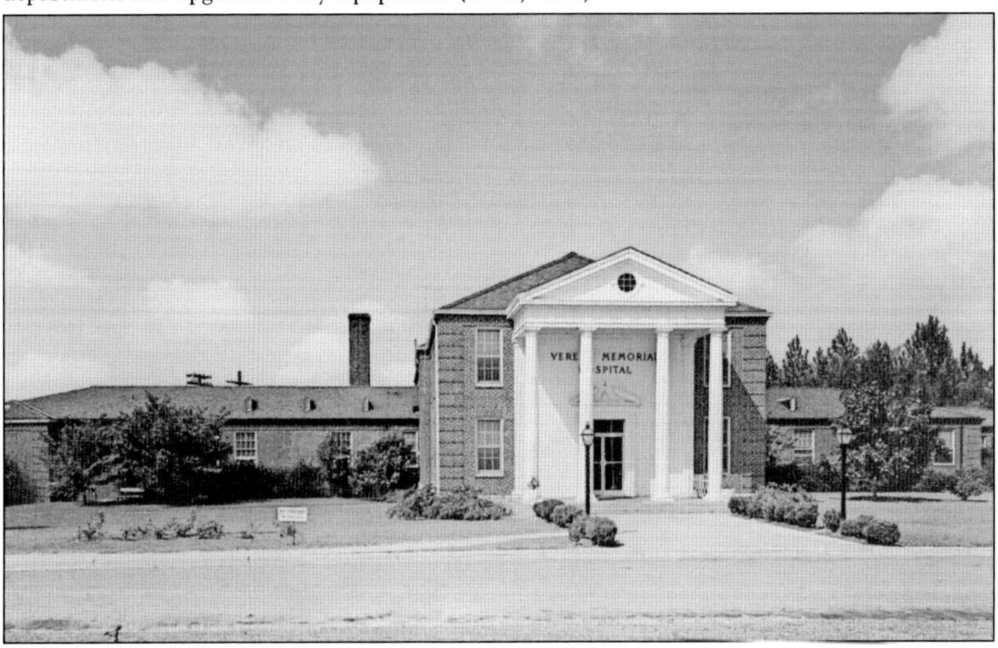

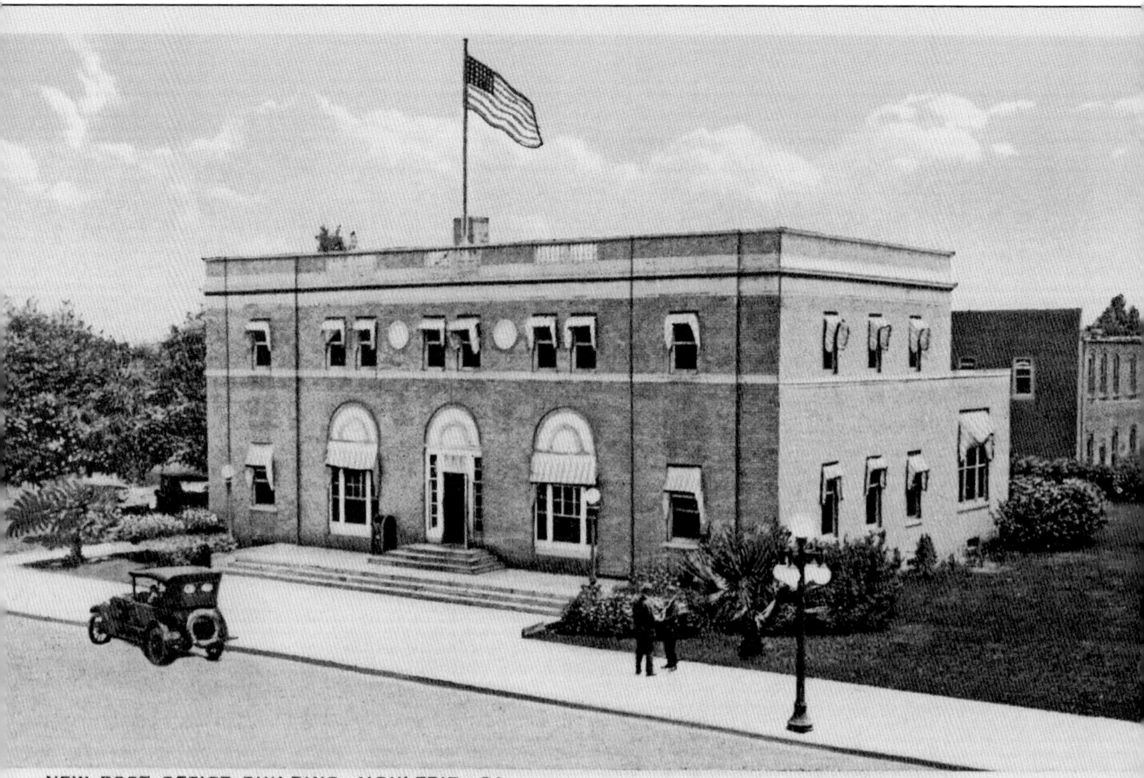

NEW POST OFFICE BUILDING, MOULTRIE, GA.

In 1912, Congress appropriated $65,000 for the construction of a new post office in Moultrie. Construction did not begin for two years and did not finish until 1919. The Federal Building, at the corner of Main Street and First Avenue NE, opened in July 1919 and served the community for 45 years. (APP.)

Two

PIONEERS

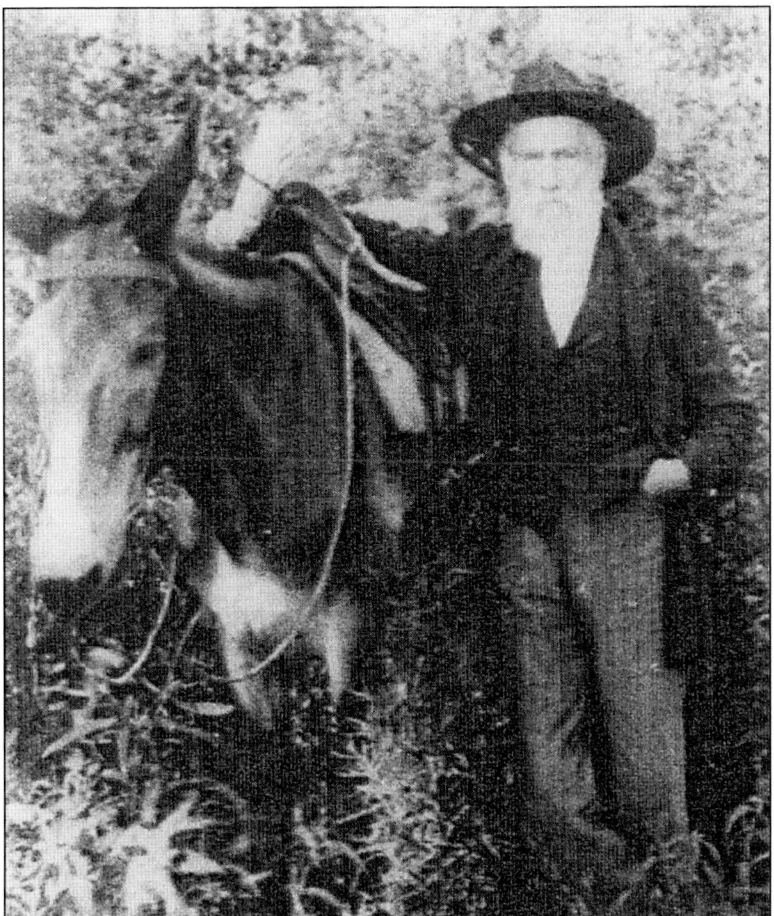

This undated photograph shows Jacob Frederick Reichert Jr., who was born in Wurtenburg, Germany, on January 22, 1820. In 1932, he immigrated with his family to Jefferson County, Florida, where he made his living farming. In the late 1840s, he moved to Thomas County, Georgia. When Colquitt County was formed in 1856, Reichert was named sheriff of the new county, and he served until 1857. He served again in 1860. (MO.)

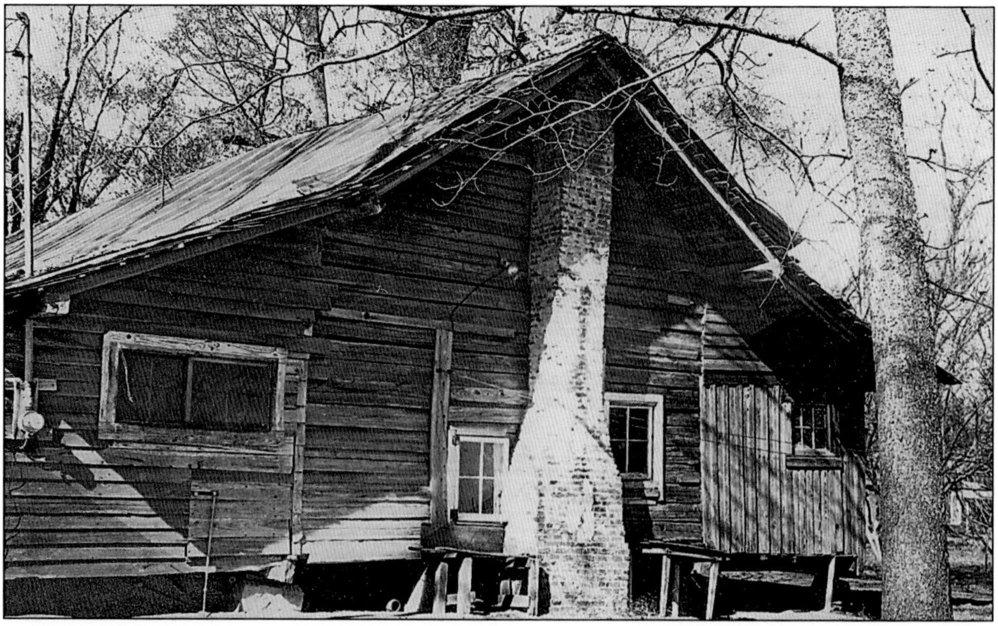

Henry Crawford Tucker built the house shown above in 1818 on land in Irwin County. That land was taken into Thomas County when it was formed, and in 1856, when Colquitt County was formed, that same land became part of the new county. The main part of the house was constructed of hand-hewn logs with half-dovetail notching. The rooms enclosed from the porch were sided with crude weatherboarding and board-and-batten siding. It was home to Elder Tucker and his three successive wives, Nancy Sapp, Margaret Watson, and Rebecca Bryant. Tucker was the father of 32 children and the grandfather of 184 children. The photograph below shows Elder Tucker and his third wife, Rebecca. (Both, MO.)

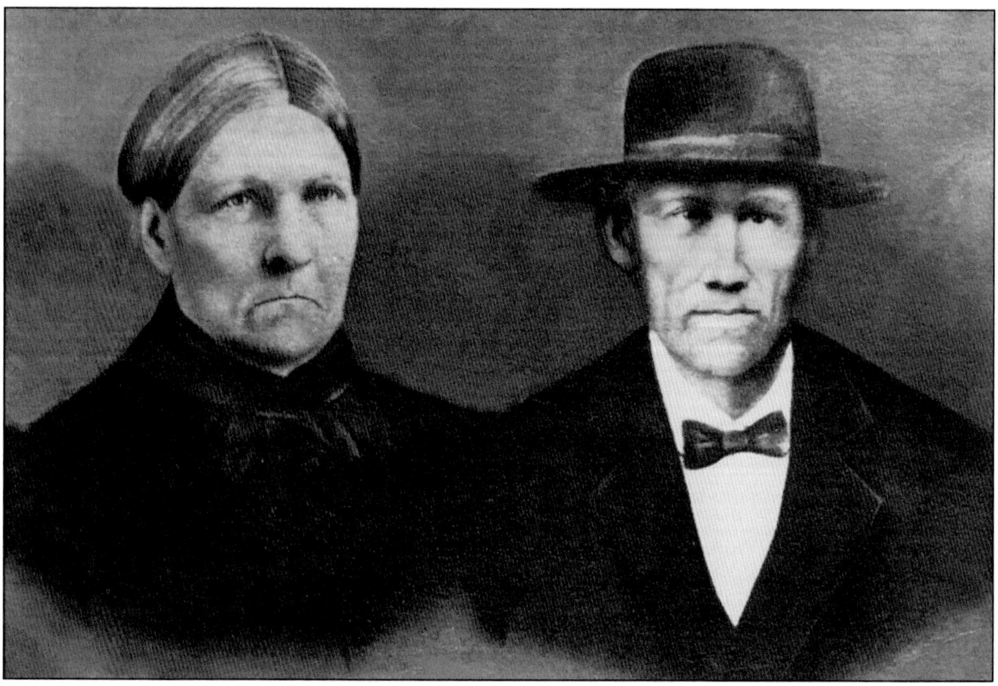

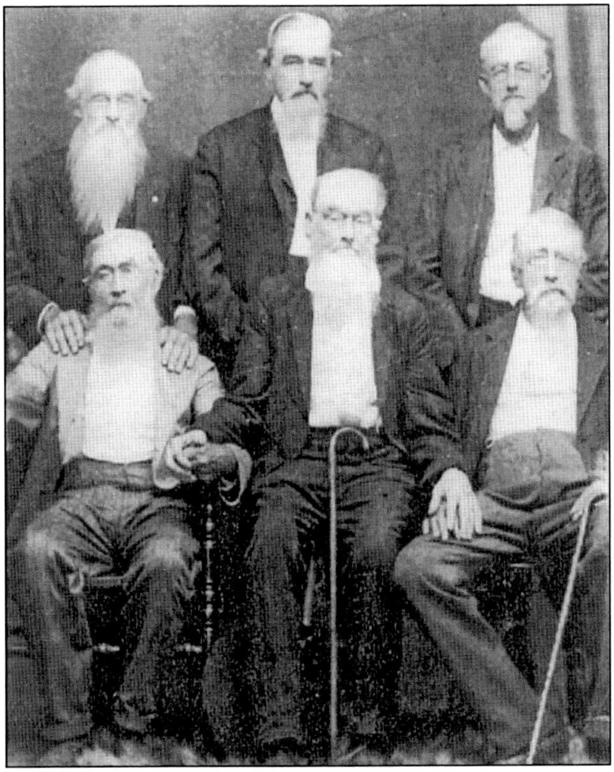

In 1905, the six living sons of James Mitchell Norman and Ruth Taylor Tillman gathered for what was to be their last portrait together. A seventh son, John Tillman Norman (1828–1891) died before this portrait was taken. All seven sons were Confederate veterans. From left to right are (first row) Joseph James Norman (1833–1908), Moses C. Norman (1823–1909), and Jeremiah Bryant Norman (1821–1908); (second row) Richard J. Norman (1836–1914), Joel Samuel Norman (1839–1926) and William Henry Harrison Norman (1842–1912). (MO.)

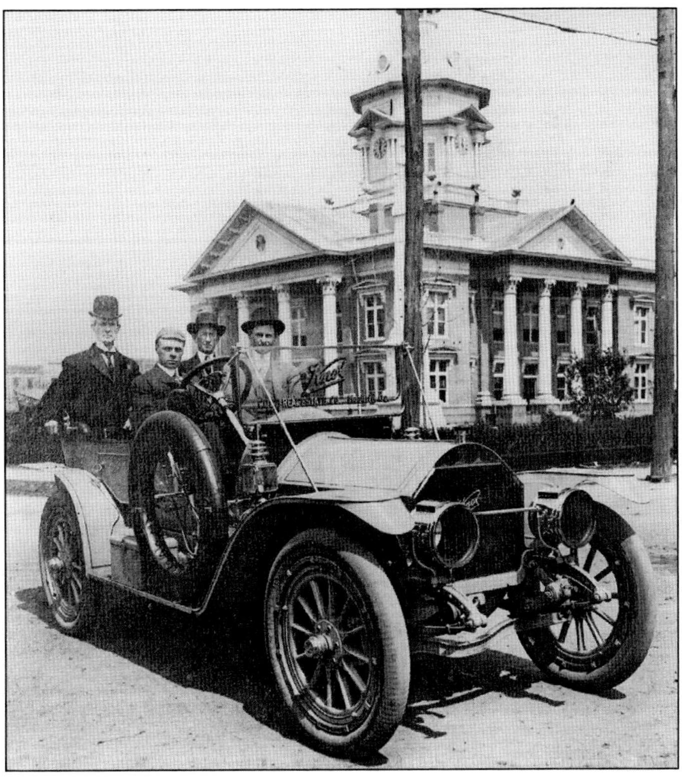

This photograph from 1910 shows several Colquitt County businessmen and a friend pausing in front of the Colquitt County Courthouse. The Knox automobile in which they are riding was purchased by W. E. Aycock at the 1910 auto show in Atlanta, Georgia. From left to right in the front seat are Johnny Toole of Atlanta and Charlie Kendall. From left to right in the rear seat are Z. H. Clark and W. E. Aycock. Aycock, Clark, and Kendall owned and operated Cobb Real Estate Company, buying and selling farmland in Colquitt County. This automobile, along with two others, was used to drive their customers while showing property. (MO.)

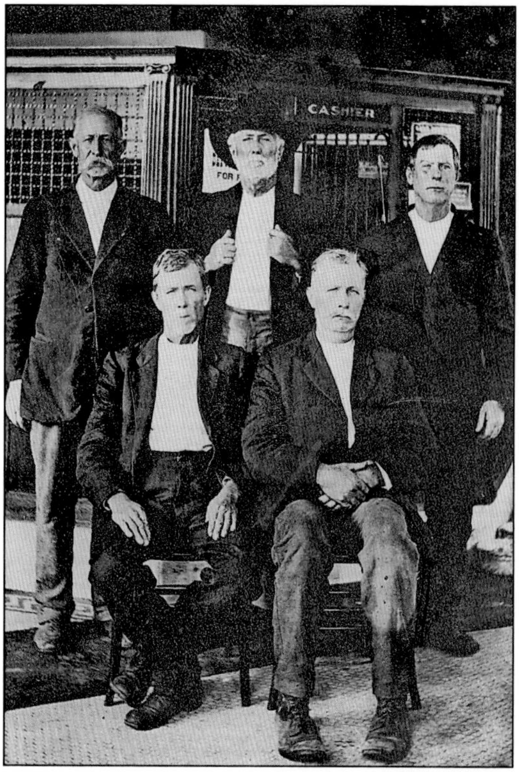

During the early days of the lumber and naval stores industries, Ellenton was a booming sawmill community. As a railroad stop between Sparks and Moultrie, Ellenton prospered. Pictured in front of the cashier's window of the Ellenton Bank, which was established in 1901, are, from left to right, (first row) J. J. Baker and Millard Baker; (second row) Absolom Baker, Richard (Dick) Baker (president), and J. M. Baker. (MO.)

Among the entrepreneurs who came to Colquitt County in the late 1800s to take advantage of the plentiful virgin pine forests were Davis Jenkins and his sons. Pictured in this 1930s photograph are, from left to right, Davis (Capp) Jenkins, Walt Jenkins, Cliff Jenkins, Davis Jenkins Jr., Watt Jenkins, and Hamp Jenkins. (Author.)

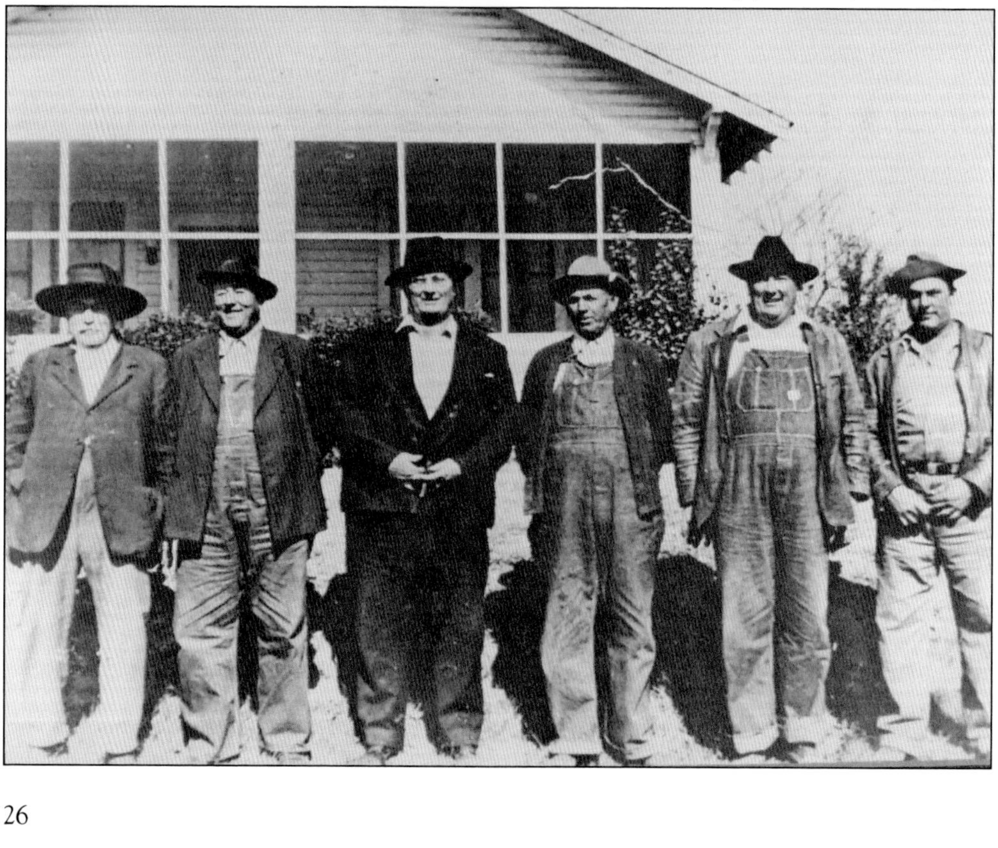

William Coachman Vereen (1859–1942) was born in Cheraw, South Carolina. He moved to Colquitt County in 1890 with his family and his in-laws, the McNeills, to engage in the naval stores business. He helped organize the Moultrie Banking Company in 1896, the Moultrie Packing Company in 1914, Moultrie Cotton Mills in 1910, and the Colquitt County Tobacco Warehouse Company. He was also active in numerous civic and religious organizations, including Vereen Memorial Hospital, First Presbyterian Church of Moultrie, local and state boards of education, Colquitt County Commission, and Moultrie Chamber of Commerce, and he also served as mayor of Moultrie. This undated photograph of "Mr. W. C.," as he was affectionately known to many, was taken during his later years. (APP.)

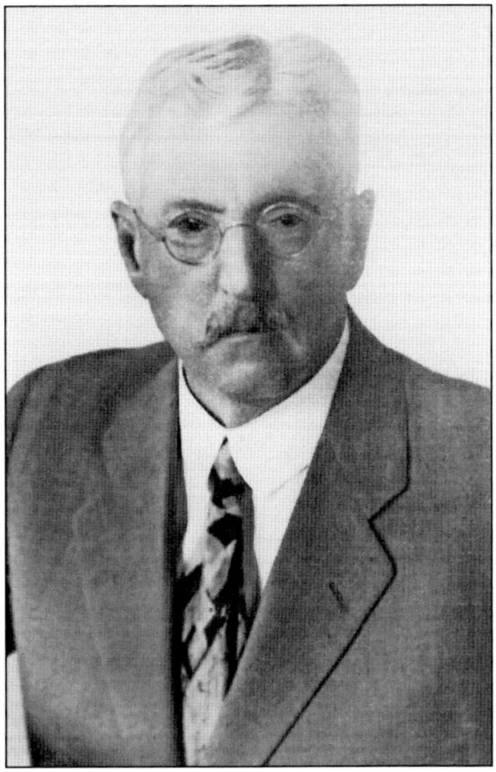

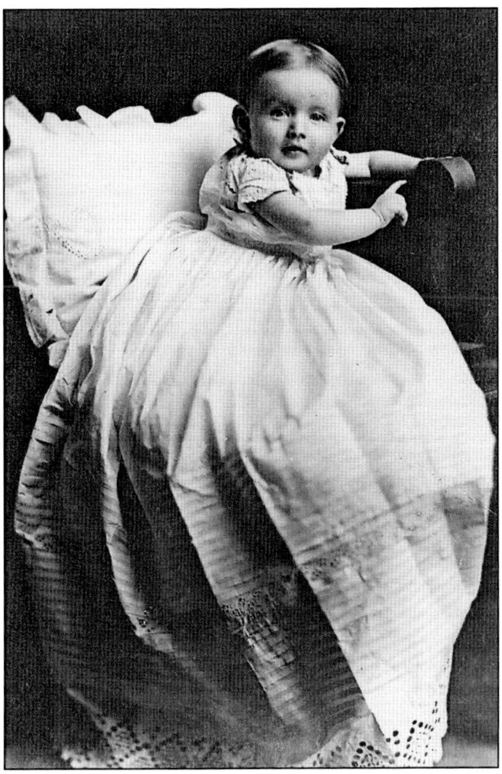

William Coachman (Bud) Vereen Jr., grandson of William Coachman Vereen, is pictured at the time of his baptism. The baptismal dress in the photograph has been worn by generations of Vereen children and is still in use today. First worn by William Coachman Vereen at his baptism at the Presbyterian church in Cheraw, South Carolina, in 1859, the dress was made by his mother, Eugenia. Born in 1913, Bud was educated in public schools in Moultrie and at Episcopal High School in Virginia. While enrolled at Georgia Tech, Bud was called home to help the family businesses of Moultrie Cotton Mills and Riverside Manufacturing, which were struggling because of the Depression. Upon his father's death, Bud assumed the presidency of both companies. He died on April 24, 1997. (MCCL.)

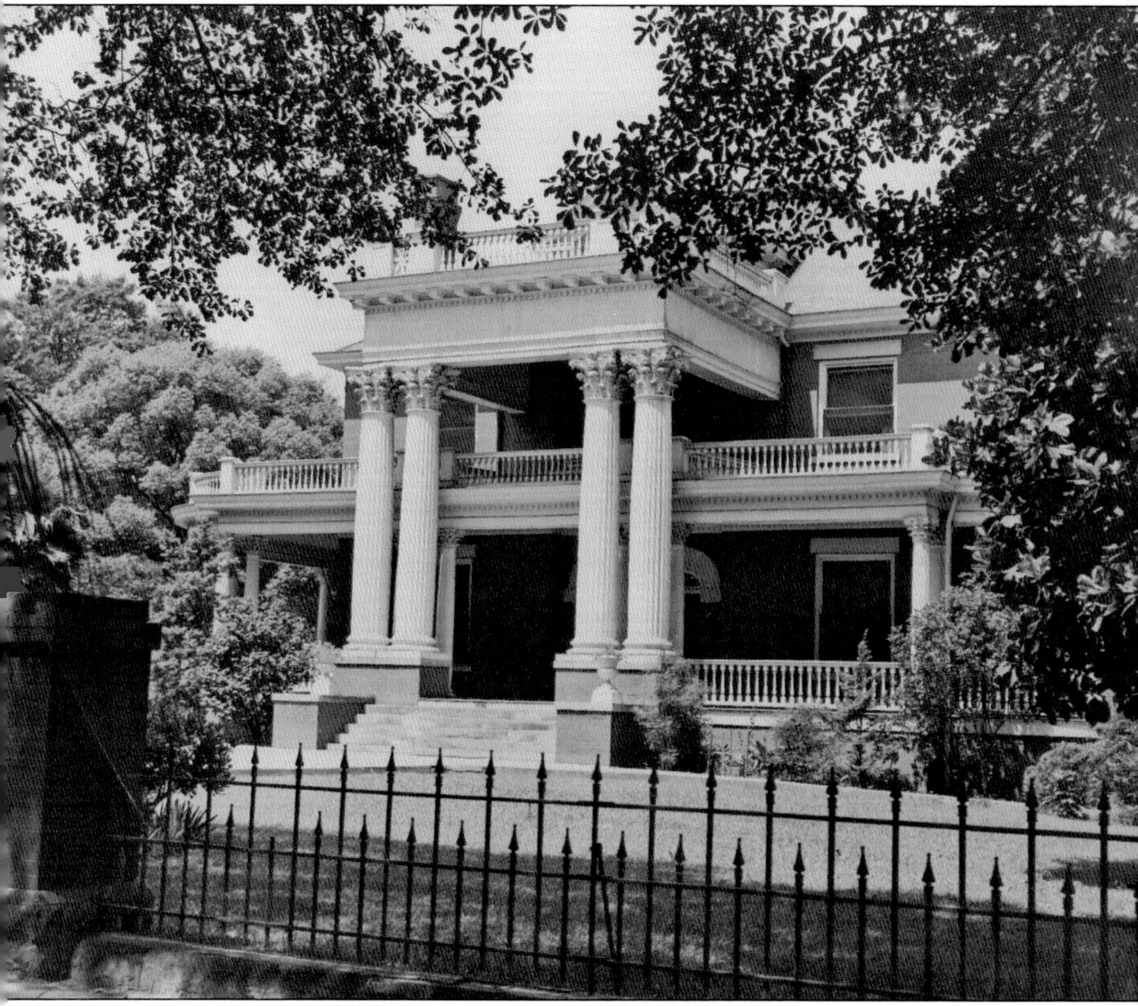

The home of William Coachman Vereen on South Main Street was built in the 1890s. The house, grounds, and outbuildings covered an entire city block. Built in the ornate fashion of the times, the house was equipped with an elevator and electricity. The house was razed in the 1950s at the wishes of the Vereen family to be replaced by the First Baptist Church. (MCCL.)

Three

BUSINESSES

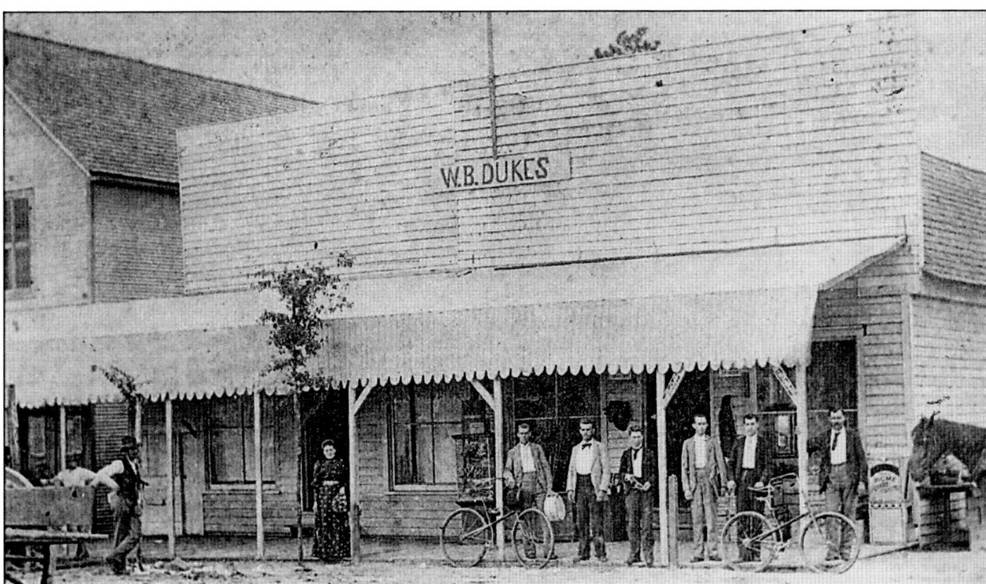

William B. Dukes, a prosperous Thomas County merchant, moved his business and his family to Moultrie in the early 1900s. Thought to be Moultrie's first department store, Dukes was located where the Friedlander Building now stands at the corner of First Street and First Avenue SE. This undated photograph was taken during the early 1900s. (MO.)

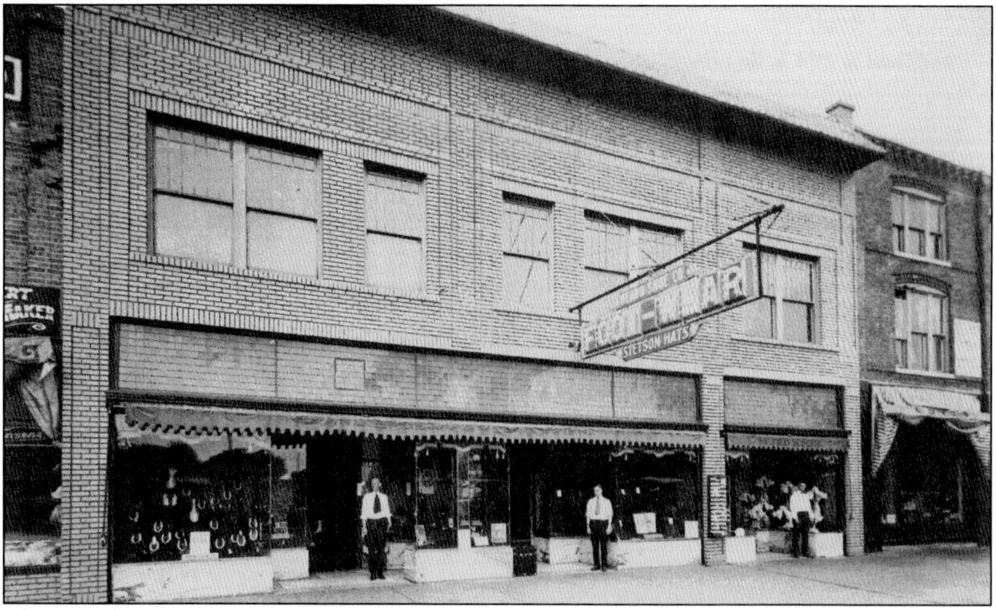

The Heard Shoe Company was on the west side of the courthouse square in the early 1900s. The street, originally named West Broad Street, was later renamed Main Street. In this undated photograph, employees of the Heard Shoe Company, which sold footwear and Stetson hats, pose outside the store. They are, from left to right, John Harvey, Alex Wicker, and Leon Fish (who died during the flu epidemic of 1918). (MO.)

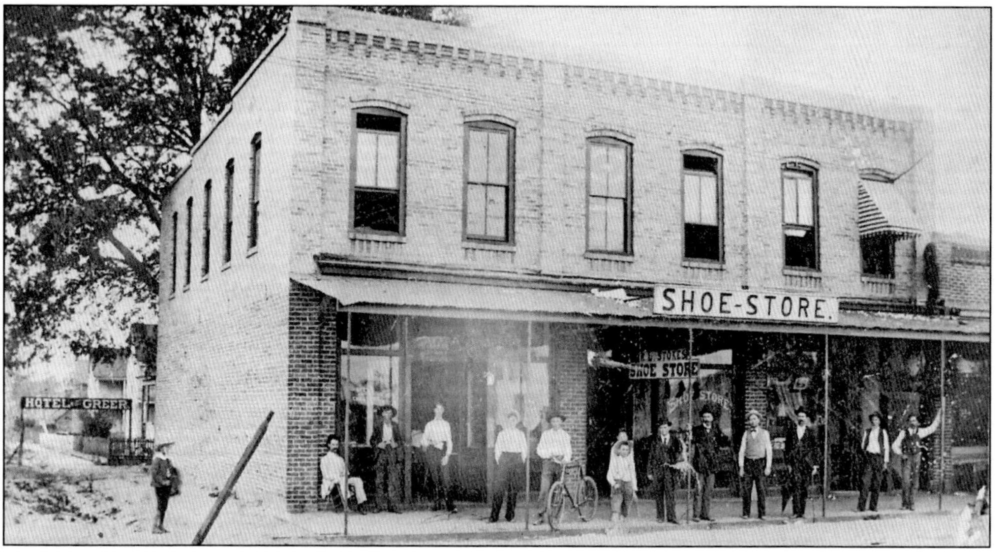

The beginning of the 20th century saw brick buildings with awnings and large signs appearing around the courthouse square. In this photograph taken between 1900 and 1910, citizens can be seen at the southwest corner of the square, where Main Street and First Avenue SW now intersect. The Huber Building was later replaced by another set of brick buildings. Dr. W. A. Blasingame Sr. (dentist) and attorneys W. A. Covington and John Smithwick occupied the upstairs corner offices. Henry Murphy and Charlie Batey ran a merchandise store in the ground-floor corner space. R. L. Stokes's shoe store was next door. The sign for the old wooden Hotel Greer can be seen at the rear of the building. (MO.)

In 1896, local businessmen W. W. Ashburn, Z. H. Clark, W. C. Vereen, M. J. Pearsall, J. F. Spivey, John McNeill, and J. B. Norman obtained a charter to form the Moultrie Banking Company, which was Moultrie's first bank. This photograph, taken in 1908, shows the new two-story red brick bank building on the northwest corner of the courthouse square. The bank occupied the first floor, with a law office and insurance company upstairs. In 1924, this structure was torn down, and a new two-story limestone building was constructed in its place. (MO.)

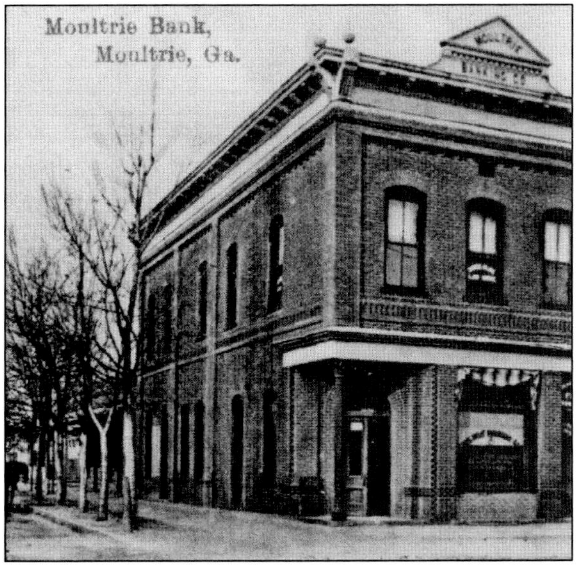

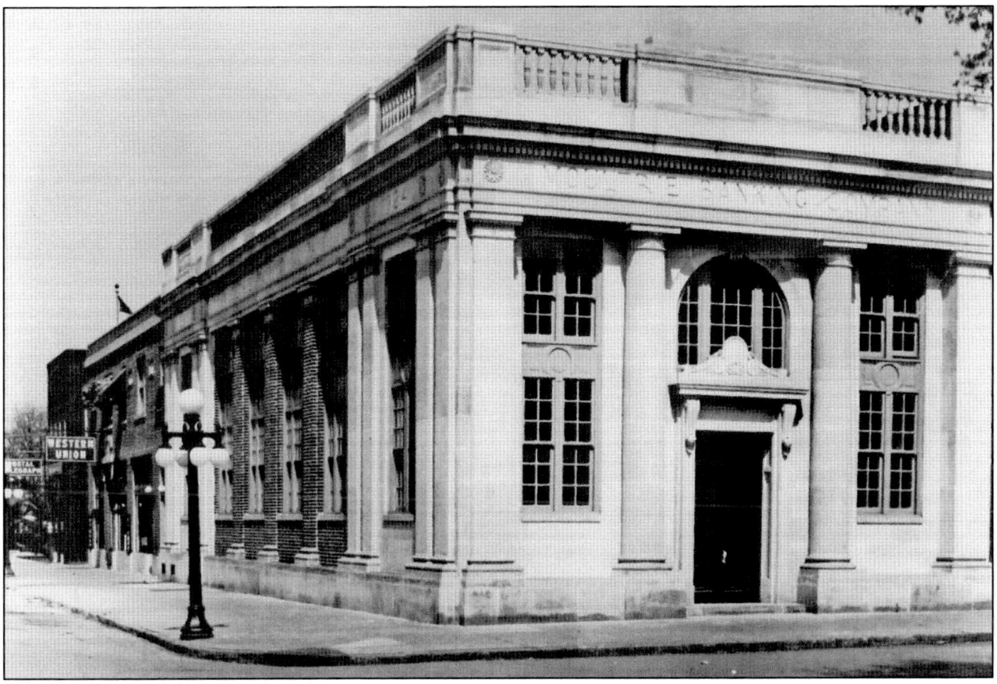

Shown in the 1940s, the facade of the Moultrie Banking Company building resembles a Greek or Roman temple, complete with Doric columns. The architect was T. F. Lockwood, who 17 years earlier had designed the nearby Carnegie Library building. Local contractor Anton Huber was in charge of its construction. Huber also built many other downtown Moultrie buildings, including the Colquitt Tower across the street and the Commercial Building a block to the south. In the 1960s, the Citizens and Southern (C&S) Bank Company purchased the Moultrie Banking Company. Because of the old building's small size and lack of space for drive-through banking, C&S moved to a new location on South Main Street in 1971. After the C&S Bank moved out, the Colquitt Loan Company moved into the Moultrie Banking Company Building and remains there today. (JMJ.)

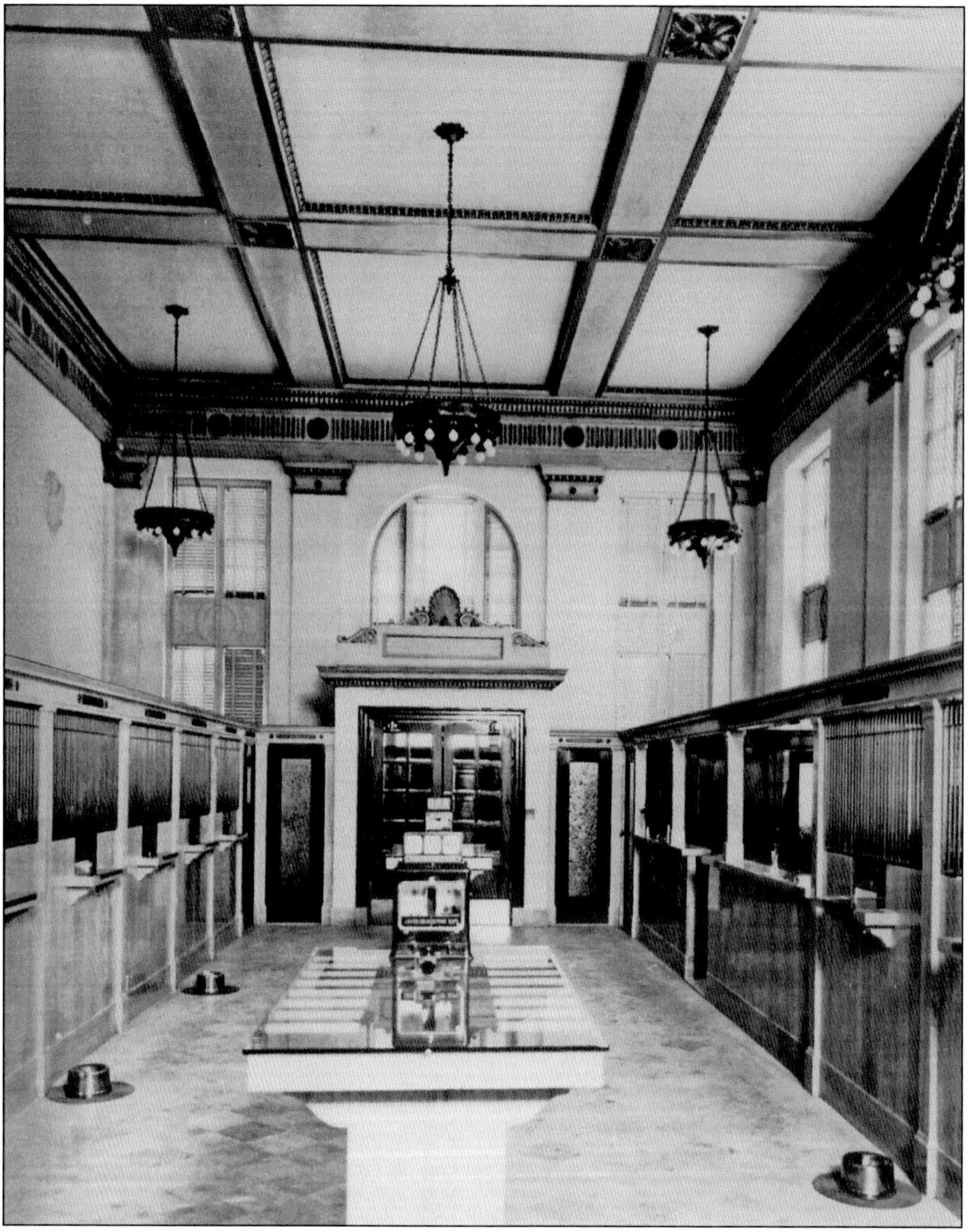

In the early 20th century, many successful businessmen in America wanted downtown office buildings that reflected their wealth and culture. However, because downtown space was at a premium, they often settled for compact adaptations of classical architecture. The Moultrie Banking Company Building incorporates a tall and narrow facade with a much greater depth. It is not a large building, but this skillful utilization of architecture creates an appearance of massiveness and security. This interior photograph of the Moultrie Banking Company Building was taken in the 1940s and is an excellent demonstration of this concept. (JMJ.)

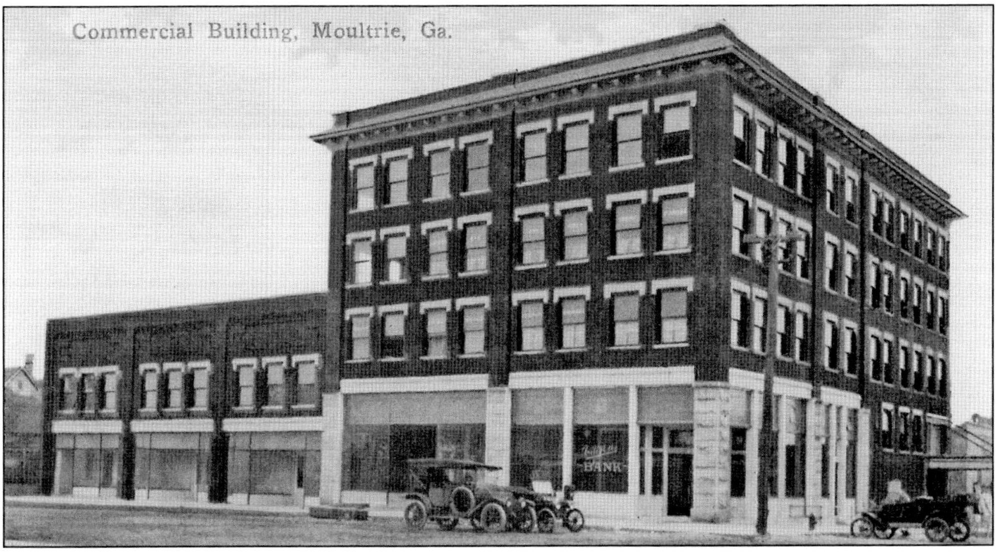

In 1912, local contractor Anton Huber built the Commercial Building on the site of a former carriage house and cotton warehouse. Originally the building was intended for use as a department store and for offices. The department store never materialized. Instead, the Citizens Bank became the building's main client, occupying the corner of the ground floor. Adjacent to the bank along Main Street were a hardware store, an auto supply store, and a furniture store. From the front, the building appears to have four stories. This is because the ground floor along Main Street was designed as prime commercial space with extra-tall ceilings. In reality, the rest of the building consists of five floors. At the time of its construction, the Commercial Building was the largest structure in downtown Moultrie in terms of square footage. Even today, it remains downtown Moultrie's largest building, surpassing even the courthouse in total floor space. (APP.)

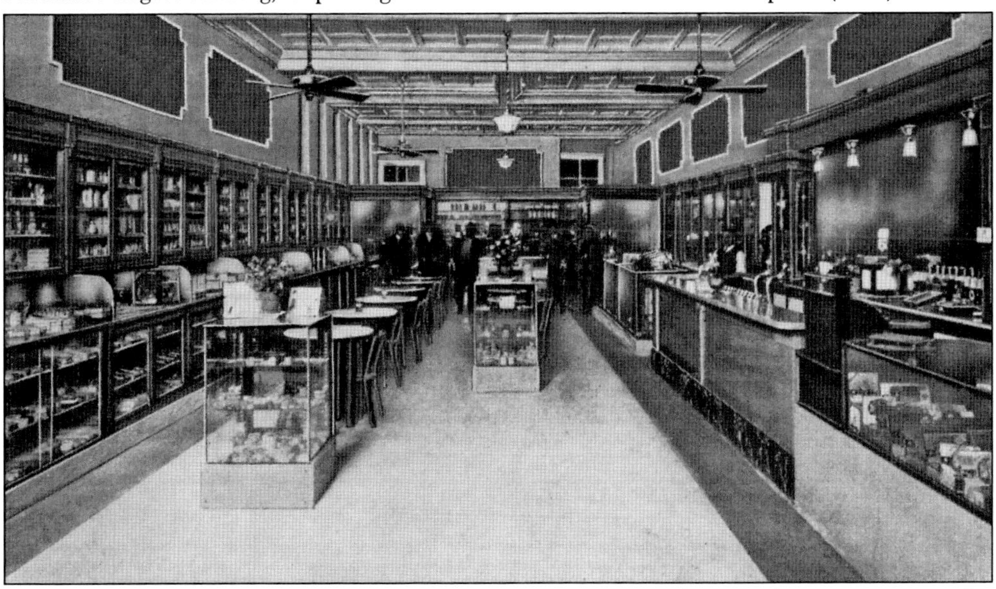

Crystal Pharmacy was originally on the southwest corner of the courthouse square, at the intersection of Main Street and First Avenue SW. This photograph shows the interior of the drugstore opened in the early 1900s, complete with a soda fountain, tables for customer seating, glass-fronted display cases, cash register, and the druggist's dispensary. (APP.)

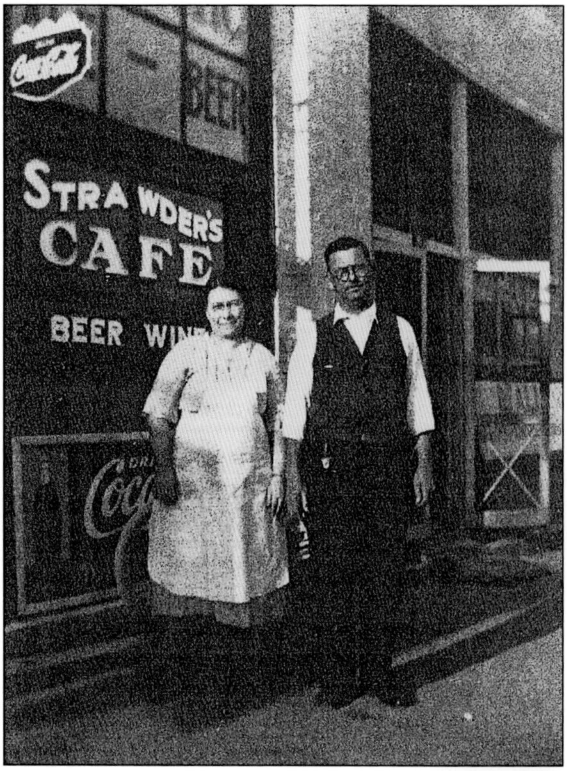

Anna Amanda "Mandy" Williams Strawder and her husband, William Richard Strawder Sr., are shown outside their café at the start of the Great Depression. The Strawders never turned down a hungry person during the Depression and treated paying and non-paying customers equally, offering them meals rounded out with their choice of pie or cake as well as tea or coffee. (MO.)

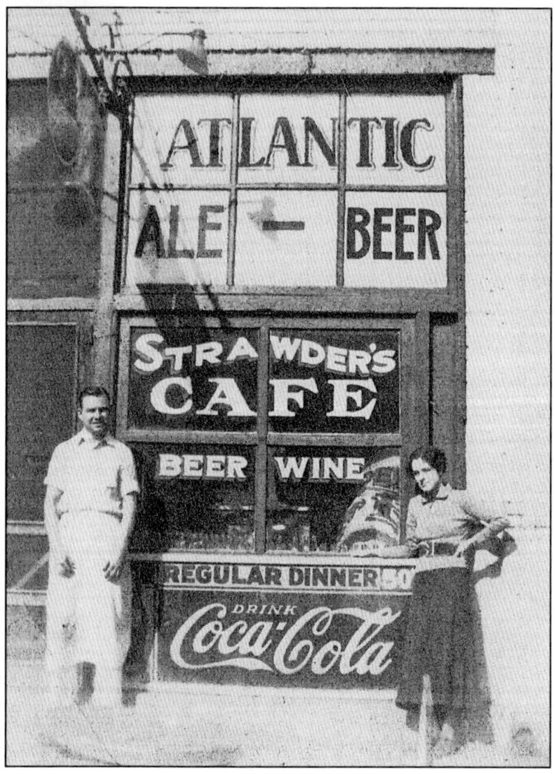

Horace Hall Strawder and his wife, Maria Stallings Strawder, stand in front of Strawder's Café on First Street NE in 1925. For $5 per week, boarders received three meals a day, complete with iced tea and pie. One could purchase a hamburger at Strawder's for a nickel or six for a quarter during the tobacco season. (MO.)

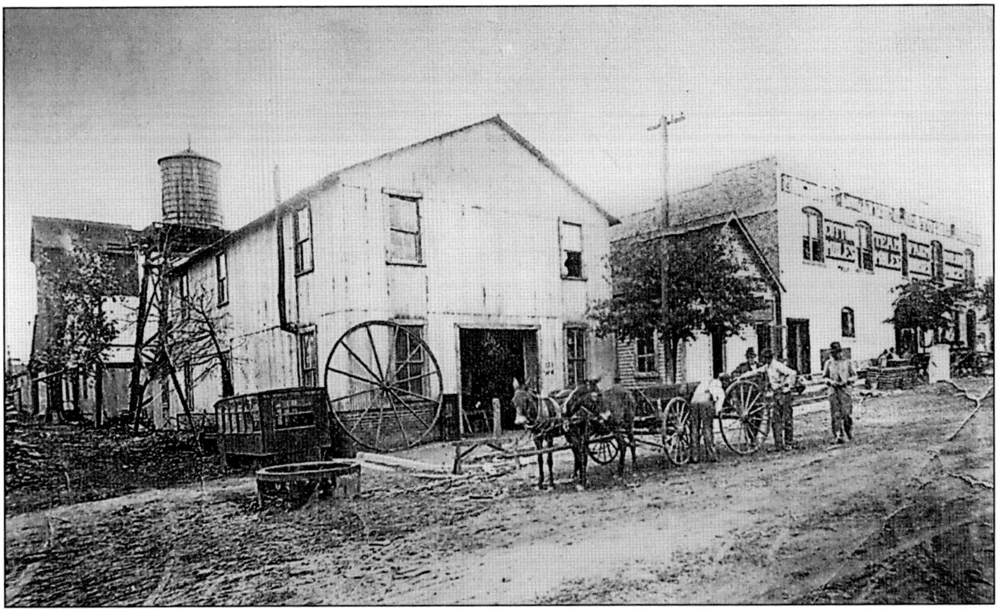

Horne's Livestock Company was located on East Central Avenue in the early 1900s. This photograph shows the livestock barn with a wagon and mule team in the foreground. Horne's sold cotton mules, team mules, farm horses, and draft horses. (MO.)

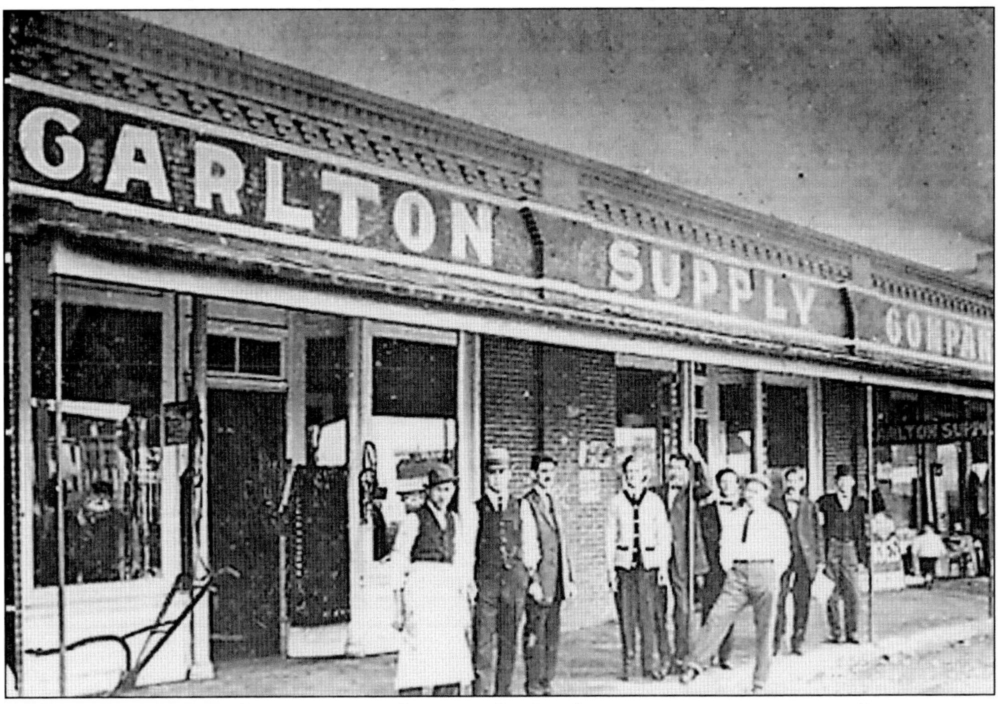

In the early 1900s, Moultrie proprietors began to display their wares in a more eye-catching manner. Carlton Supply Company, in the middle of the block on the south side of the courthouse square, carried everything from shoes to plows and horse blankets. Posing in this 1908 shot are, from left to right, J. B. Pinckard, William Dupriest, Estill Campbell, Charlie Webb, M. V. Robbins, W. T. Cooper, T. E. Williams, and two unidentified men. (MO.)

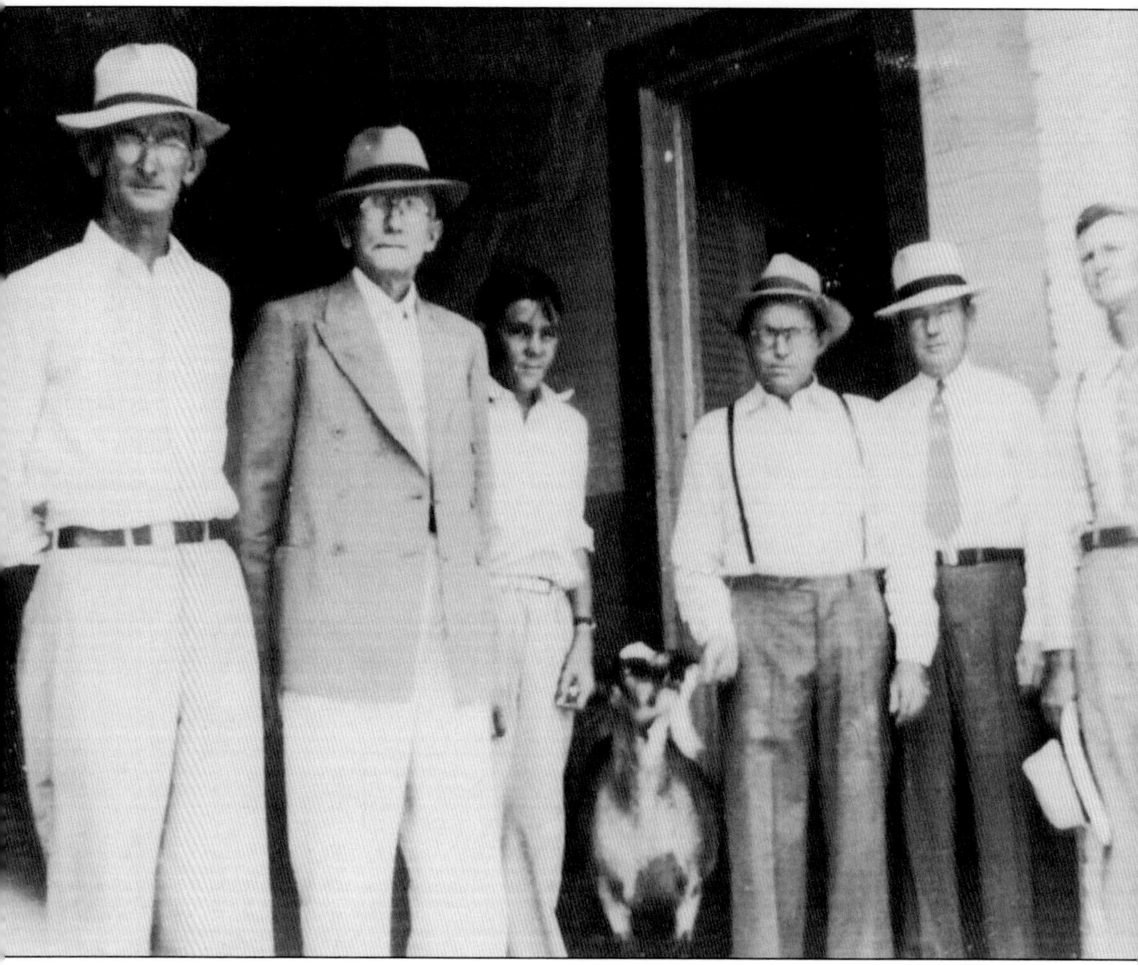

In 1921, J. L. Holman Sr. moved to Moultrie to manage a livestock company owned by his father. Located on East Central Avenue, it was the largest mule and livestock business in South Georgia and was the first to finance mules. Pictured above are the "men at the stable" (a phrase used by locals to describe these employees) during the late 1930s. John Lindsay Holman Sr. is third from the right, and his son, John Lindsay Holman Jr., is third from the left, with J. L. Sr.'s pet goat, Bill, between them. The other men are unidentified. (TPH.)

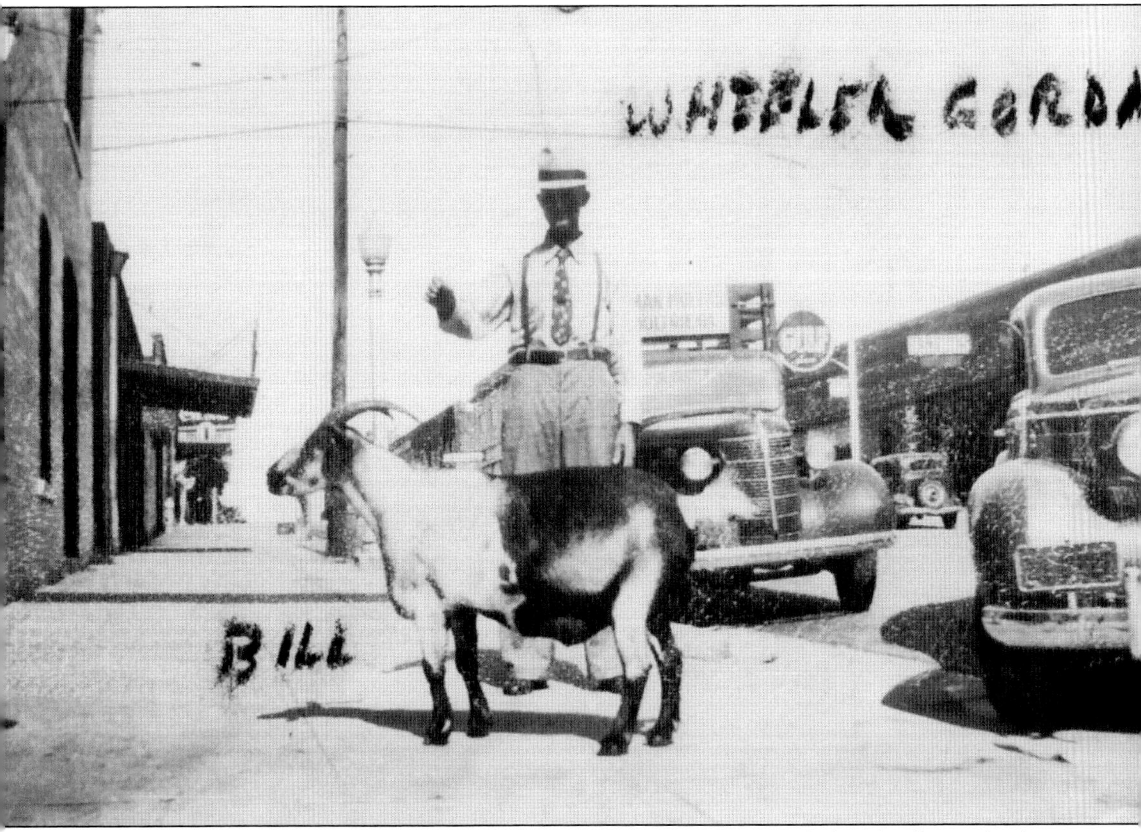

Bill, J. L. Holman Sr.'s pet goat, is pictured in the late 1930s. Standing behind Bill is Wheeler Gordan, one of the employees of the Holman Mule Company. According to family stories, Bill slept under Mr. Holman's desk and was as well trained as a dog. Bill knew the exact time of day when children who lived on the east side of town would be returning home from Central Elementary School. The children had to walk down the street in front of the mule barn, and Bill would wait for them at the corner above the barn so he could nibble on the leftover crumbs in their lunch pails. Bill would walk down the block with the children, but would not cross the street at the end of the block. Instead, he would return to the mule barn to wait for them the next day. (TPH.)

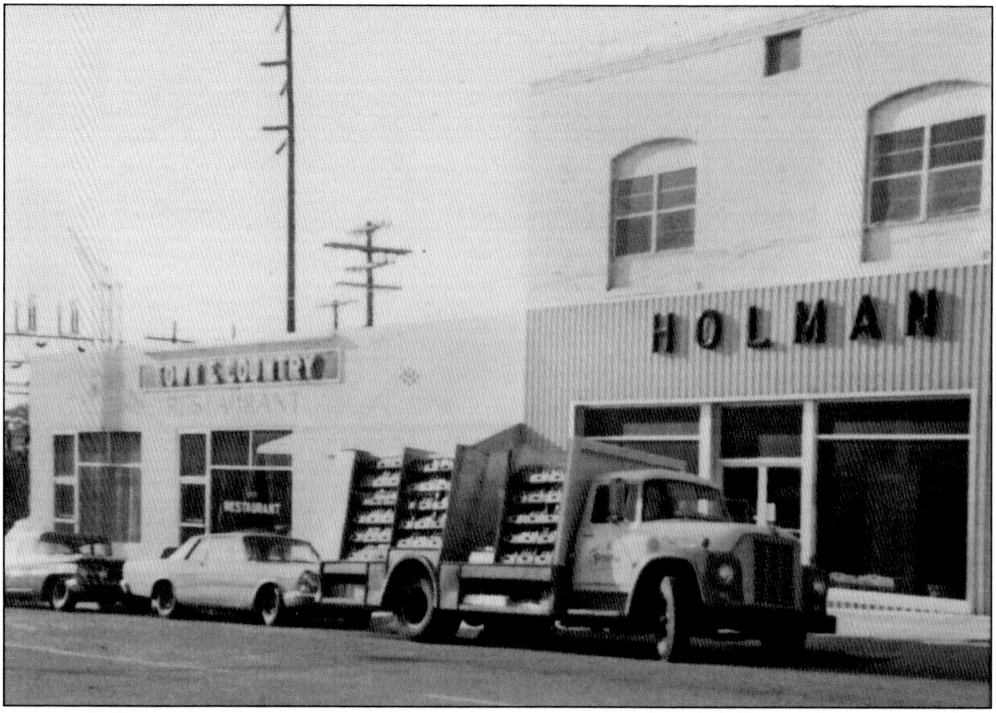

After World War II, the company changed with the times and became a hardware and supply company. Shown here in the 1950s, Holman Supply Company can be seen next to the Town and Country Restaurant. (TPH.)

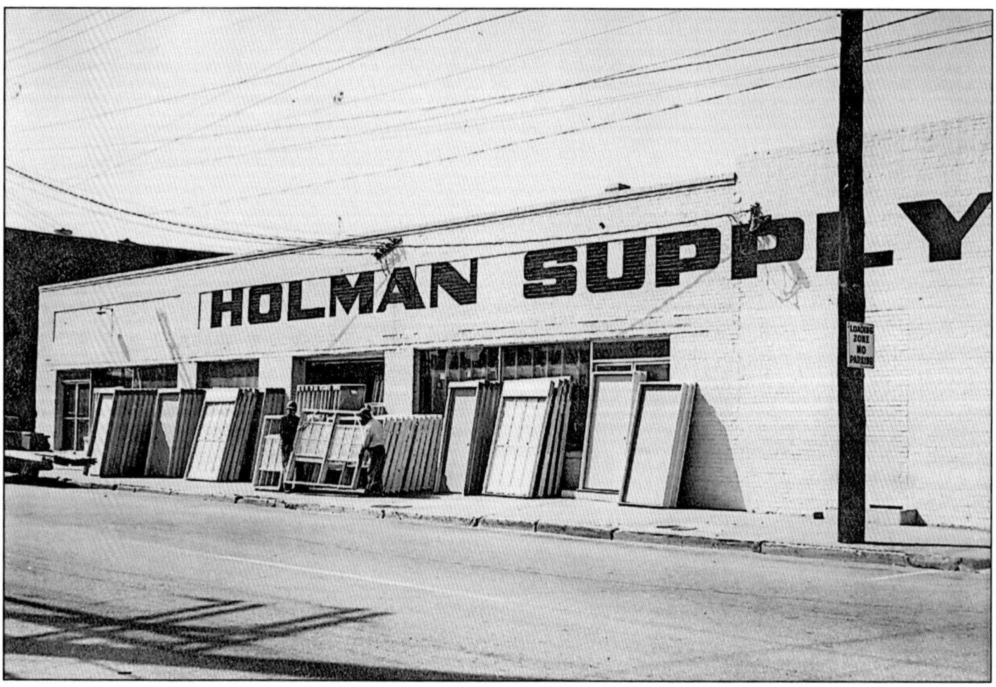

Holman Supply Company is shown as it existed until 1972, when a new warehouse, office, and showroom were built. Windows and door facings are displayed on the sidewalk. (MO.)

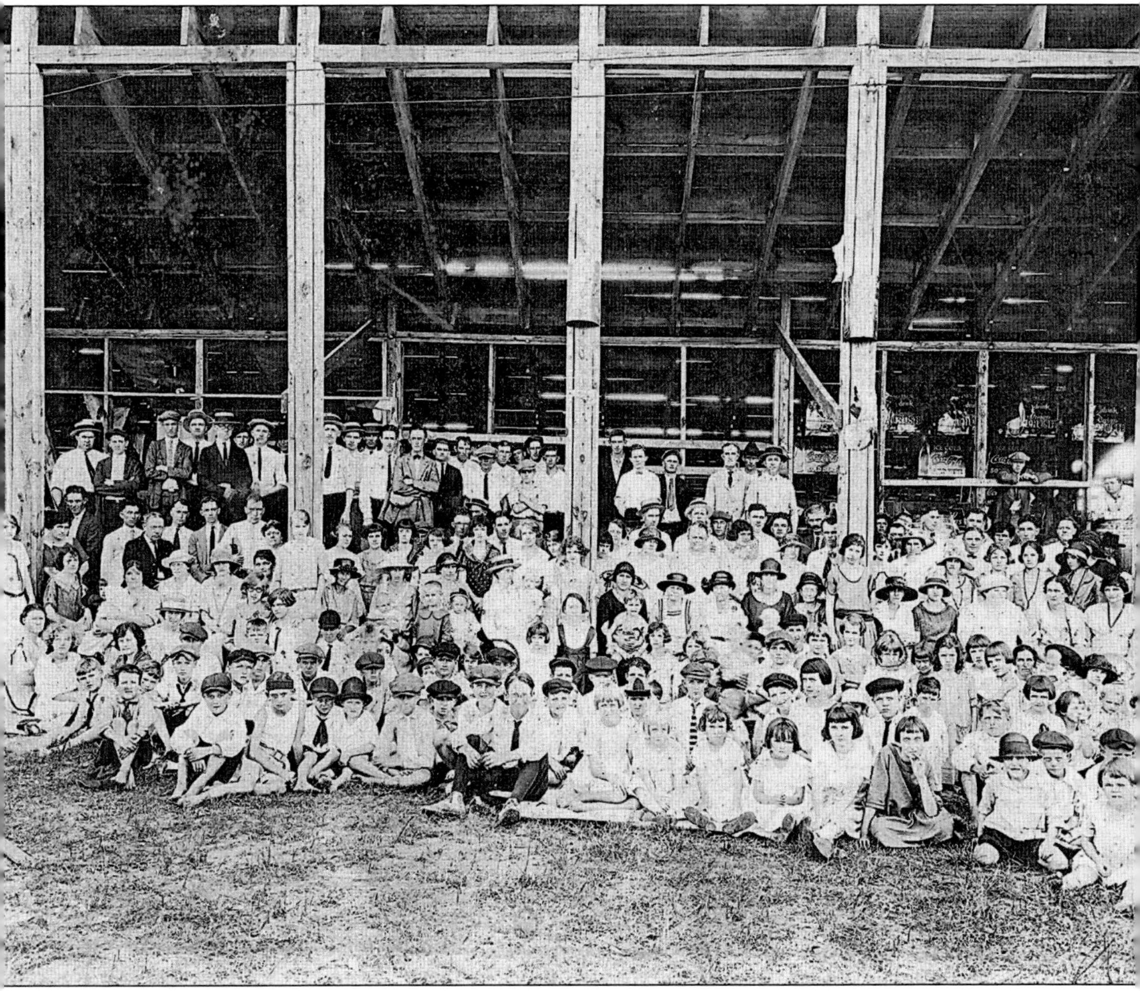

In this 1927 photograph, Swift and Company employees and their families celebrate at a company-wide barbecue. The event was held at the old fairgrounds in the southwest section of Moultrie, in an area known as "Pill Hill." (MO.)

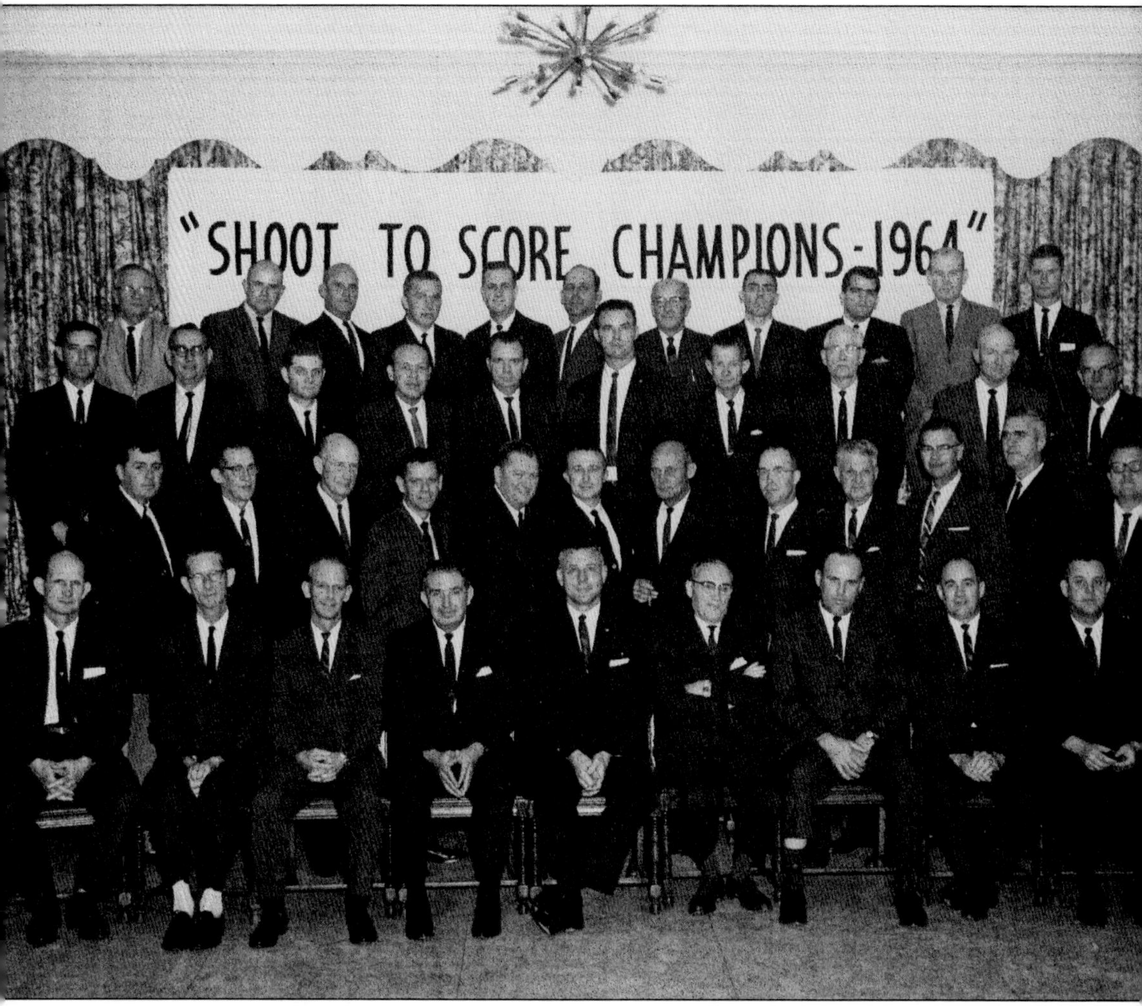

Employees of Swift and Company shown in 1964 are, from left to right, (first row) Walter Beasly, George Ohlinger, Henry Knox, Verlon Jones, Bill Jones, Clarence Killebrew, Bob Byers, Bob Perry, and Jim Knight; (second row) Virgil Mims, Herb Walker, Frank Conway, Tom Sheffield, John Carlton, Junior Young, Wilburn Tucker, Carroll Akridge, Lloyd Spinks, Jack Spivey, Ray Hendricks, and Wallace Duncan; (third row) Wayne Tillman, Jay Oxford, Marvin Martin, Bill Hayes, Julian Simpson, Ivan Clayton, Bill Martin, Coy Parham, Jerry Norman, and Paul Long; (fourth row) Wallace Gay, James Weaver, Clyde Isom, Marvin Tillman, Truett Cannon, Daniel Pussiegur, Floyd Beers, Joyce Cox, Woody Adkins, Ken Shockley, and Leverne Royals. (MO.)

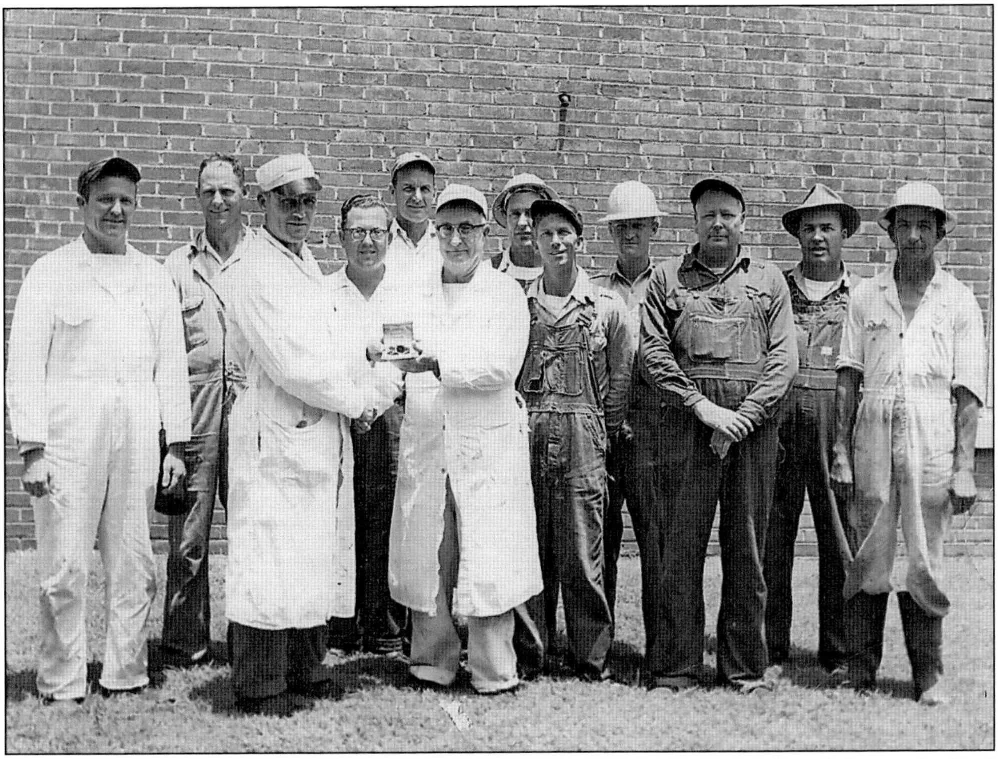

The Freezer Gang, photographed in July 1957 at Swift and Company, are, from left to right, Earl Weldon, Tony Spurlin, Clyde (Piggy) Isom Sr., James (Chubie) Stanfield, P. C. Carter, J. B. Cox, C. H. Buckner, Talmadge (Wormy) Drinkard, Marvin Harrison, Dallas Truitt, Lester (Curly) Reynolds, and H. M. Waldon. (MO.)

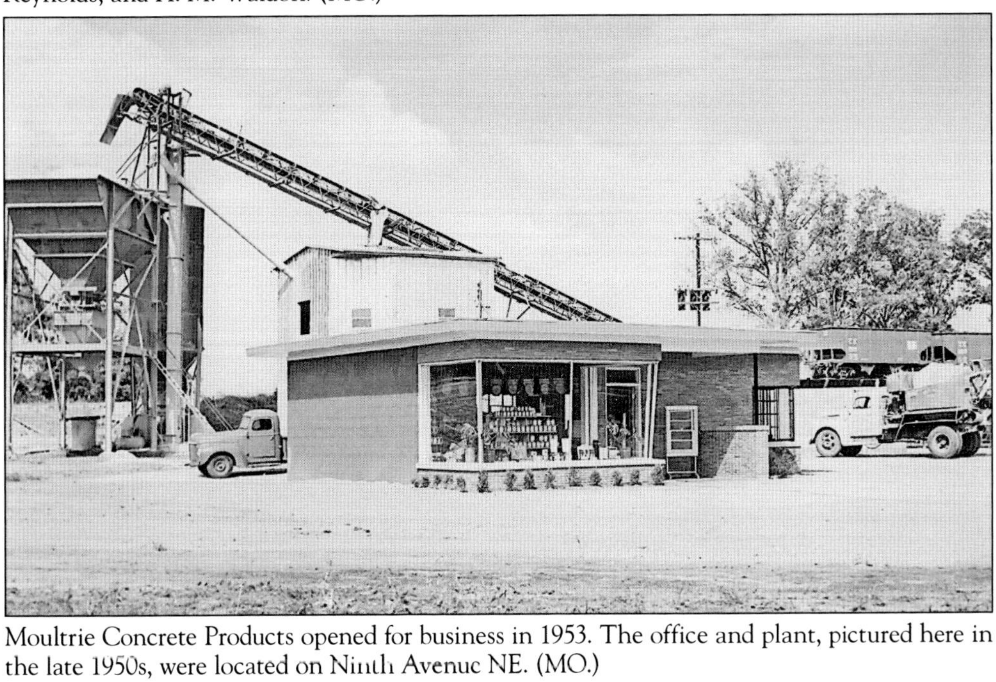

Moultrie Concrete Products opened for business in 1953. The office and plant, pictured here in the late 1950s, were located on Ninth Avenue NE. (MO.)

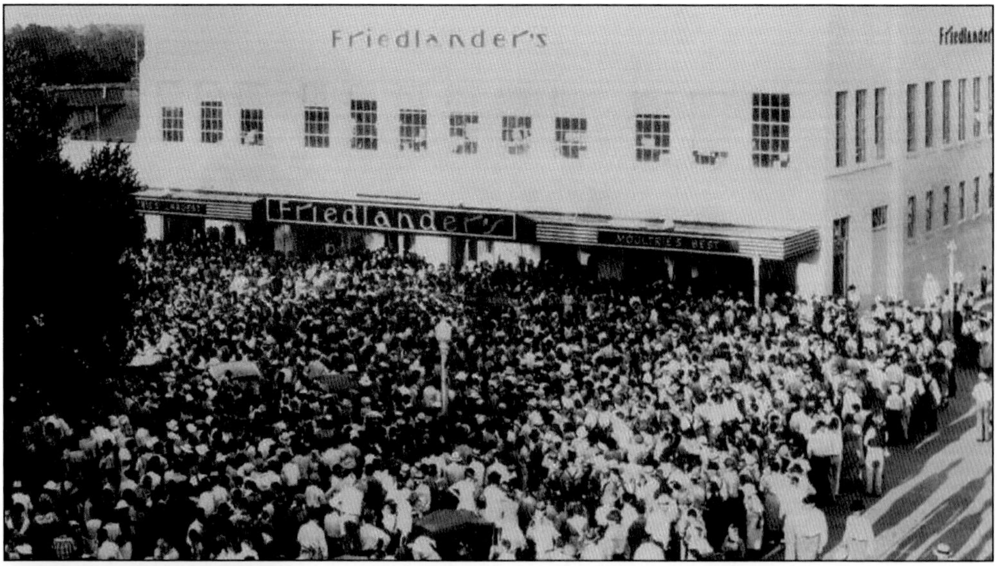

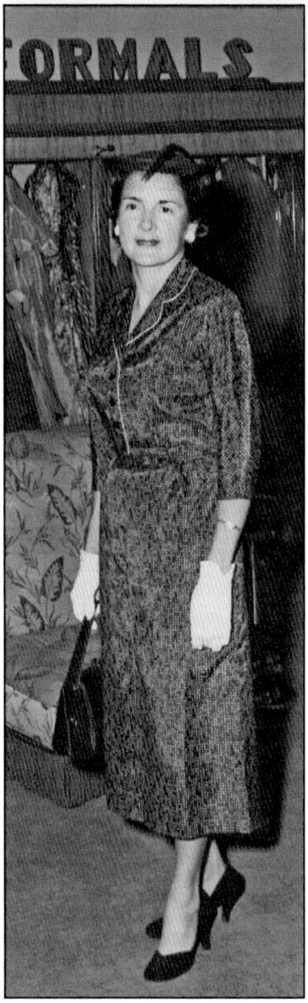

Friedlander's Department Store was founded in 1909 by Louis Friedlander. Located on the east side of the courthouse square, Friedlander's began as a small dry goods store and eventually blossomed into a chain of stores throughout South Georgia carrying a wide selection of fashion merchandise. The Moultrie store featured an open interior on the first floor with a raised mezzanine visible in the rear. An elevator, the only one in a public building in Moultrie at the time, carried shoppers to the second floor, where women's fashions and formals were sold. The photograph above shows a large crowd gathered in front of the downtown landmark building during a 1940s promotional event. The unidentified lady at the right models fashions representative of items carried in the store during the 1950s. (MSP.)

G. G. Henderson founded his business, named Henderson Furniture Company, House Furnishings, and Funeral Directors, in 1901. Although this combination of products and services seems highly unusual today, during the early days of the 20th century, it was not uncommon. Originally located on the east side of the courthouse square, Henderson moved his furniture business to the location pictured here on West Central Avenue, just one block off the square on the west side, in the 1950s. (MO.)

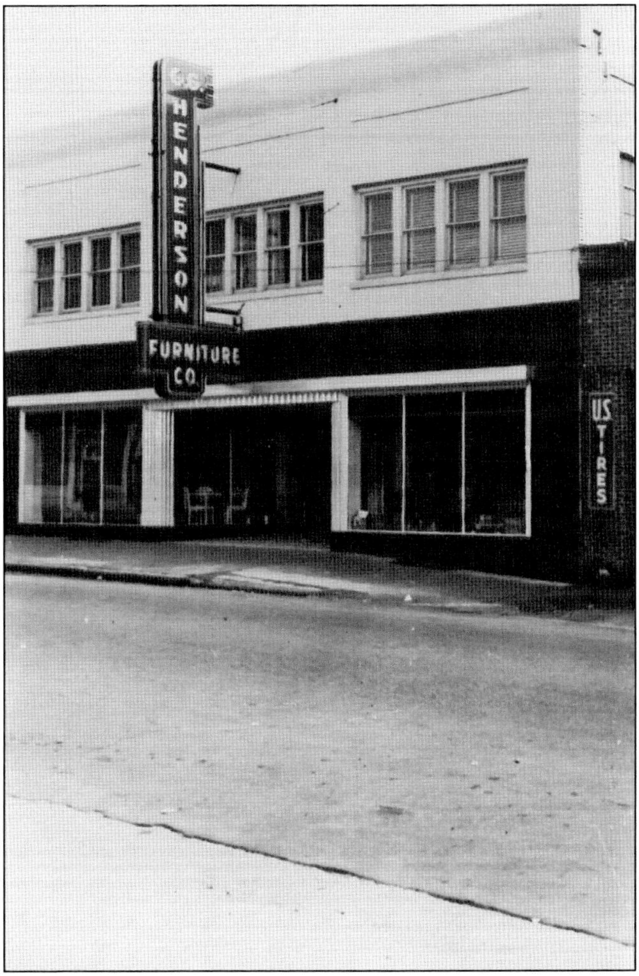

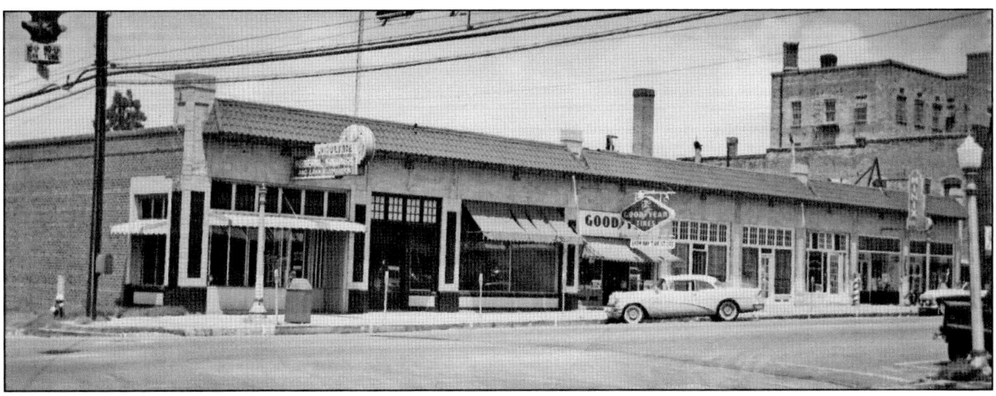

This 1950s view of Main Street shows the storefronts in the block directly south of the courthouse square. The corner business on the left was Moultrie Federal Savings and Loan. The Goodyear Tire Store can be seen in the middle of the block. To the right was a barbershop and Minix Drug Store. The combination of locally owned businesses and national franchises was common in Moultrie at an early date. In the background, the upper floors of the Commercial Building can be seen. (MO.)

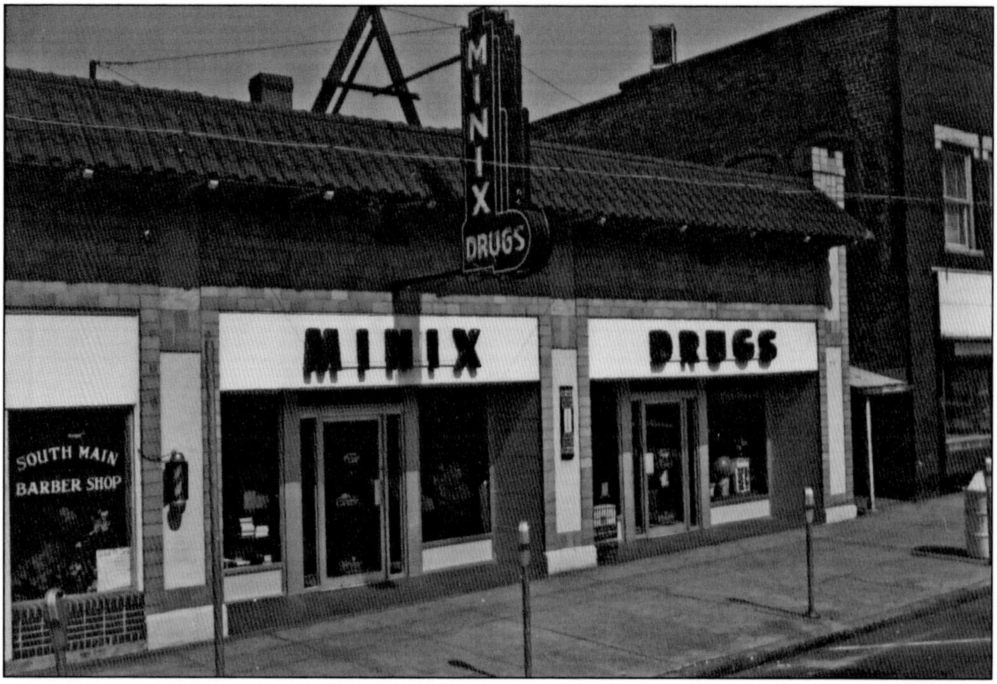

This closer view of Minix Drug Store was taken during the same time period as the photograph on the previous page and shows more detail of the storefront. There were two entrance doors and plenty of display area behind the wide expanse of front windows. The South Main Barber Shop can be seen to the left. (MO.)

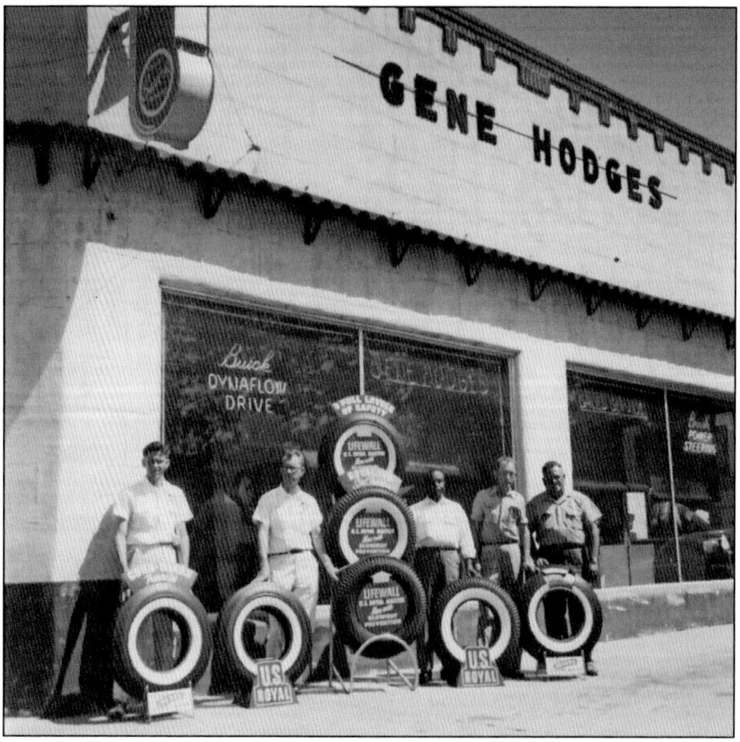

Automobiles were seen on Moultrie streets as early as 1902, but the first automobile dealership did not open until 1909. At that time only 12 to 15 vehicles were in operation in the entire county. By October 1927, one local dealership established a sales record by selling 50 new and 83 used cars in one month. This photograph, taken during the 1950s, shows unidentified employees of the Gene Hodges Buick dealership in front of the showroom on First Street SE. (MO.)

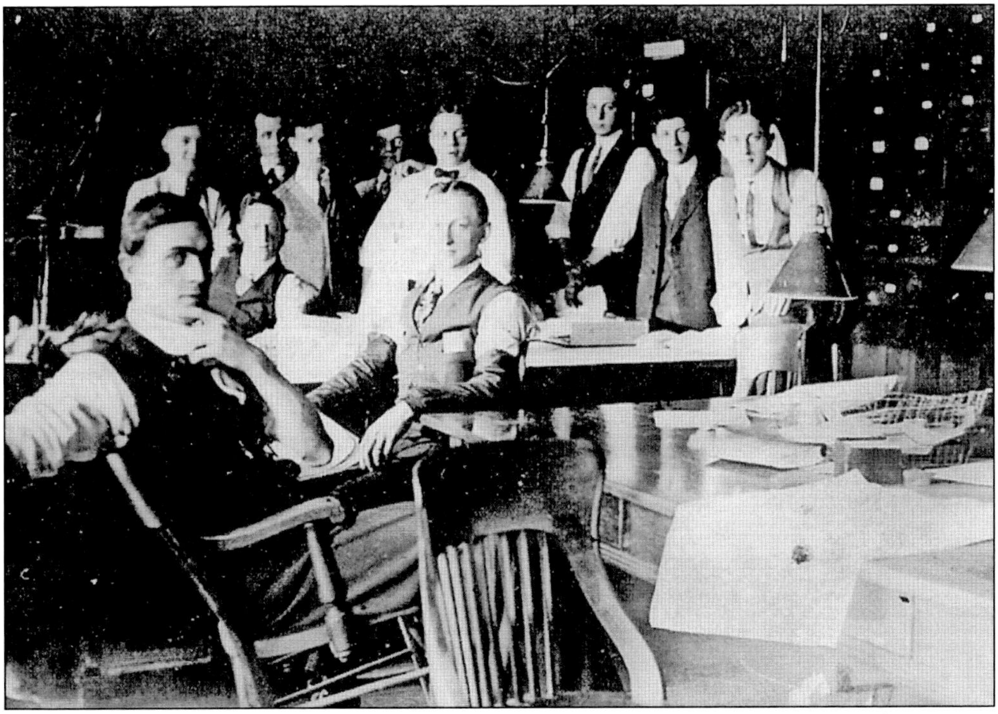

The first edition of the *Moultrie Observer*, the local newspaper, was printed on March 15, 1894. Until 1905, only a weekly edition was published. On June 19, 1905, a daily publication schedule began in addition to the weekly. The weekly edition was discontinued in December 1988. This photograph of unidentified staff members of the *Moultrie Observer* was taken in 1911. (MO.)

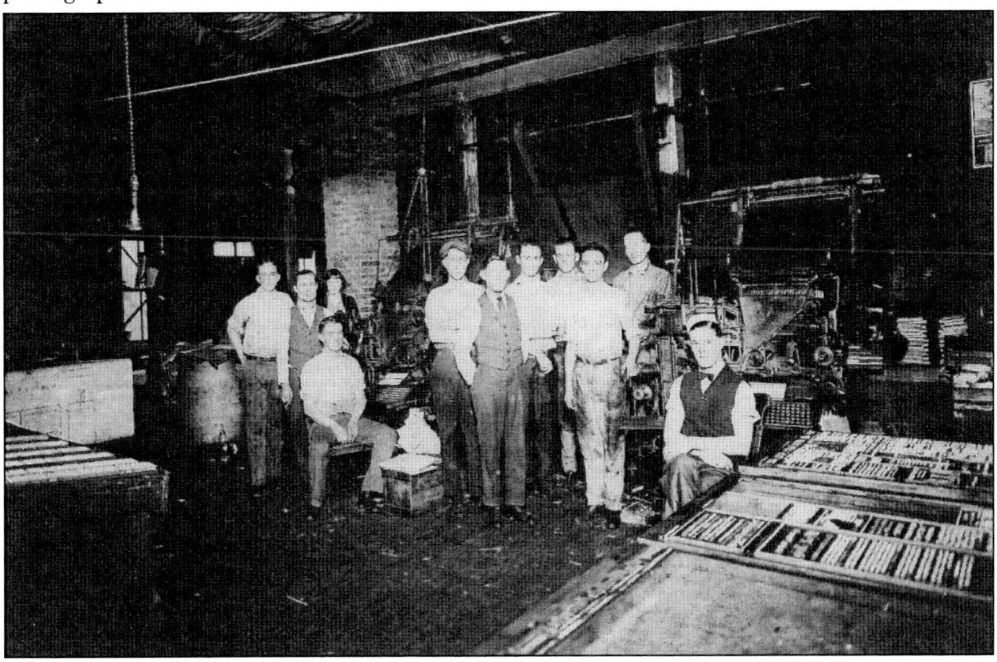

The printing press for the *Moultrie Observer* is shown in 1911. The employees of the local newspaper are unidentified. (MCCL.)

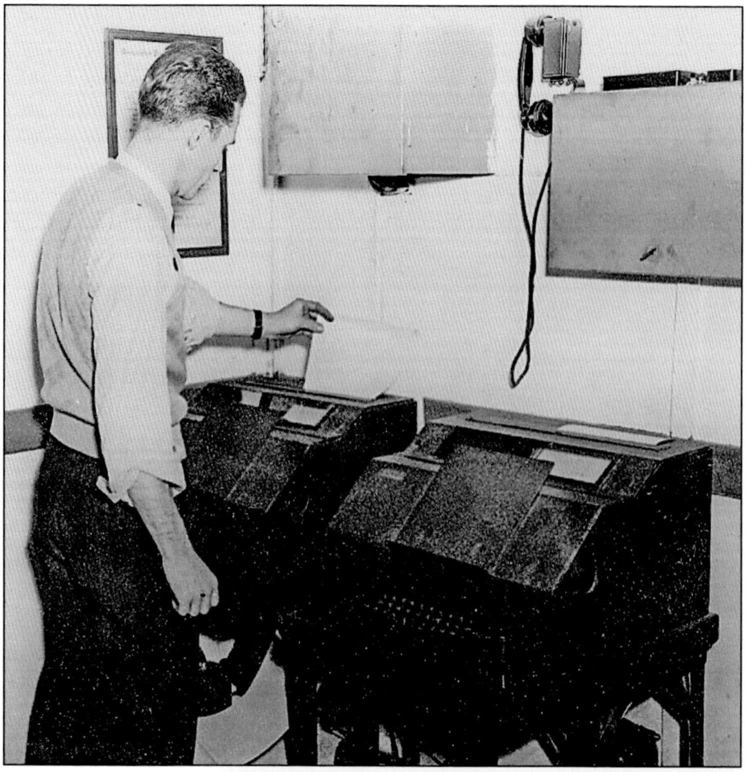

Former *Moultrie Observer* editor W. D. (Bill) Avera is shown taking copy from the Associated Press wire printer in this late-1940s photograph. (MO.)

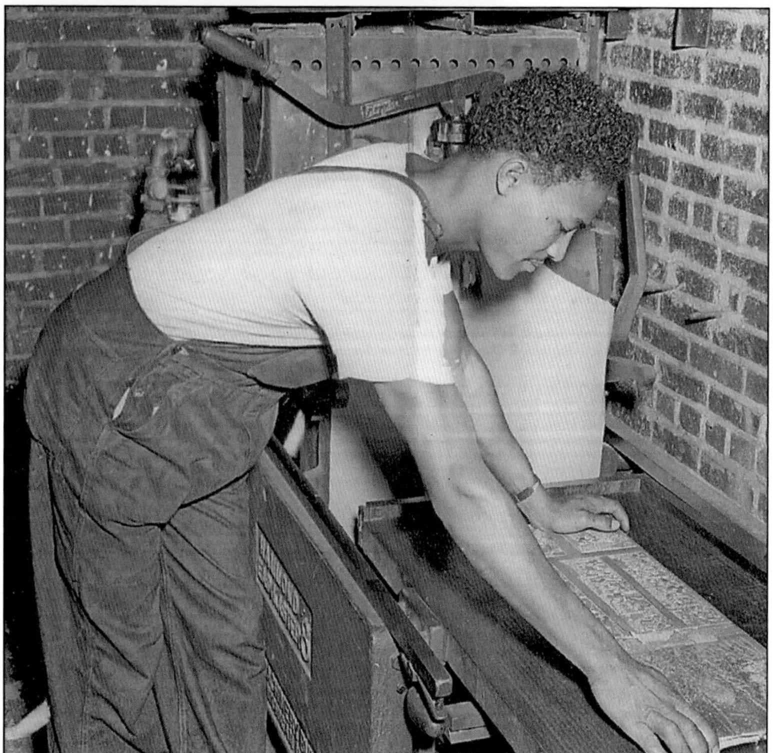

This unidentified pressman proofs a page galley of the *Moultrie Observer* before it was placed on the press for the day's run. The photograph was taken in the late 1940s. (MO.)

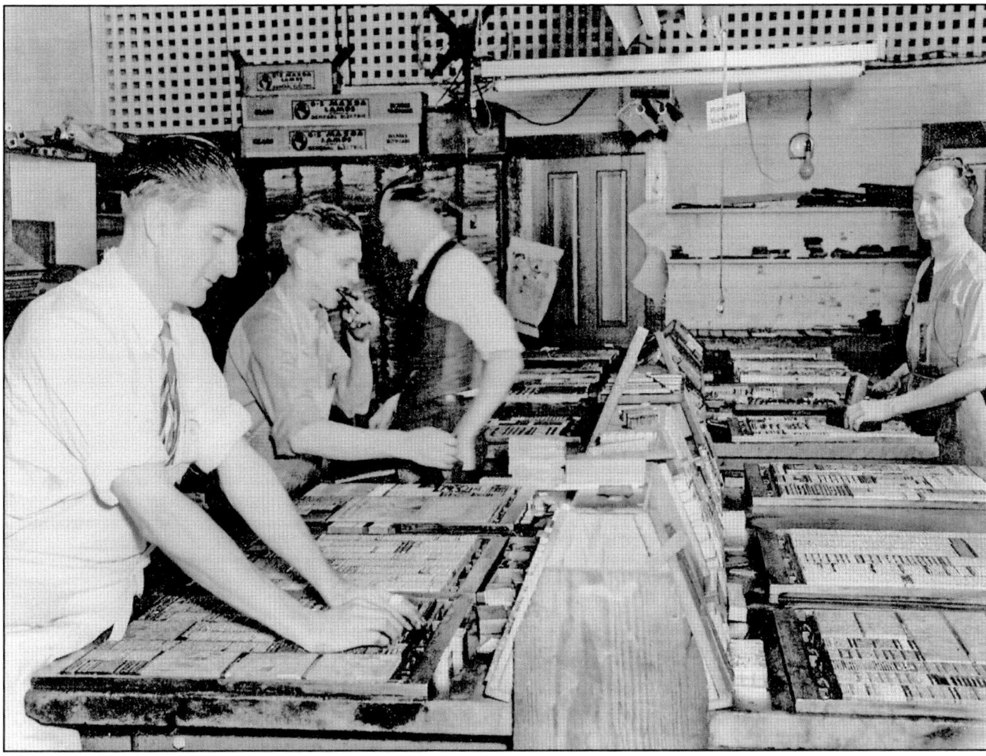

In this photograph taken during the late 1950s, unidentified typesetters for the *Moultrie Observer* are blocking the pages of an edition of the newspaper. (MO.)

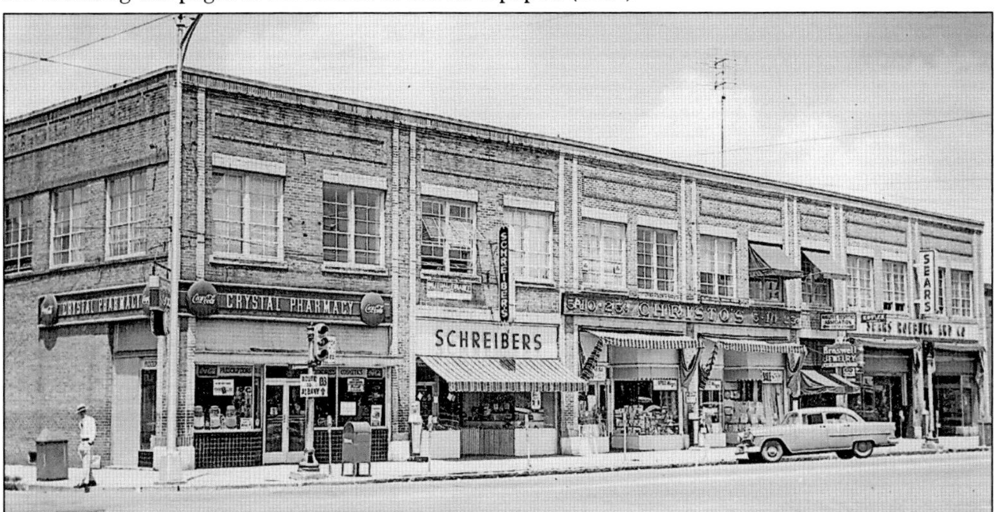

A mid-1950s view of the storefronts on the west side of the courthouse square demonstrates the variety of shopping experiences available to Moultrie residents during the period. Crystal Pharmacy, on the corner, was later moved to a location further south on Main Street and is still in operation today. Schreiber's was a men's clothing store owned by a local family. Christo's Dime Store carried a wide variety of products. Braswell's Jewelry Store, owned by a local businessman, sold and repaired jewelry and watches. Nationally known stores such as Sears Roebuck, in the middle of the block, could also be found in the downtown commercial area. (MO.)

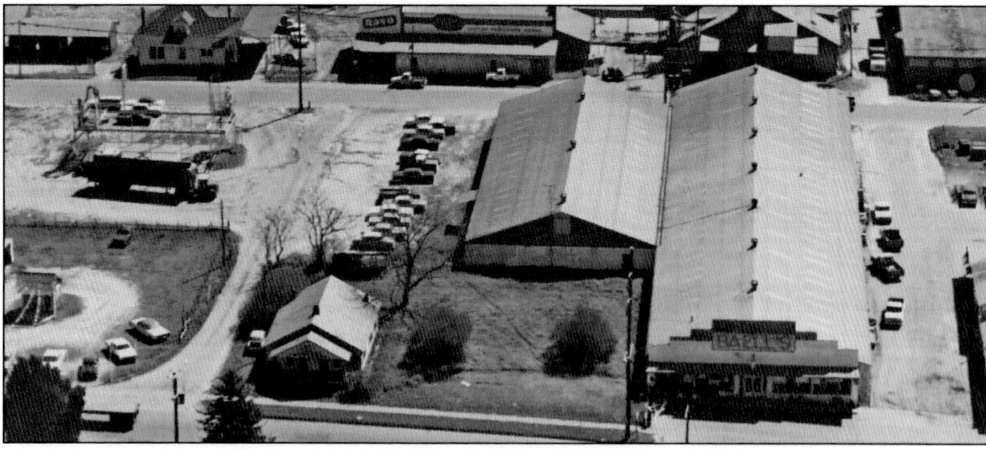

James Jesse Baell bought out an Attapulgus, Georgia, general merchandise store on January 2, 1923, and renamed it Baell Mercantile Company. The small store in a sawmill town prospered because residents shopped close to home, having few means of transportation to a larger town. However, the Great Depression radically changed the economy of South Georgia, and by 1935, the Baells realized for their business to thrive, they needed to relocate to a community with a more diversified agricultural base and a more vibrant economy. James "Sugar" Baell and his wife, Tabitha, moved to Moultrie and rented a building at 119 East Central Avenue, across the street from the Holman Mule Company. Their business grew, and in 1954, Sugar Baell built the new store pictured here at 550 First Street NE. Ravo Peanut Oil Company can bee seen behind Baell Mercantile. (MCCL.)

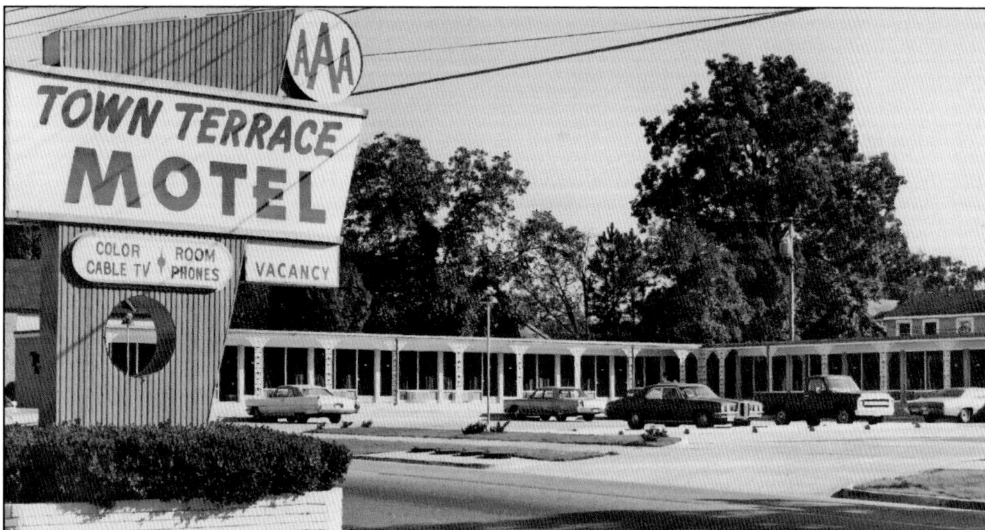

Forty new motel units were added to the public accommodations of Colquitt County when the Town Terrace Motel was built in 1954 on South Main Street. Shown in the 1970s, the Town Terrace was the first motel built in the county. It boasted color cable television, room telephones, and a pool. In 1970, thirty new units were added. These units were factory manufactured and placed on site for completion. C. O. Smith Industries, a mobile home manufacturing company that opened in Moultrie in 1969, manufactured the units at their Modular Structures Division of Peachtree Housing. This is an excellent example of a locally produced product being used to solve local needs. (MCCL.)

Four

EDUCATION

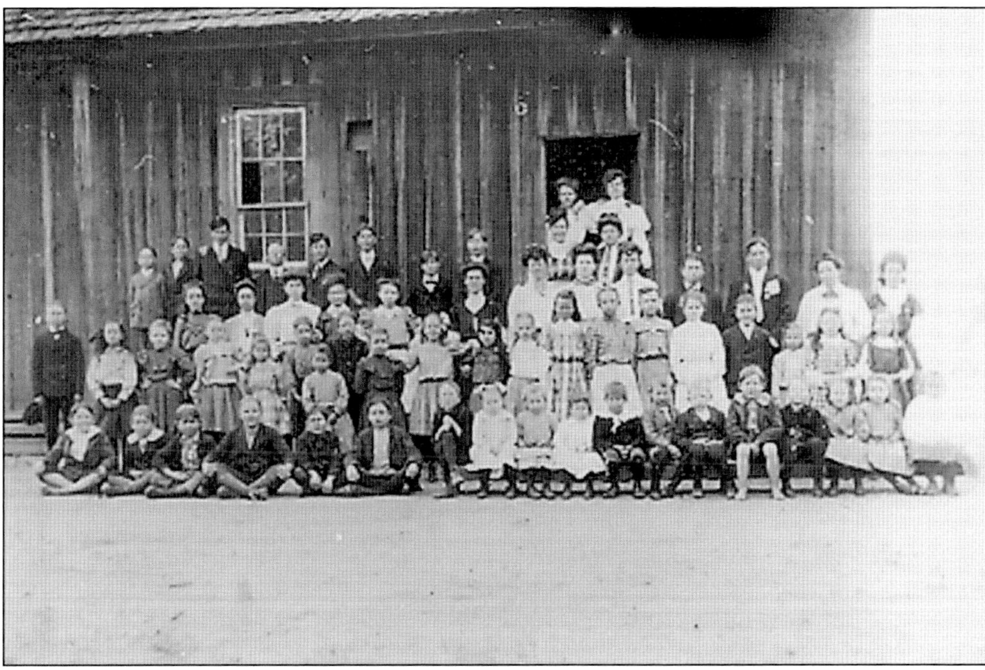

Prior to the 1920s, the education of rural children was not presented in an organized or equal manner. With no centralized governing body to provide for uniform education, each community was responsible for the educational opportunities afforded to its children. Most schools were one-room buildings where children of all ages were taught by one professor or "school marm." The upkeep of the buildings, salaries of the teachers, and learning materials were all financed by those in the community who were financially able to contribute. Wealthier communities built more comfortable school buildings and provided better salaries for the teachers. However, most rural schools were always in jeopardy of closing because of the shortfall of operating funds. This unidentified rural school in Colquitt County was typical of those found in the area around 1900. (MO.)

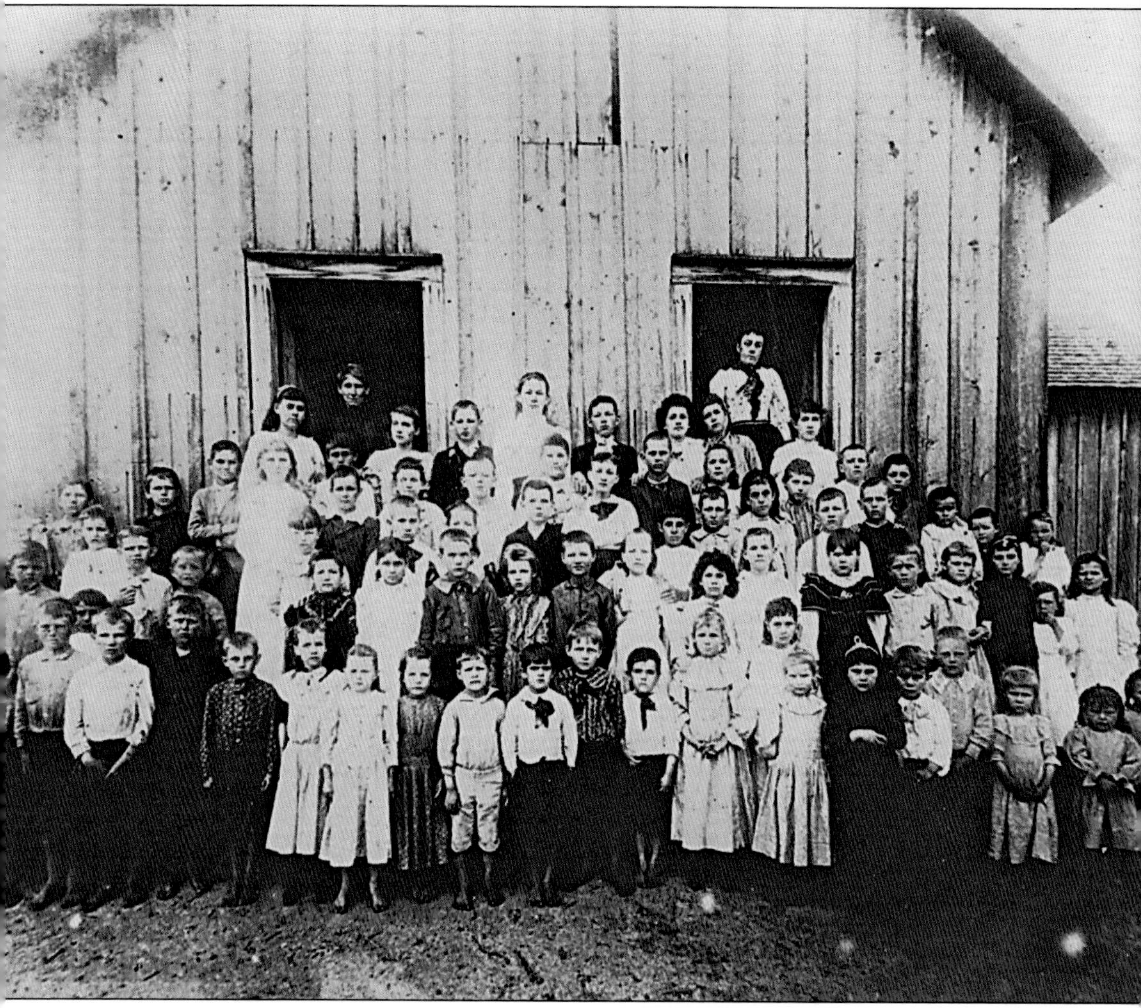

This photograph of the student body and teachers of the Collegiate Institute, the predecessor of the Moultrie Public School System, was taken in 1895 in front of the city's first school building. Prior to this time, classes met in churches, homes, and log cabins. Ellen McNeill was a teacher at the school, and Mamie McFadden was the assistant principal. Students at the school included Edith Boswell, W. T. Blanton, Abner Suber, Bessie Daniel, Bessie Boswell, Georgia Millsap, Lydia Whitley, Richard Millsap, Estelle Campbell, W. J. Vereen, Hattie Holmes, Cora Daniel, Willie Gregory, Nona Smith, Jimmie Hall, Jess Thomas, Brye Thomas, John Duggan, Tommie Hall, Wilson Millsap, Gart Anderson, Amos Faison, Maggie Blanton, Bobbie Melton, Max Webb, and Jim Holmes. (MO.)

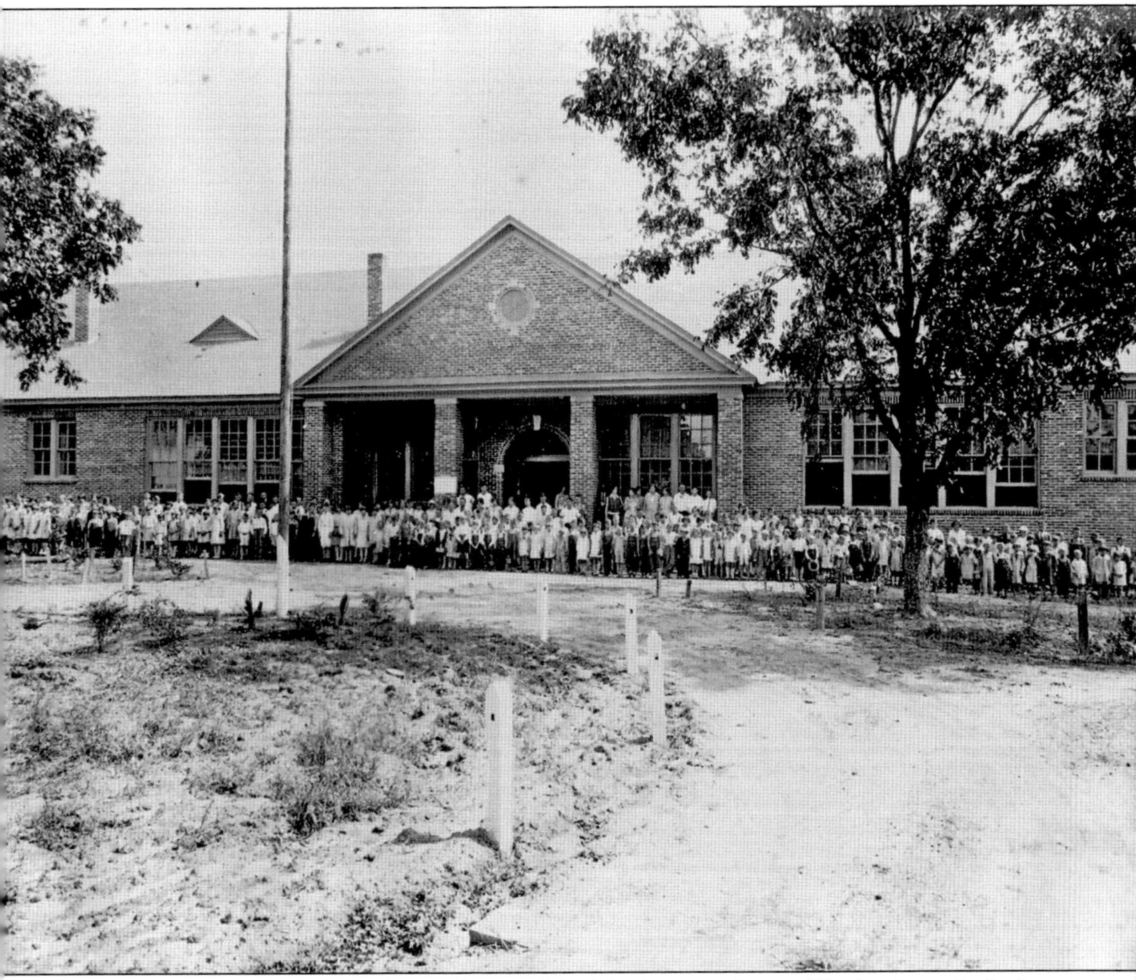

Okapilco School is located 5 miles northwest of the Moultrie city limits. The land on which the building sits was secured from Dr. C. G. Watson and had previously been used for agricultural purposes. Swift and Company donated $60,000 toward the building program, and construction was completed in 1927. This photograph shows the student body assembled in front of the school in 1927. (MO.)

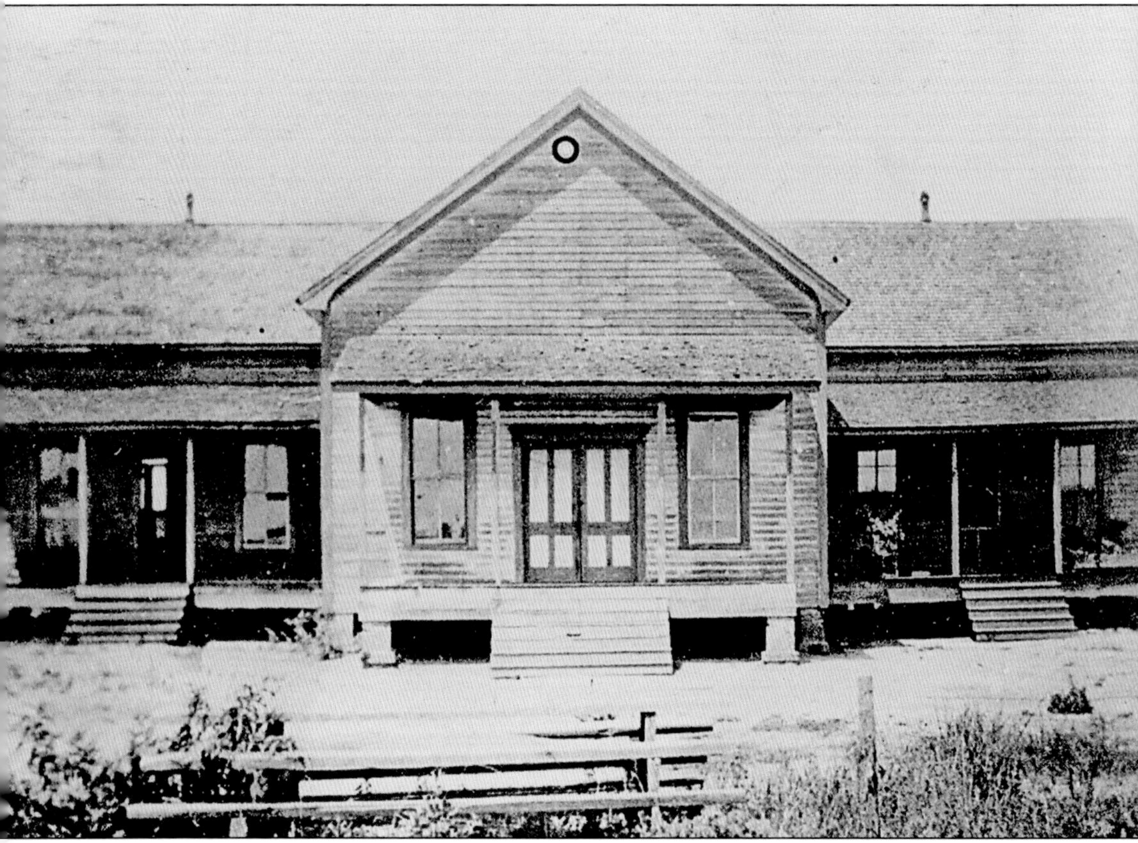

Rocky Ford School was a three-room school and employed three teachers, unlike most of the other rural schools in the county, which had only one room and one teacher. The students shared the duties necessary for the operation of the school by sweeping the floors, drawing water from the well, and building a fire in a potbellied stove with wood carried from home. This building was no longer used when Rocky Ford School consolidated with Okapilco in 1927. Part of the original building remains in use today as a private residence. (MO.)

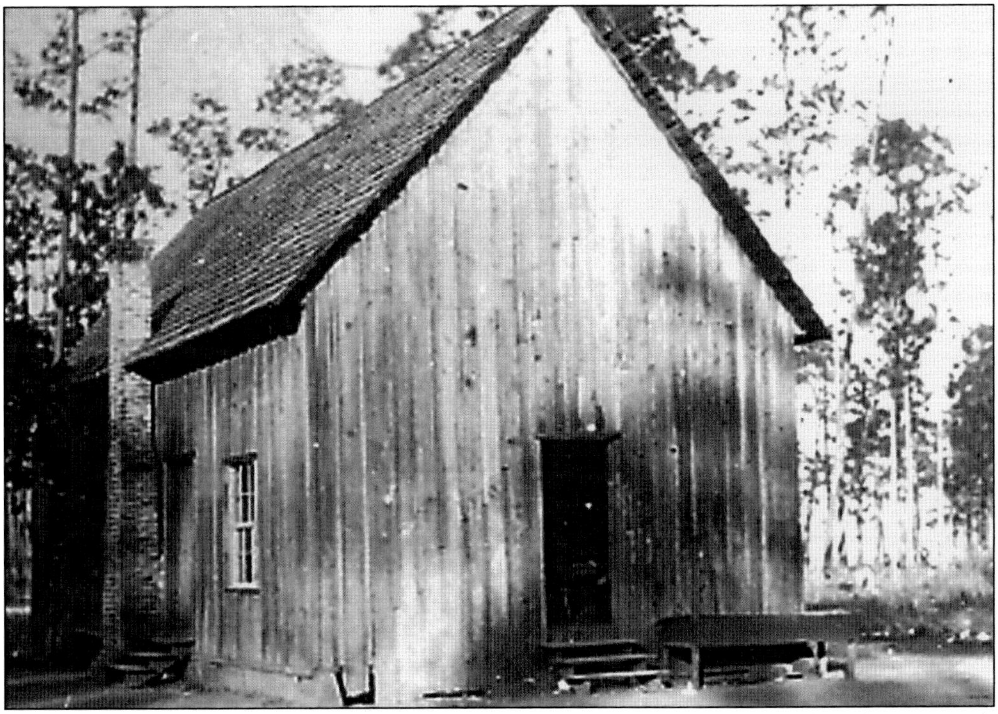

Rose Hill Community is located in the western part of Colquitt County on the Thigpen Trail. The first school in the community was a one-room subscription school named Collier–Rose Hill, pictured above. The students sat on backless benches on opposites sides of the room for their lessons and also played in separate areas outside. In the early 1900s, Collier School was consolidated with McNeil School and was moved into the larger building below. The students lined up each morning at the start of the school day and marched single file to the church for morning prayers. They marched back to the schoolhouse for classes. (Both, MO.)

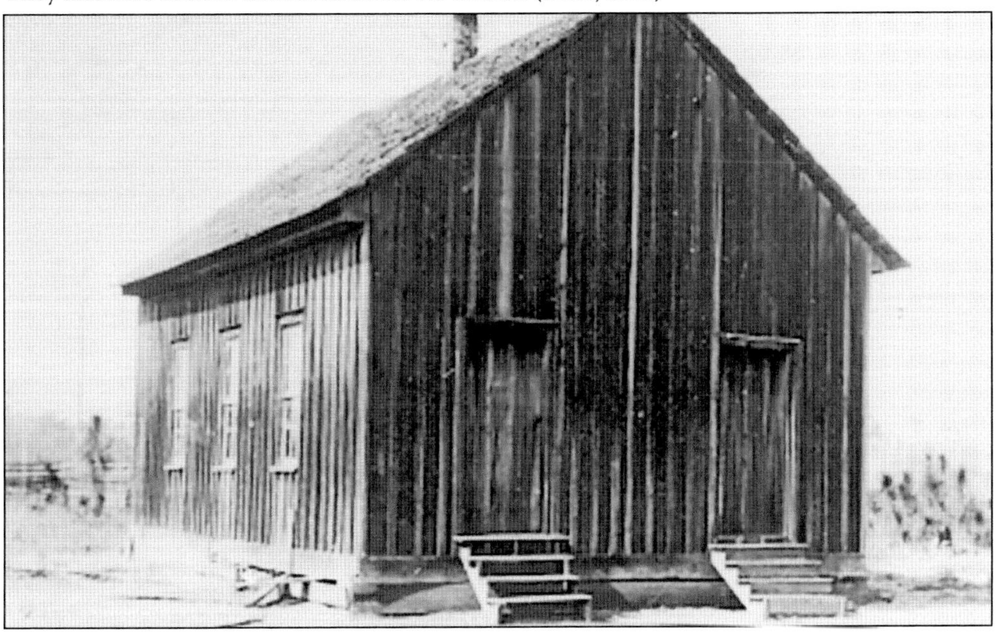

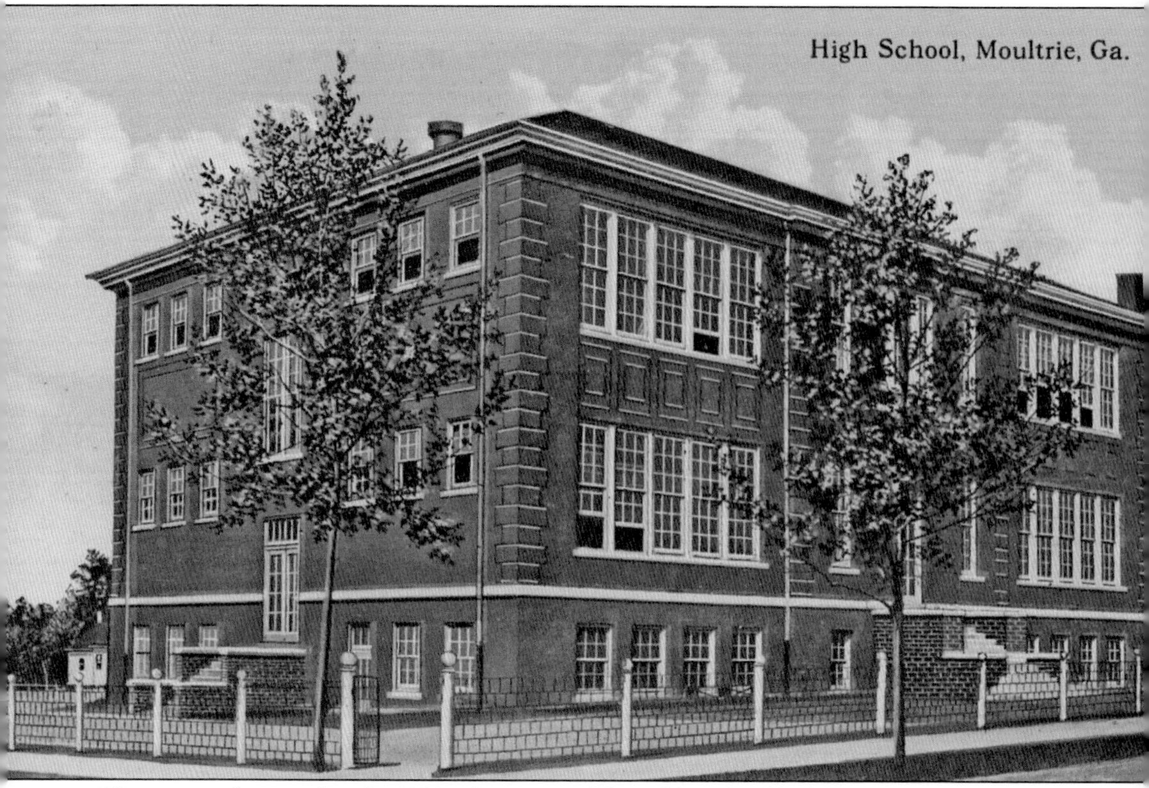

This postcard, printed in the 1930s, shows one of the public school buildings within the city limits of Moultrie. This is in stark contrast to the one-story wooden school buildings located throughout the rural areas of the county. (APP.)

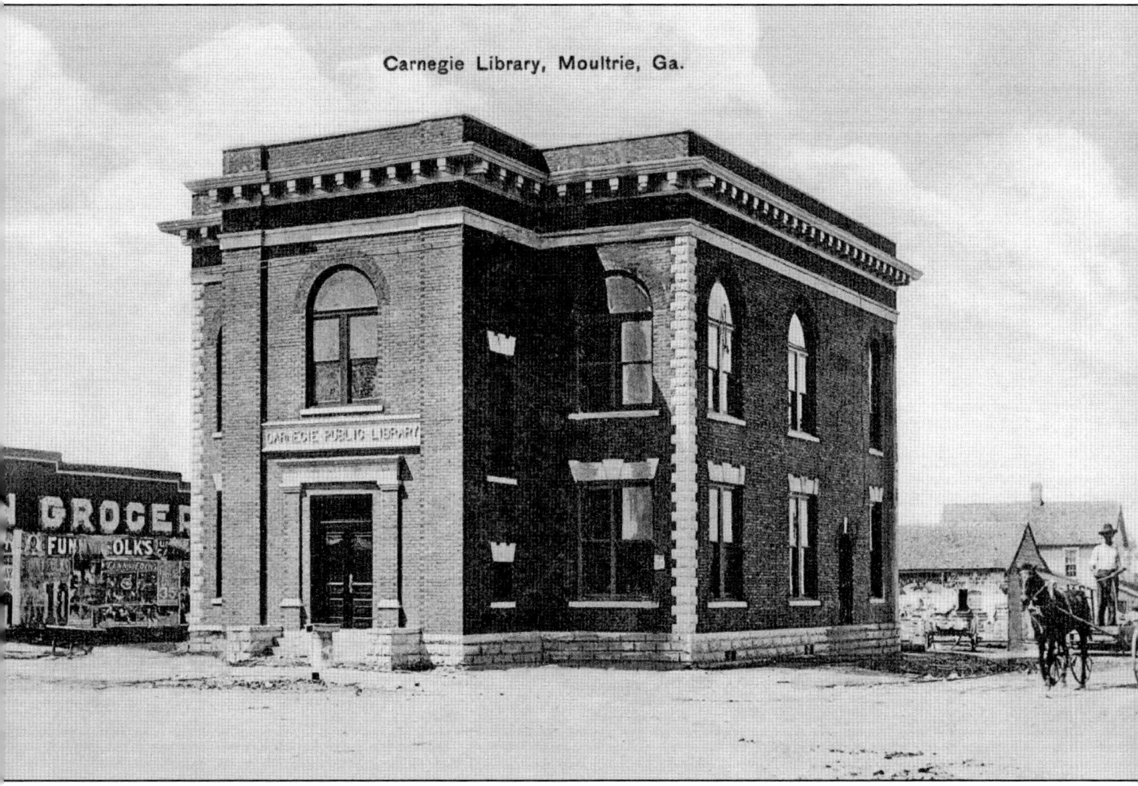

The Carnegie Library, shown in 1908, was established on January 1, 1907, when the first board of managers was appointed. C. B. Allen, C. W. Pidcock, W. H. Barber, W. C. Vereen Jr., E. Howell, J. B. Norman Jr., J. F. Monk, W. A. Covington, and Z. H. Clark were the appointees. Howell, the commissioner of schools for the county, had convinced Andrew Carnegie that the economy and population of Colquitt County would support a library. The building was formally opened on May 29, 1908, and was located at the corner of Main Street and First Avenue NW. Jennie McKenzie, wife of W. C. McKenzie, was the first librarian. (APP.)

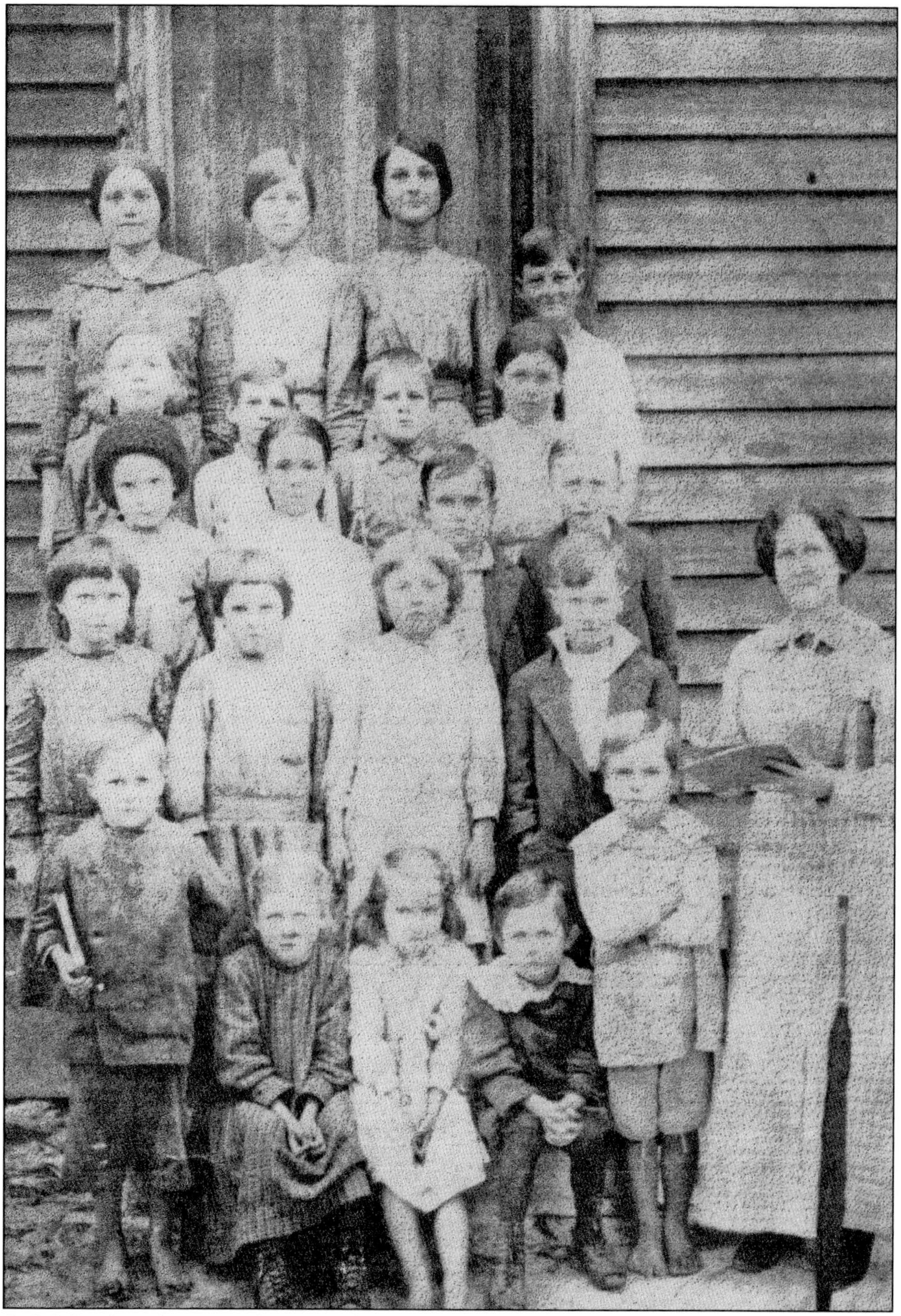

Bethel School students are shown in this photograph, taken in 1916 or 1917. From left to right are (first row) Irvin Howell, Clyde Cooper, Eva Massey, Irban Alligood, Hoke Stanaland, and teacher Georgia Jenkins; (second row) Grace Stanaland, Marie Cooper, Rossie Alligood, and Howard Massey; (third row) Ida Belle Howell, unidentified, Austin Howell, and Wiley Thelmer Vinson; (fourth row) Dewey Alligood, Clifford Cooper, Charlie Cooper, and unidentified; (fifth row) Annie Alligood, Louell Cooper, Edna Lloyd, and Carl Lloyd. (MO.)

Nancy Ethel Adams, pictured here in 1936, came to Moultrie in 1905 to take charge of a fifth-grade class whose teacher had resigned. Adams served the school system for 51 years—longer than any other educator—as a teacher, principal, and guidance counselor. She served as the high school principal from 1924 until 1950. (MSP.)

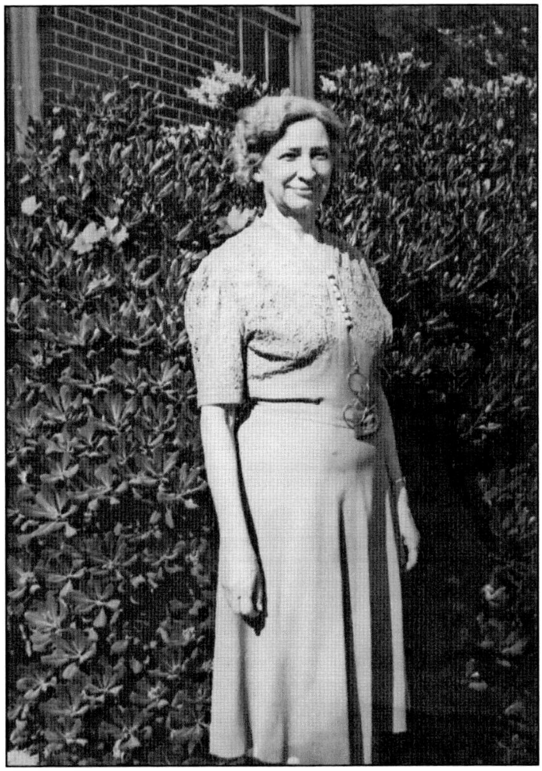

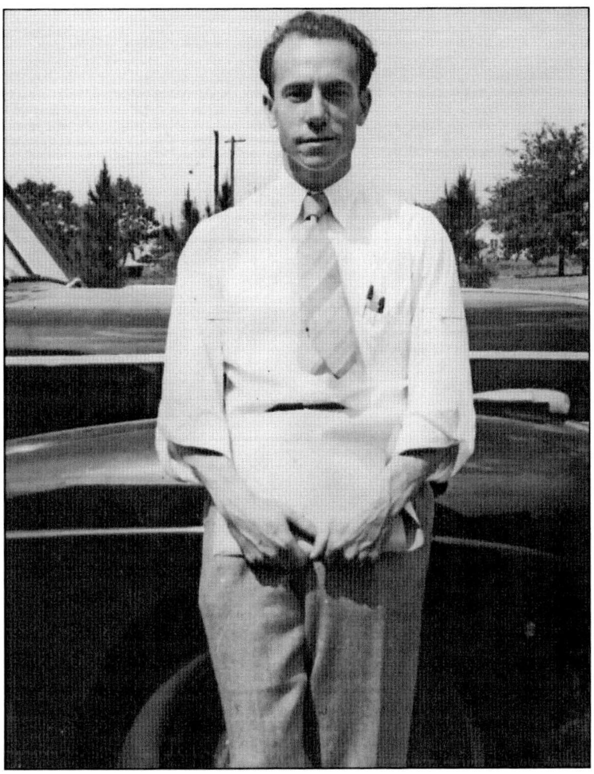

J. G. Thomas, pictured in 1938, was the agricultural instructor at Moultrie High School for several years. (MCCL.)

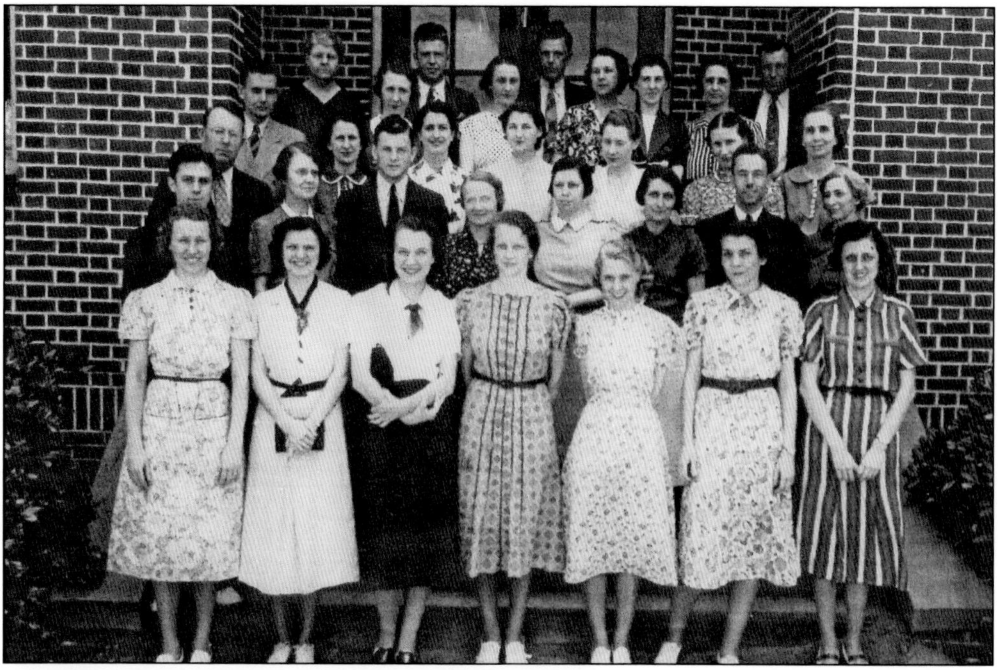

The faculty of Moultrie High School is shown on the steps of the school during the 1938–1939 school year. From left to right are (first row) Adrian Wills, Catherine Mallory, Myra Jenkins, Floy Simpson, Florence Knight, Marion Thorpe, and Harriet Wright; (second row) Thomas Mahler, Erin McMechan, A. T. Dorminey, Bessie Sanford, Gladys Espy, Ethel Parrish, J. G. Thomas, and Ethel Adams; (third row) W. H. Moseley, Eleanor Pryor, Eugenia Whirehead, Ella Levie, Cooper Bell, Juanita Miles, and Louise Brown; (fourth row) Ralph Head, Mary Waldrop, Juanita Clements, Winifred Rogers, Virginia Kirkland, Annie Belle Rion, and Grant Gillis; (fifth row) Margaret Ragan, Huey Murphy, and C. H. (Pop) Jennison. (MCCL.)

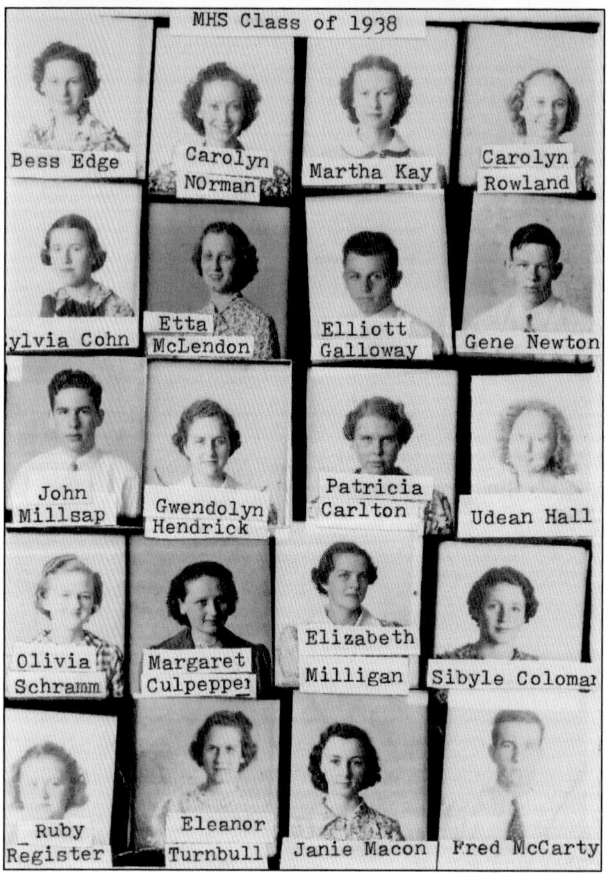

Members of the graduating class of Moultrie High School in 1938 are pictured with their names below each student. (MCCL.)

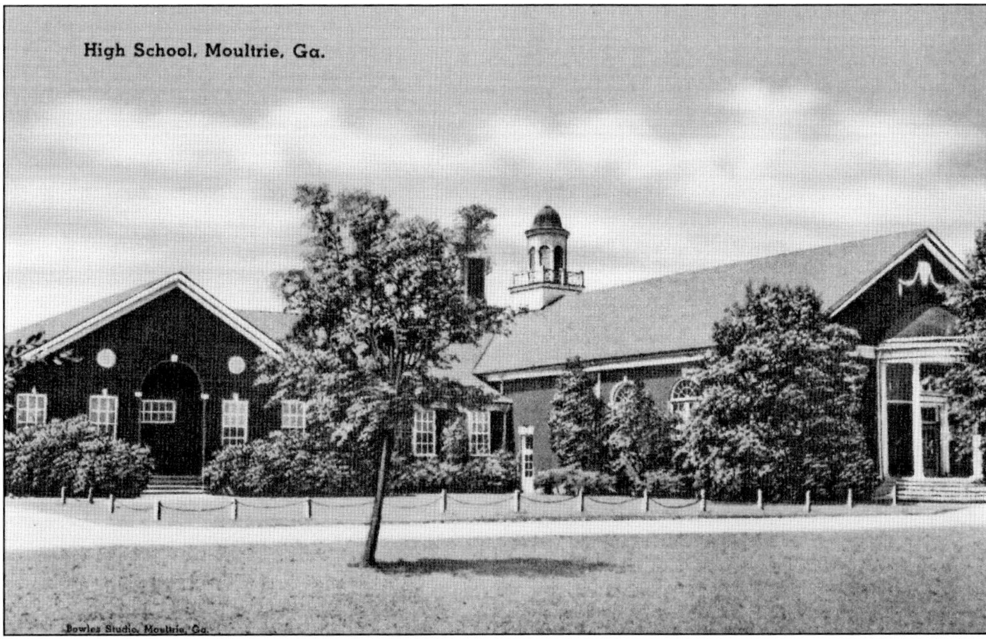

The postcard above, printed in the 1930s, shows Moultrie High School, which was built in 1925. Featuring an auditorium (the section of the building to the foreground under the cupola) with stage and theater seating, classrooms, a library, and administrative offices, the building served a variety of purposes over the years. A new high school was constructed in the 1960s, and this building was used to house the junior high school until 1977. At that time, the title to the building was given to the Moultrie Service League, and a fine arts center was established. It is still used for that purpose. The 1930s aerial view of the high school below shows the entire campus, which included a gymnasium at the rear of the campus and several tennis courts. (Both, APP.)

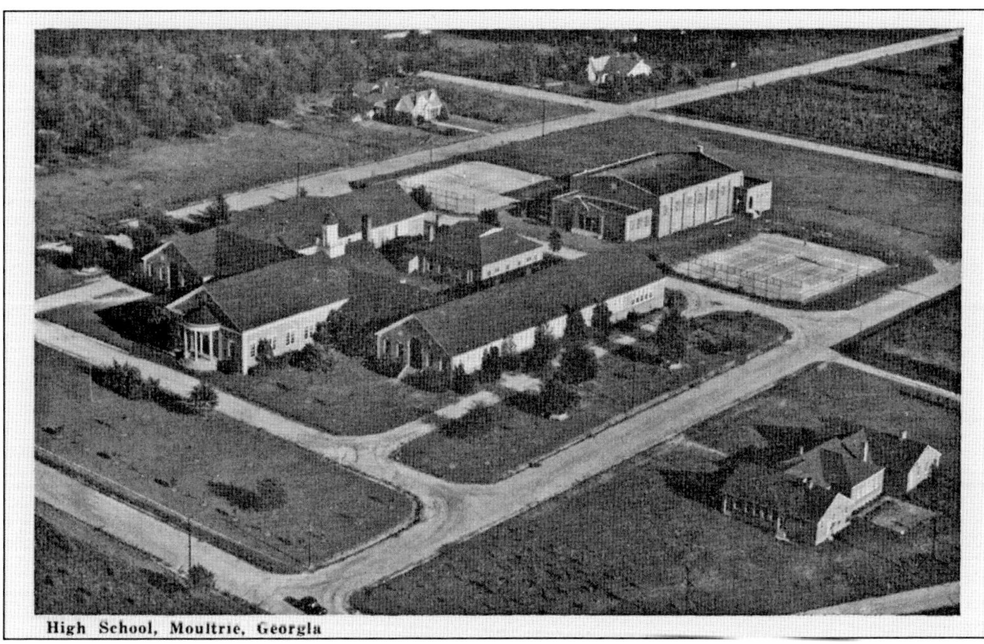

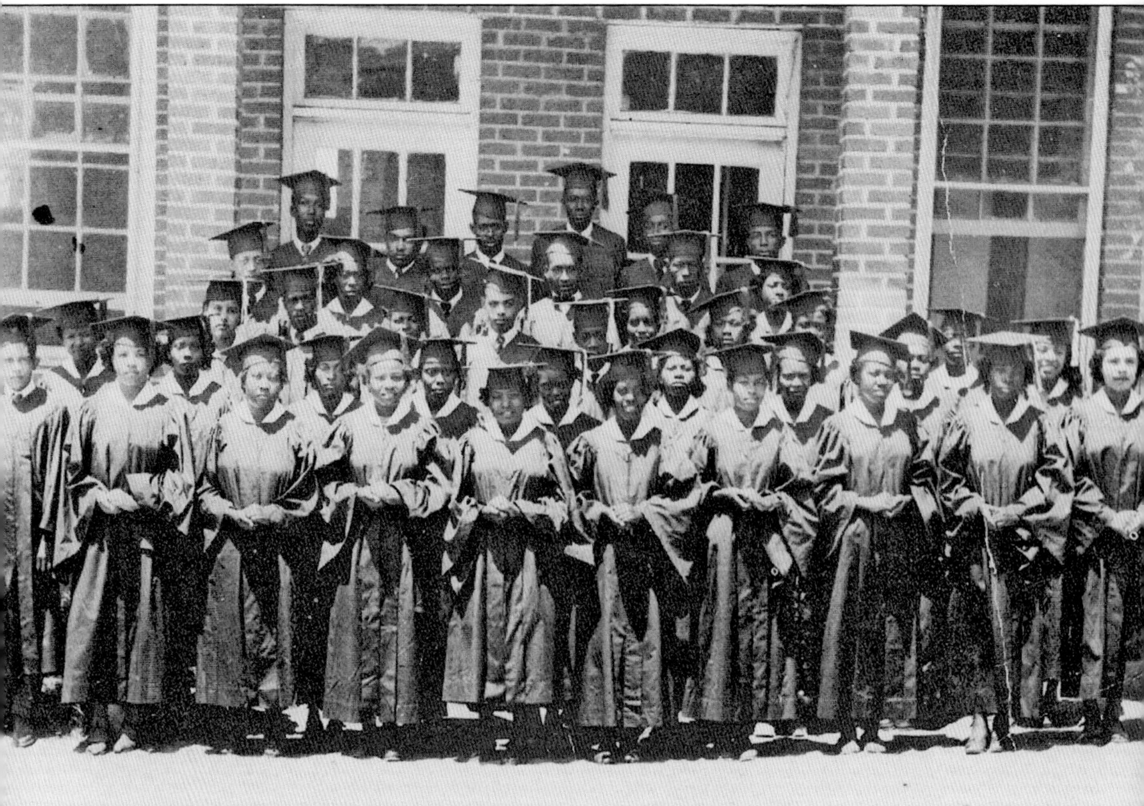

At the beginning of the 20th century, black children in Moultrie were usually educated in churches or homes. In 1907, the CME church operated a private school for African American children in the northwest section of Moultrie. In 1920, a new school was built at Seventh Street and Third Avenue NW and was named for William Bryant, a principal in one of the black schools. This building burned in 1925 and was rebuilt in 1926. A new high school was completed in 1938 and remained in operation until desegregation occurred in 1964. This photograph shows the graduating class of William Bryant High School in 1947. (MO.)

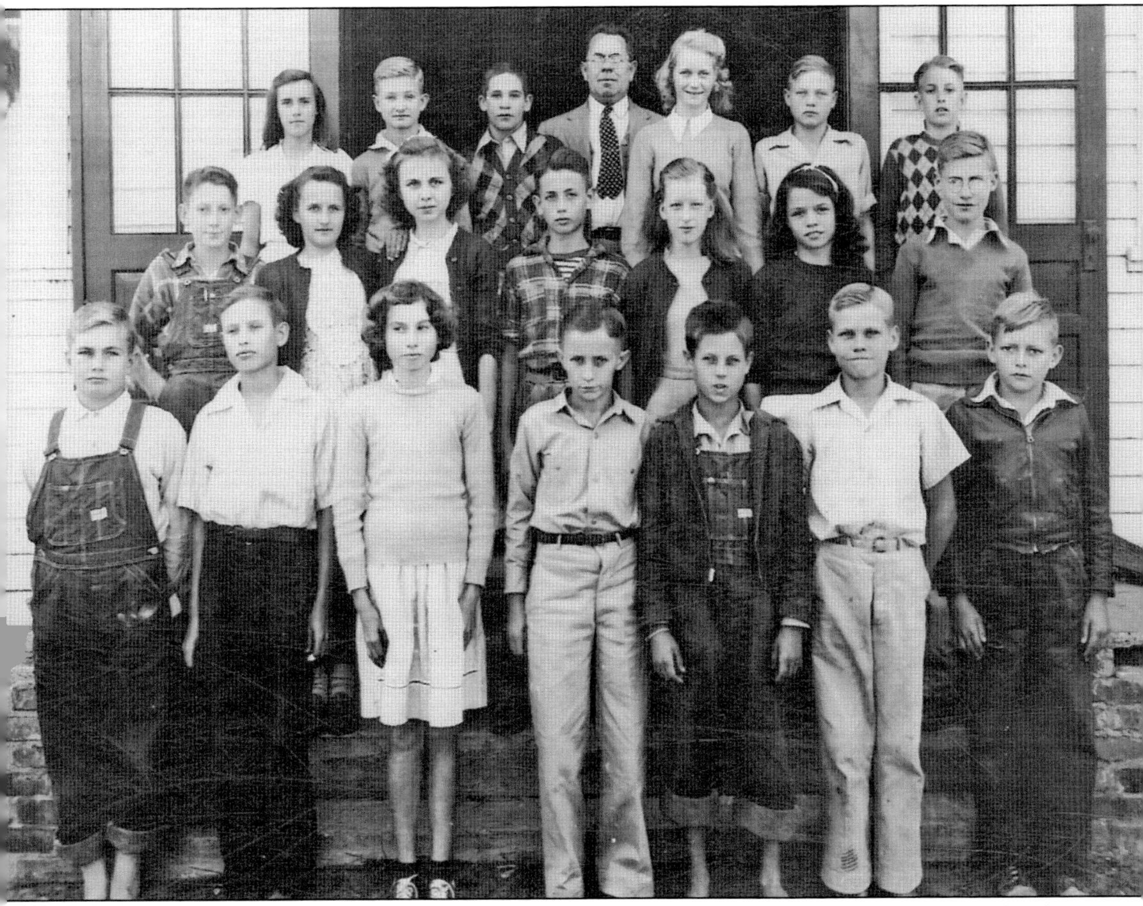

This photograph shows the seventh-grade class of Sunset School during the 1945–1946 school year. Pictured from left to right are (first row) Thomas Williams, David Green, Zetra Carden, Johnny Motley, Donald Harper, Frank Flowers, and Raiford Flowers; (second row) Thurl Smith, Gatha Cooper, Margie Lewis, Gene Ellington, Sylvia Murphy, Alma Curls, and Fred Giles; (third row) Mary Elizabeth Gray, Darol Horne, Hugh Don Ohern, Mr. Rooks (the principal and seventh-grade teacher), Bessie Lee Wilson, Robert Nix, and Lamar Goff. (MCCL.)

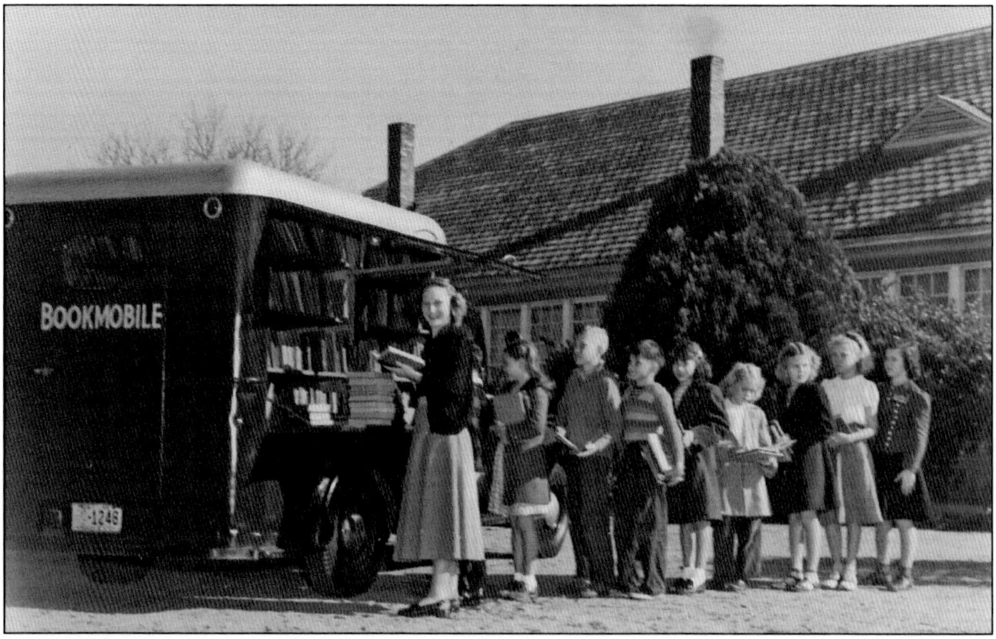

In the 1940s, the library staff realized that children and adults in the rural areas wanted library services. Because money was in short supply and building libraries in communities around the county was too costly, bookmobile service was started. These small vans would carry the library to citizens in the county so that they could enjoy the same services as city residents. In this photograph, taken on December 10, 1948, Catherine M. Bryant, bookmobile driver, is shown with a group of children at Okapilco School. The children standing in line are, from left to right, Joe Ellis, Othelle Hall, Wayman Walker, Charlie Prince, Betty Fay Jones, Peggy Alderman, Elizabeth Rossman, Iris Bell, and Marie Jones. (MCCL.)

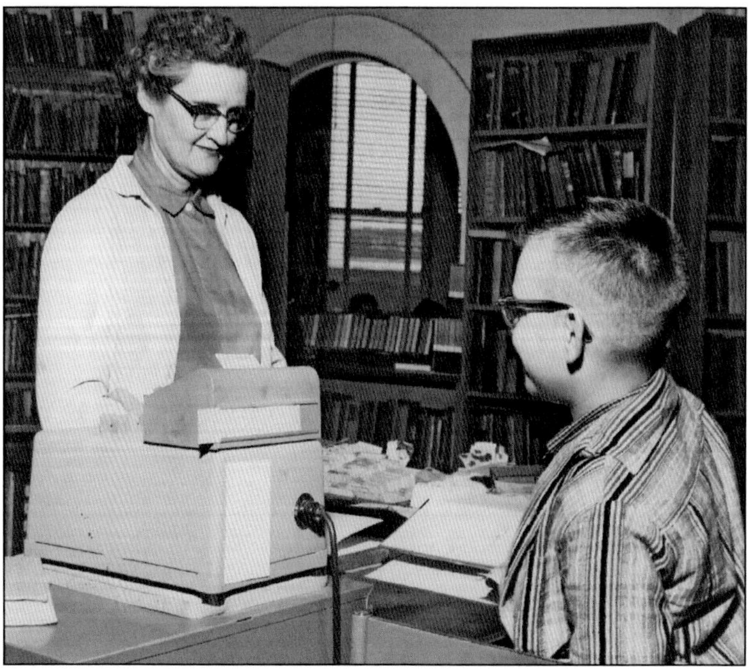

In the 1950s, librarians struggled to keep up with nationally accepted library standards of service. Budgets for the library had not expanded to keep up with the expanding use of materials and services. Library director Anna E. Schinkel used all of her energy and creativity to procure needed funds. In this October 1959 photograph, Hazel Wade checks books out for an unidentified young patron. (MCCL.)

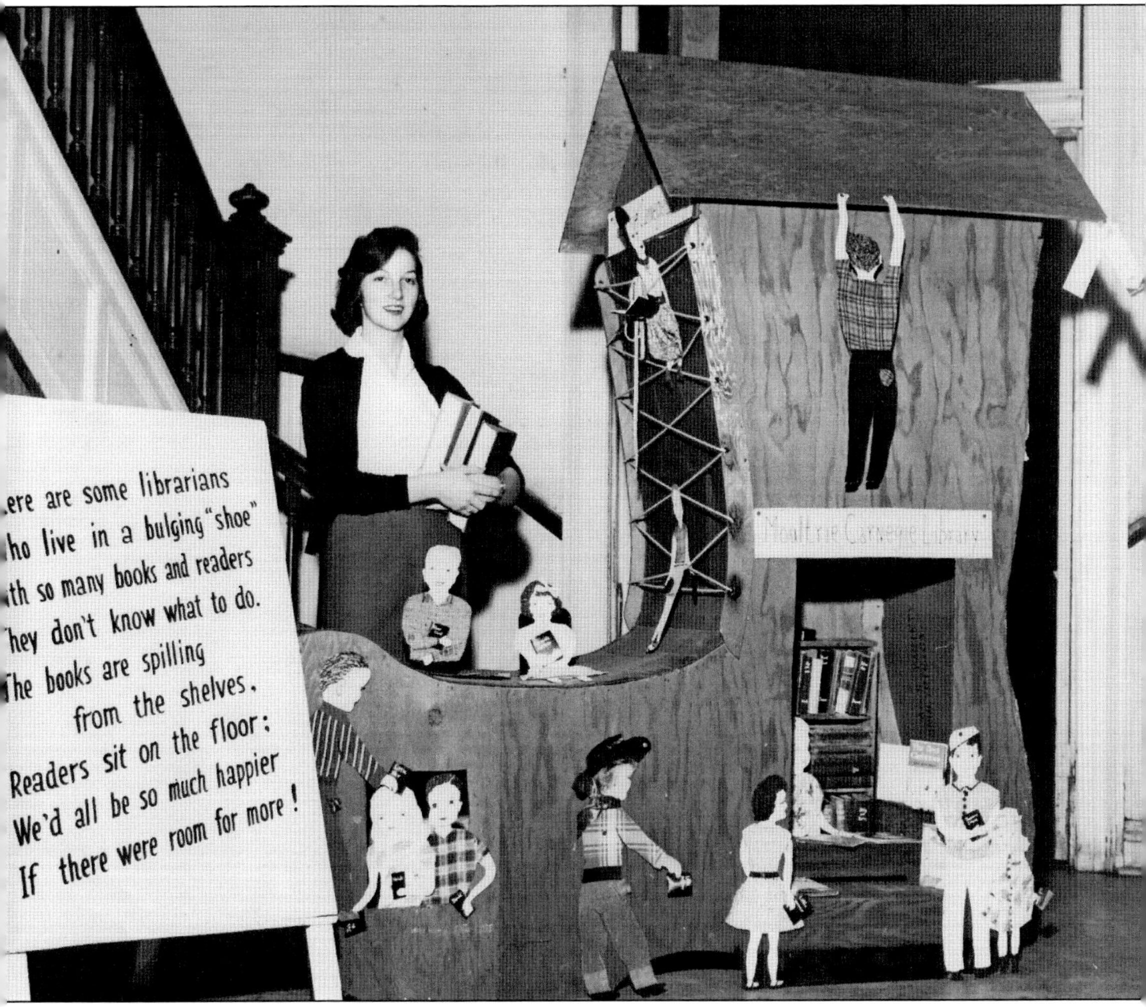

By 1960, when this photograph was taken in the entrance hall of the Carnegie Library, the library was experiencing problems in many areas of service. The interior space of the library was not adequate to serve the ever-expanding number of patrons. The roof was in disrepair, so much so that library staff members held umbrellas over the bookshelves during rainstorms to protect the books. Anna Schinkel and library board members spoke at many civic and church meetings to make the citizens aware of the problems and gain support for additional funds. Here Carolyn Railey, the student library assistant, poses by an exhibit comparing the problems at the library to the problems of the old lady who lived in a shoe. The exhibit was used at the county fair to gain the support of residents. (MCCL.)

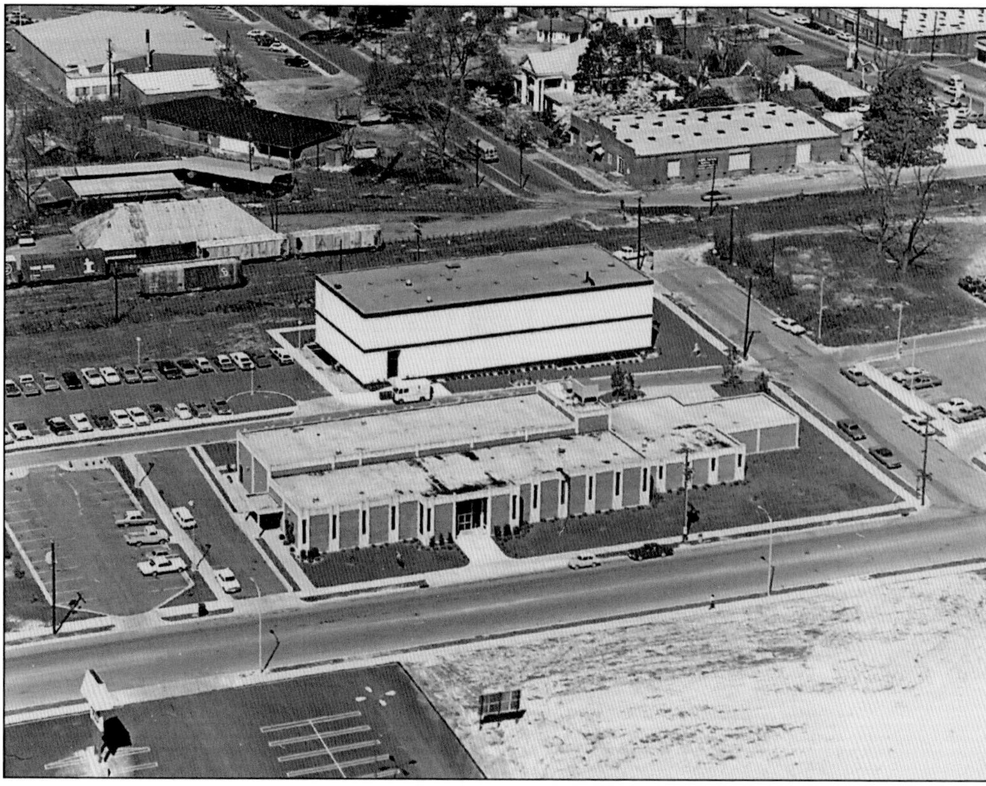

In 1963, the citizens of Colquitt County passed a bond issue to raise matching funds for a federal grant to build a new library. The new building, shown above shortly after opening, was completed in 1965. Located on Fifth Street SE, the Moultrie–Colquitt County Library contained 17,500 square feet of serviceable area to more adequately serve patrons. The building was designed by local architect William Frank McCall and was built by contractor Paul Summerford at a cost of $250,000. The photograph below shows the interior of the new library at its opening. (Both, MCCL.)

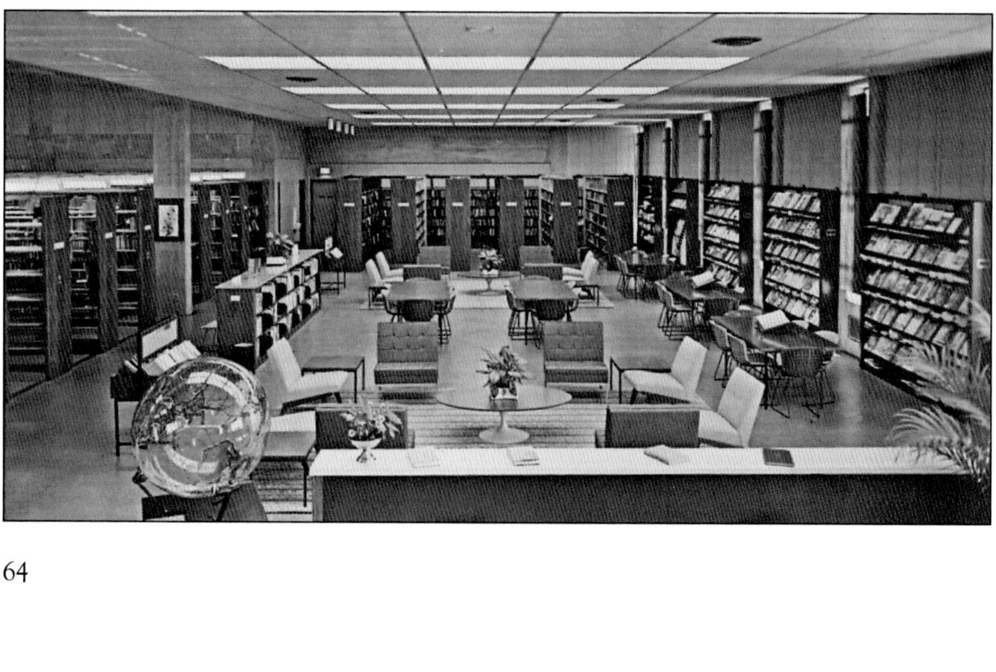

Five

Churches and Organizations

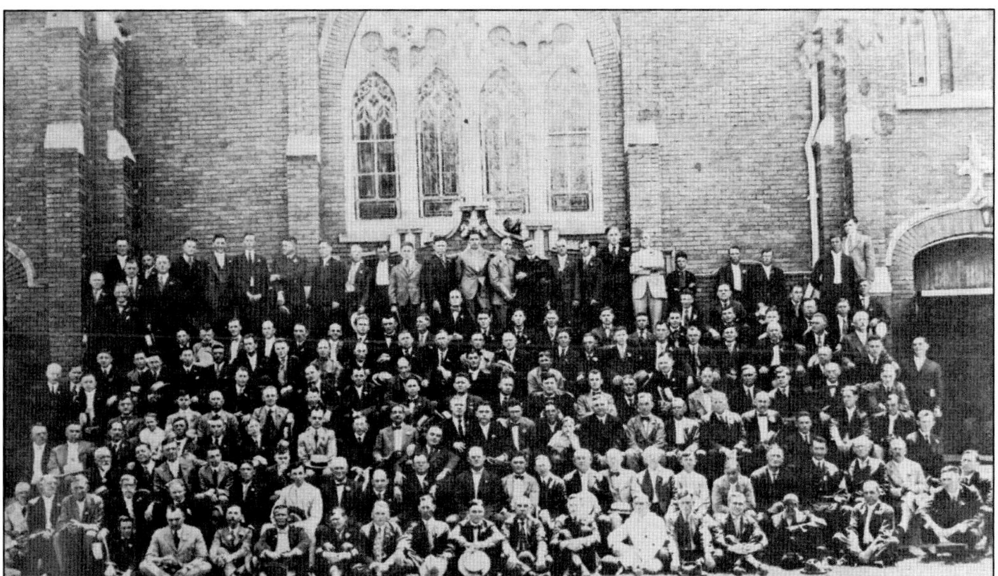

Moultrie churches have been noted for many years for their interdenominational and community-wide activities and cooperation. This photograph, taken in the 1920s, shows the members of an interdenominational Sunday school class posing in front of the First Presbyterian Church on Fifth Street SE. The class was taught by W. C. Vereen, a founding member of the Presbyterian church. This class included 163 men from virtually all denominations and even included men of Jewish faith. The class continued for several years, until Vereen's failing health and eyesight forced him to quit teaching. (FPCM.)

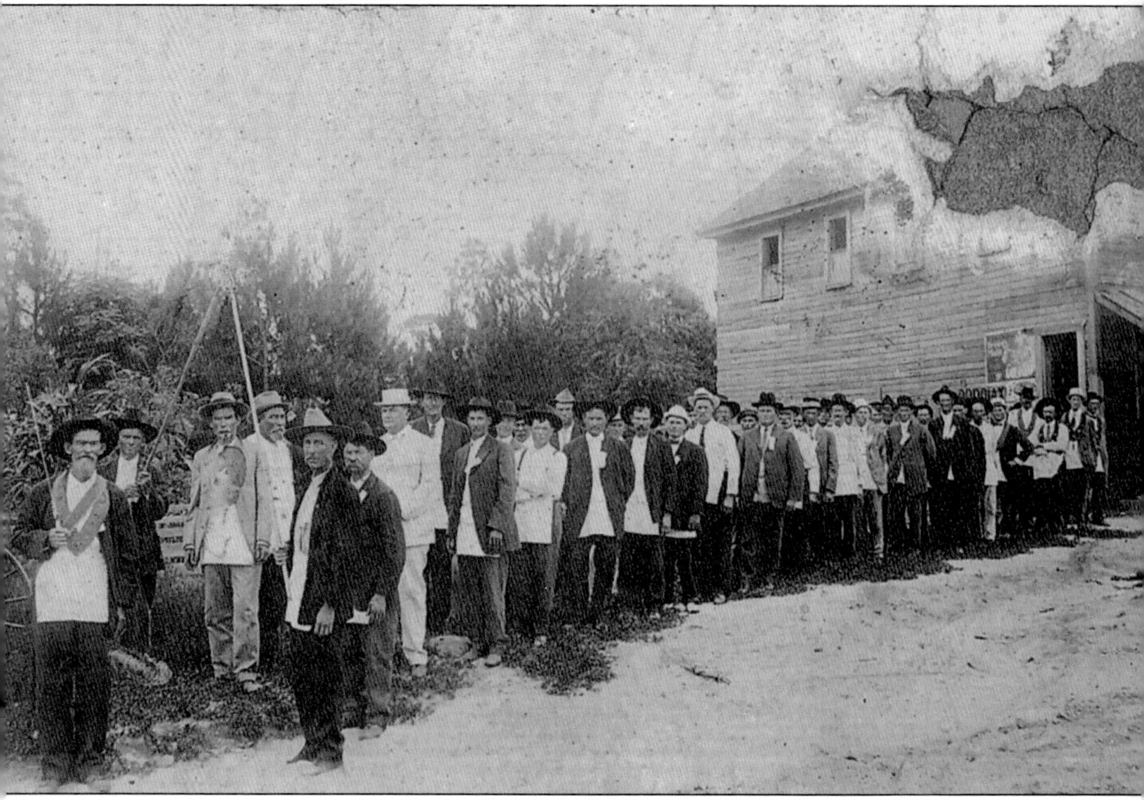

In this photograph, members of the Autreyville Masonic Lodge are gathered after a meeting between 1895 and 1910. (MO.)

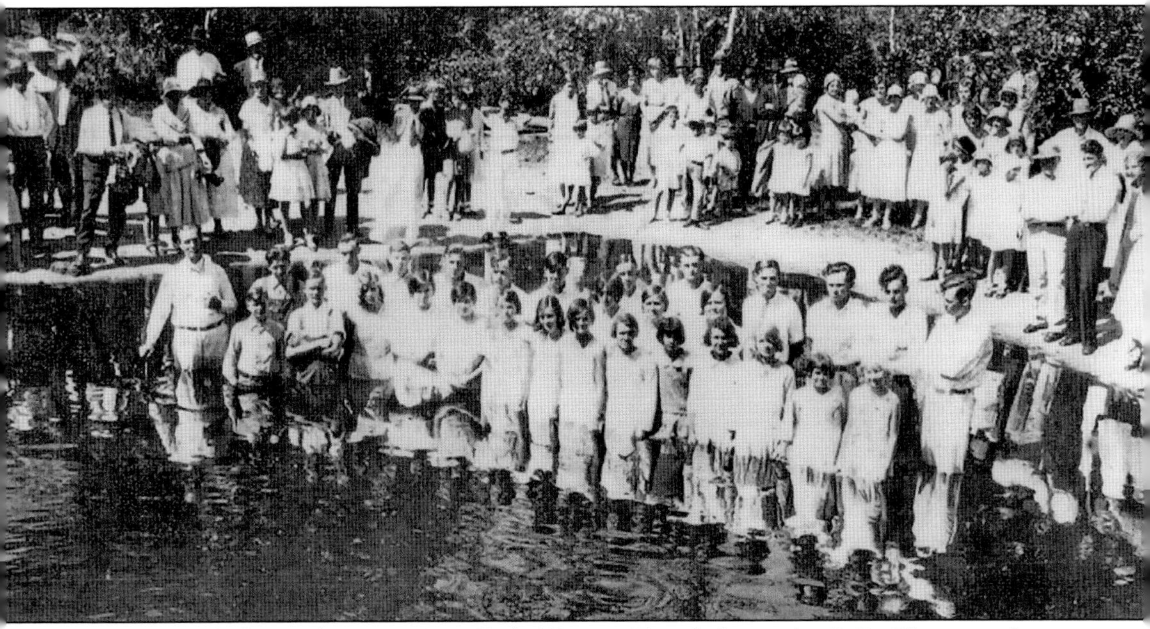

This photograph shows a baptism at New Bethel Baptist Church during the 1940s. Those standing in the water for the service are, from left to right, (first row) Pastor Charles Moore, Eulie Lastinger, Thomas E. Howell, Lena Mae Howell, unidentified, Montine Rawlings, three unidentified, Susie Holland, Odelia Strickland, two unidentified, Anna Laura Beck, and Truda Mae Key; (second row) Zulicka Autrey, Grace Sherman, and Lucy White; (third row) Ray Scarboro, Ervin Howell, Harold Duniva, Ronald Howell, Ed Presley, unidentified, J. P. Alligood, Preston Lastinger, Roy Beck, Coy Alligood, and Mason Lastinger. (MO.)

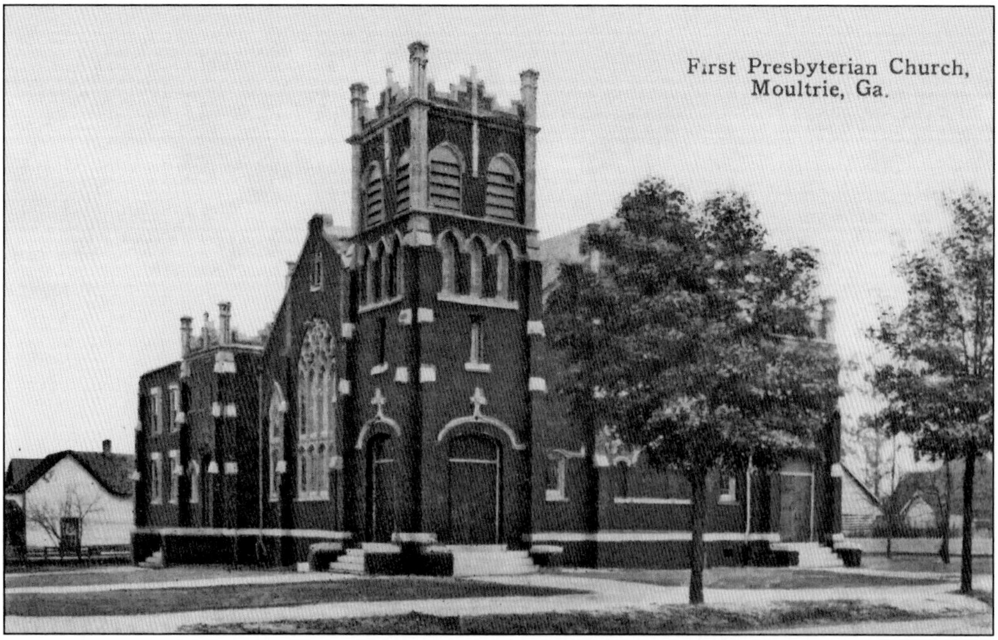

The First Presbyterian Church of Moultrie was organized on October 3, 1892, by 16 charter members. Most had migrated from South Carolina to Moultrie. Rev. T. J. Allison acted as moderator for the first meeting. William Coachman Vereen and William B. McPhaul were elected as ruling elders. John A. Milsap and James McKay were elected as deacons. The first church building was located on West Central Avenue. The building in this photograph was the third erected by the congregation. It was dedicated on October 6, 1912, and is still in use today. (MO.)

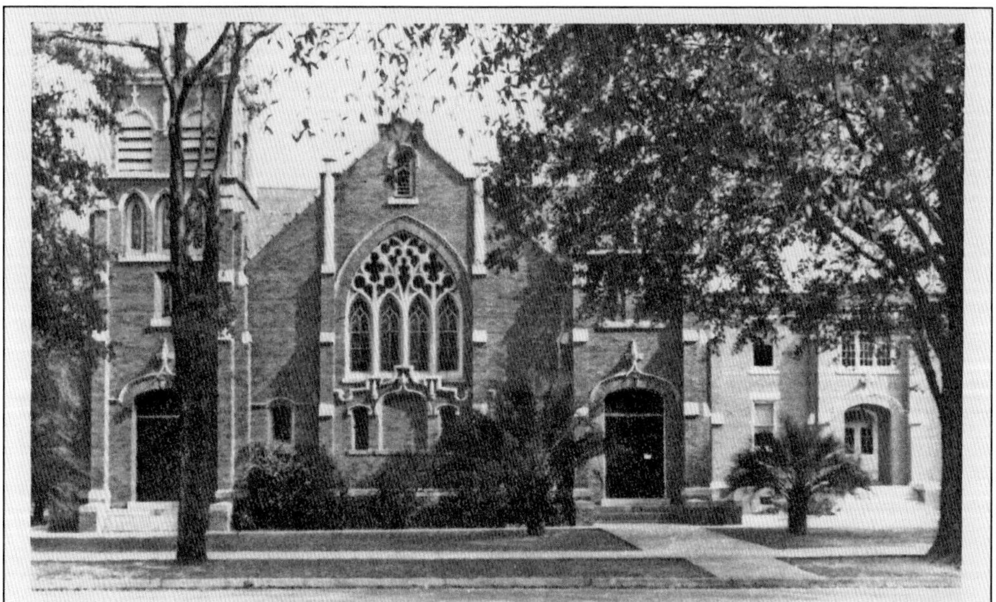

By 1931, the congregation had grown so large that an educational building addition was necessary. This view of the church shows the addition, which was named in honor of Ellen Vereen, to the right of the sanctuary. (APP.)

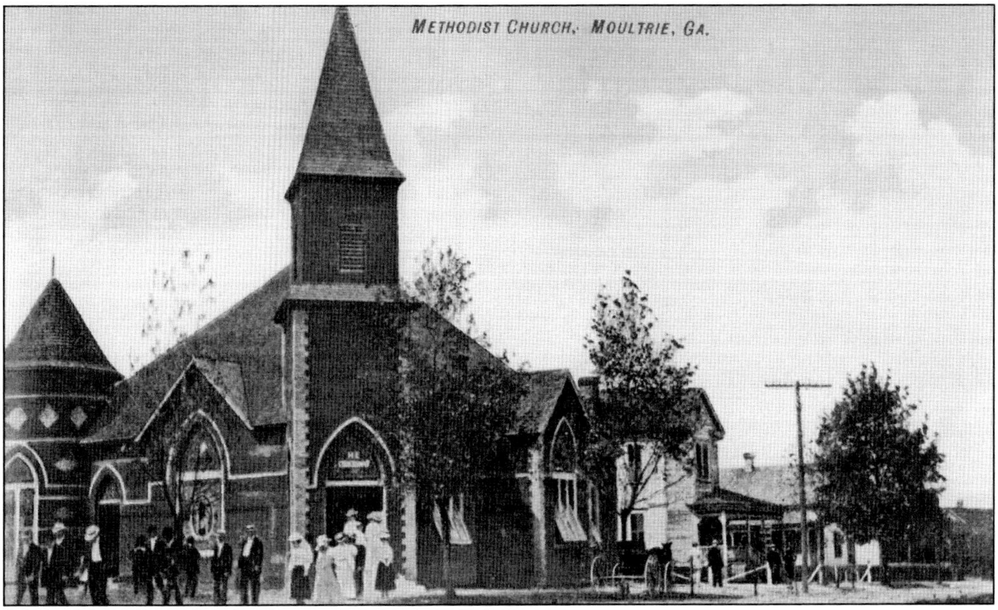

In 1878, a Methodist church was established in Colquitt County under the leadership of Caroline Culpepper Cooper. Services were held in homes until a frame building was erected in 1883. Growth in the membership lead to a new building, and in 1900, the Methodist congregation constructed the first brick church in Moultrie on the corner of First Street NE and First Avenue. Shown in this picture in the early 1900s, the unusual design featured a turret, bell tower, and stained-glass window. (APP.)

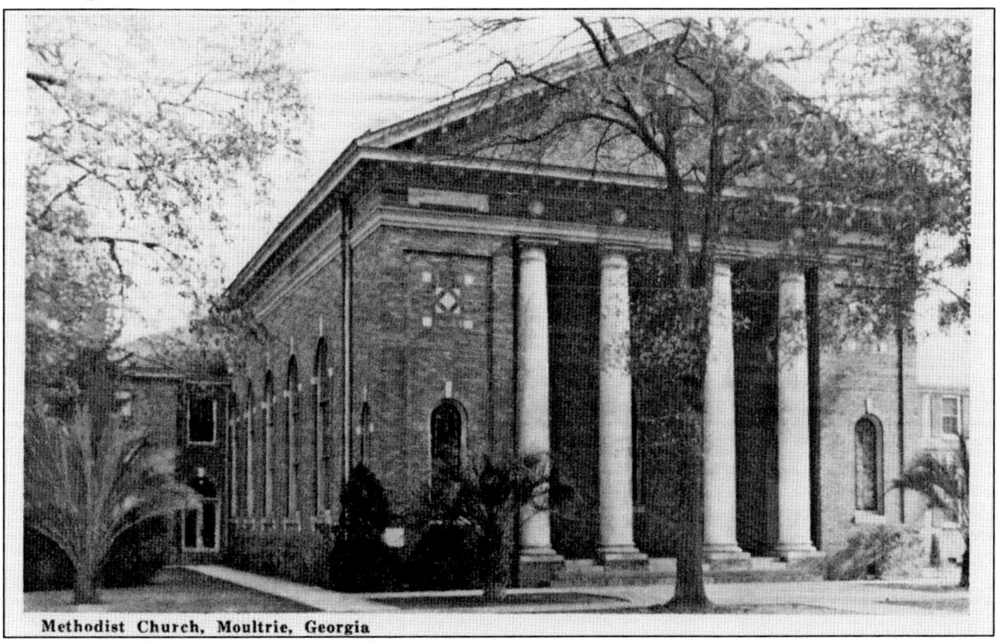

In 1916, the congregation built a larger church on First Street SE, on land donated by Mr. and Mrs. M. M. Kendall. Through the efforts of Mrs. T. E. Lewis, the beautiful stained-glass windows from the previous building were moved to the new structure. Shown in the 1950s, the building is still in use today. (APP.)

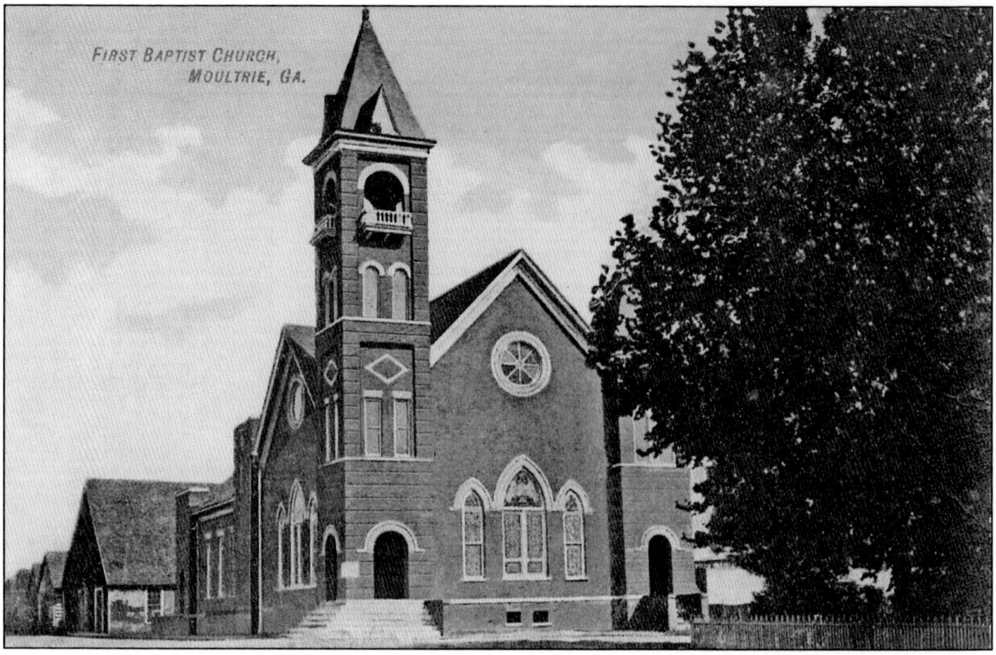

From humble beginnings as a Missionary Baptist church and a membership of nine people in 1880, the First Baptist Church of Moultrie grew into a large congregation. In September 1905, the church pictured here was dedicated on the corner of South Main Street and Second Avenue SE. The sanctuary seated nearly 1,000 people and cost close to $21,000. A debt of only $3,500 remained when the dedication service was held, but the offering taken at the dedication service was enough to pay that debt. (APP.)

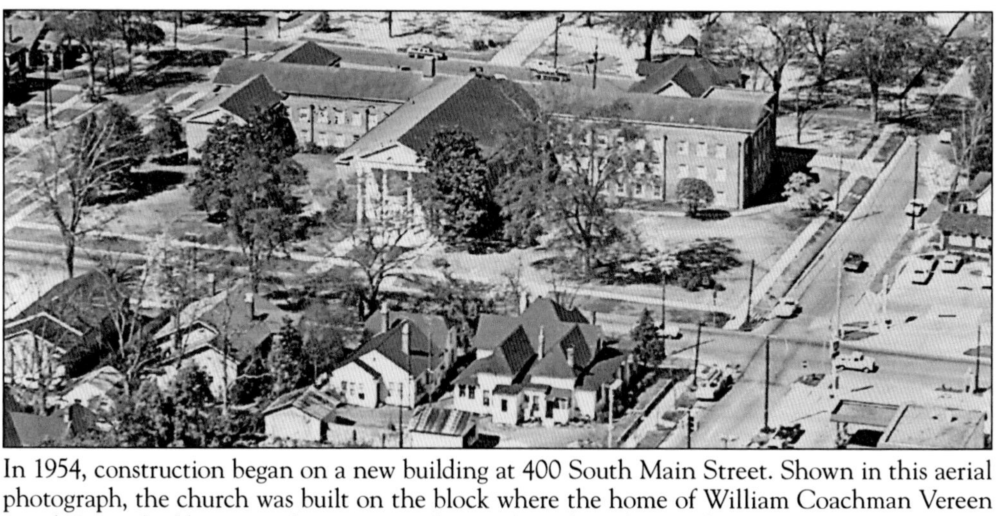

In 1954, construction began on a new building at 400 South Main Street. Shown in this aerial photograph, the church was built on the block where the home of William Coachman Vereen stood. Several additions and renovations have taken place during the ensuing years to provide for a growing congregation. This building is still in use today. (MCCL.)

Six

Sports

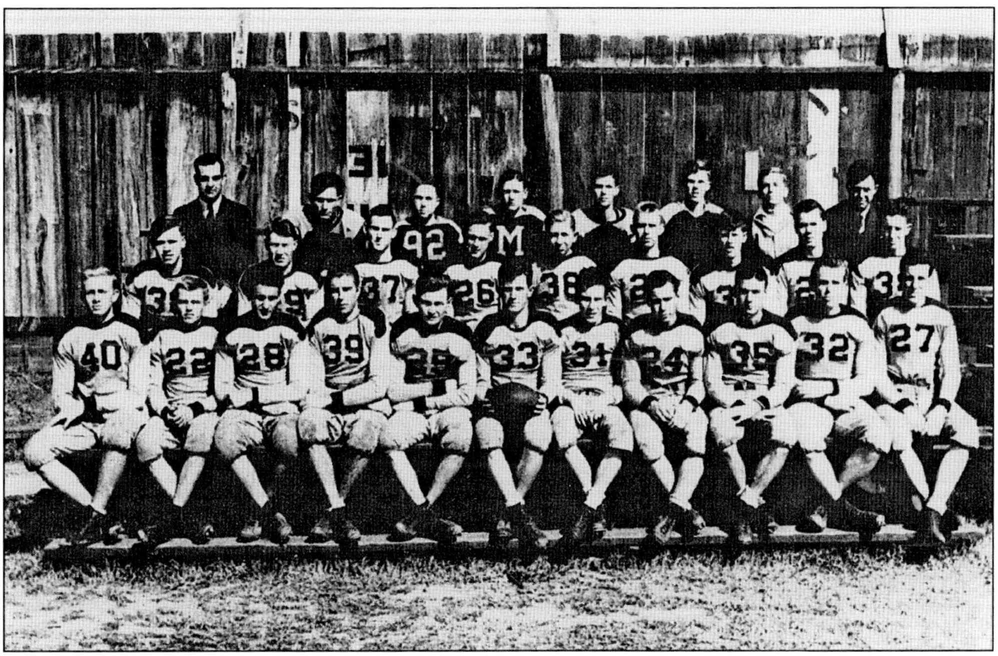

The members of the 1937 Moultrie High School football team are, from left to right, (first row) Robert Kinnard, Elliott Galloway, Pete Carlton, Myrtice Goff, Joe Norman, George Anchors, Allen Clements, R. E. Bannister, John B. Weaver Jr., Jim Taylor, and Fred McCarthay; (second row) two unidentified, Red Gobbles, Ernest Campbell, Claude Tucker, "Rat" Willis, Marion Turner, Cleon Newton, and ? Hall; (third row) coach Dode Phillips, James Spivey, Junior Tucker, William Scroggins, two unidentified, ? Beard, and assistant coach Red Murphy. (MO.)

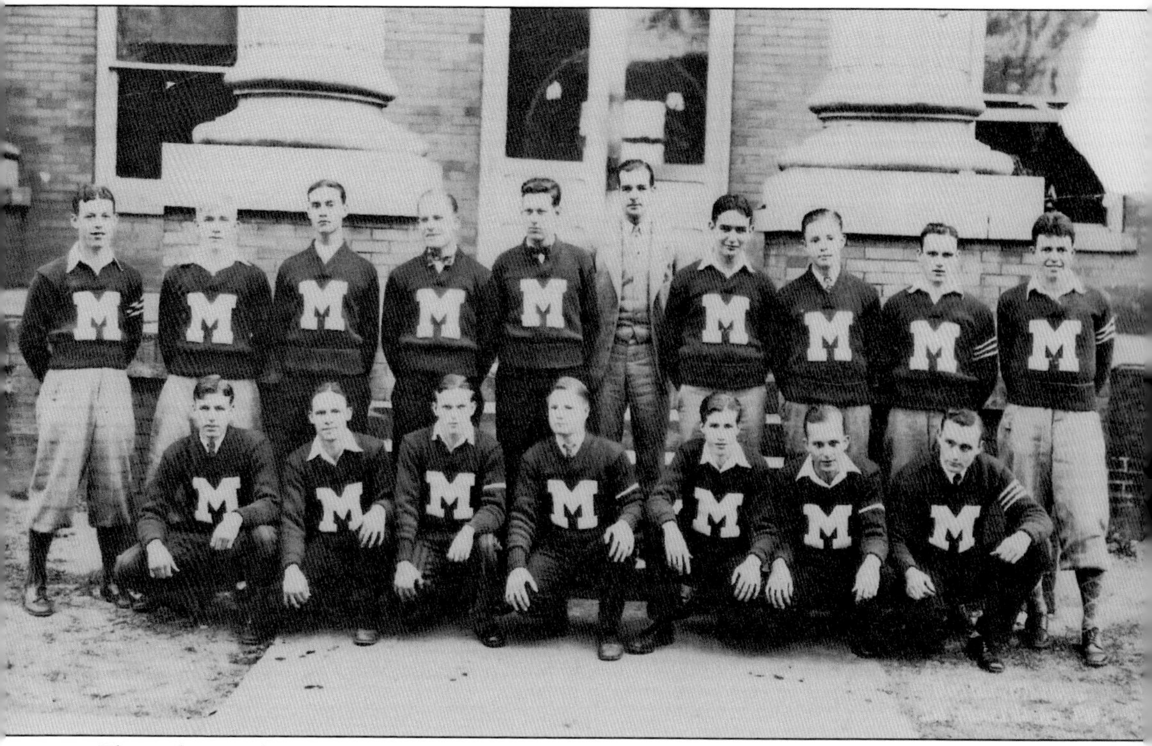

The ambition of every young man who played football for Moultrie High School was to earn his varsity letter and become a member of the "M" Club. The members for the 1927–1928 school year are shown proudly displaying their letter sweaters. The only identified man in the photograph is Arthur "Sid" Hunt, who is second from the right in the first row. (MCCL.)

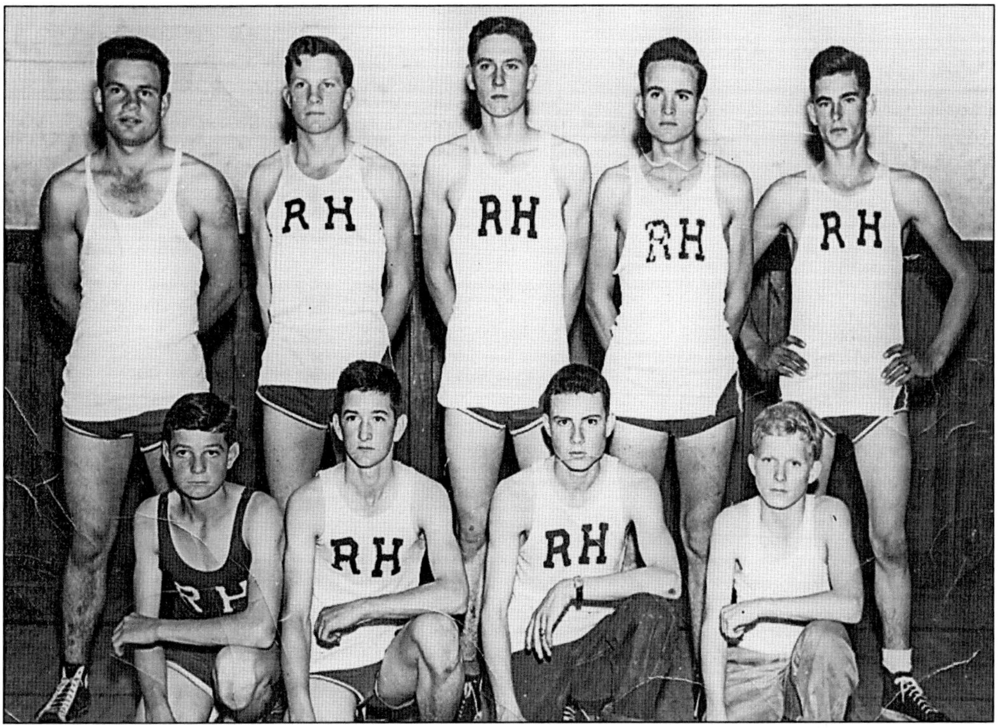

Members of the Rose Hill School basketball team for the 1942–1943 school year are, from left to right, (first row) Wallace Hall, Larry Stephenson, Ed Crosby, and Buddy Richardson; (second row) A. J. Williams, Jack D. Hall, Shelby West, Ralph Perkins, and Snooks Redman. (MO.)

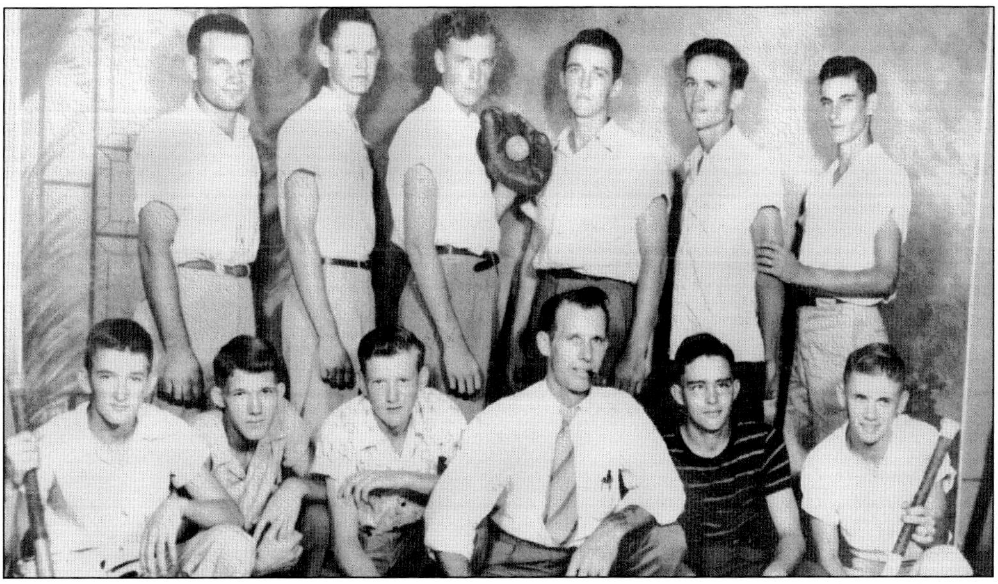

Members of the 1946 Moultrie YMCA baseball team are, from left to right, (first row) Larry Stephenson (shortstop), James Bonner (left field), ? Dampier (right field), H. L. Bonner (manager), Billie Murphy (outfield), and Lindsey Ayers (pitcher); (second row) A. J. Williams (catcher), Don Williams (first base), Harold Allegood (pitcher), Allen Dawson (outfield), Wallace Hall (third base), and Lavarrah Redman (second base). (MCCL.)

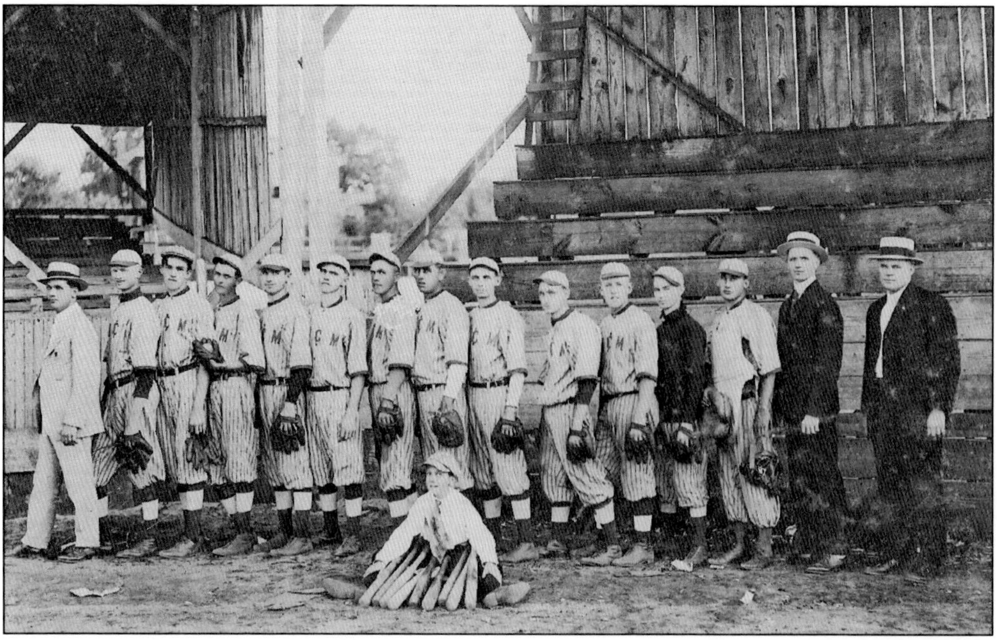

Businesses and organizations fielded baseball teams, as did the public schools. These undated photographs show players from teams other than the public schools. The team in the photograph above is believed to have been organized by the Moultrie Cotton Mills in the early 1920s. The team below is believed to be a City of Moultrie team from the 1930s. (Above, OCC; below, MCCH.)

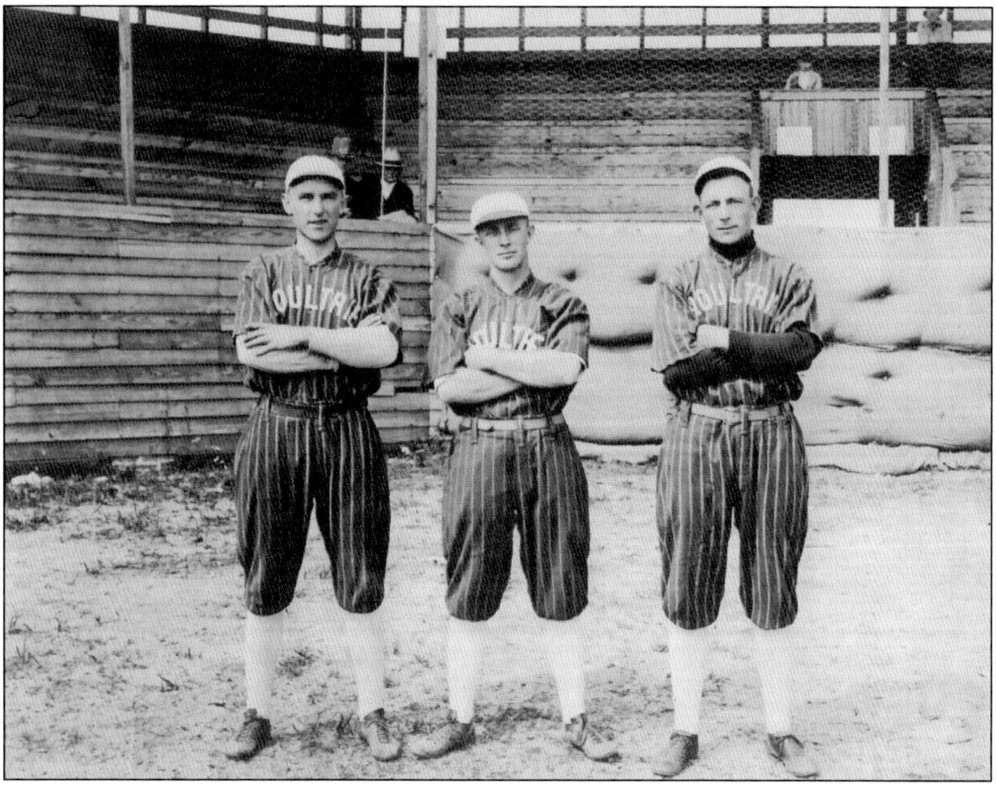

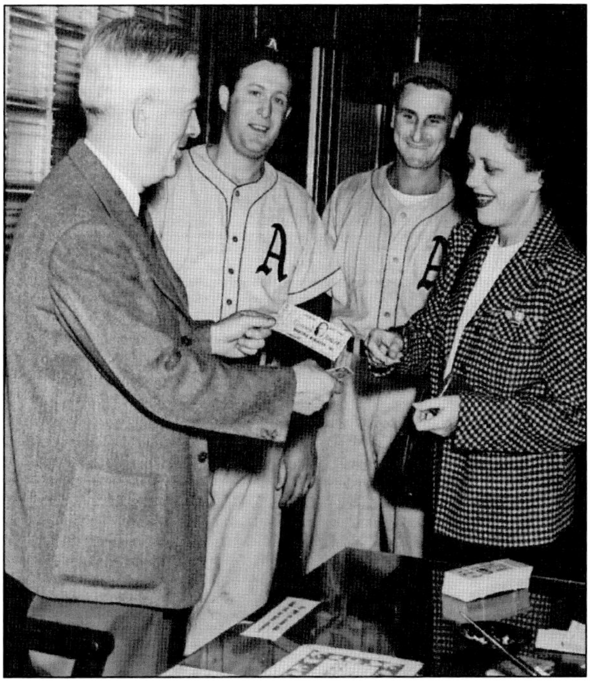

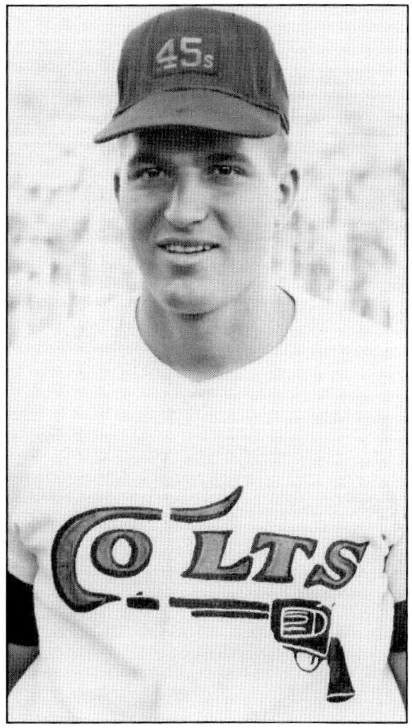

From 1935 until 1963, professional baseball teams played in Moultrie as part of the Georgia-Florida League. The promotional photograph at left above was taken in 1948 and featured administrative personnel and players from the Moultrie A's. Pictured from left to right are Henry Cohen, Bill Peterman, Ken Rhyne, and Helen Hall. One of the players on the Colt .45s was one of Moultrie's native sons. Shown in a promotional picture is Tommy Tucker, above right. (Above left, MCCH; above right, WG.)

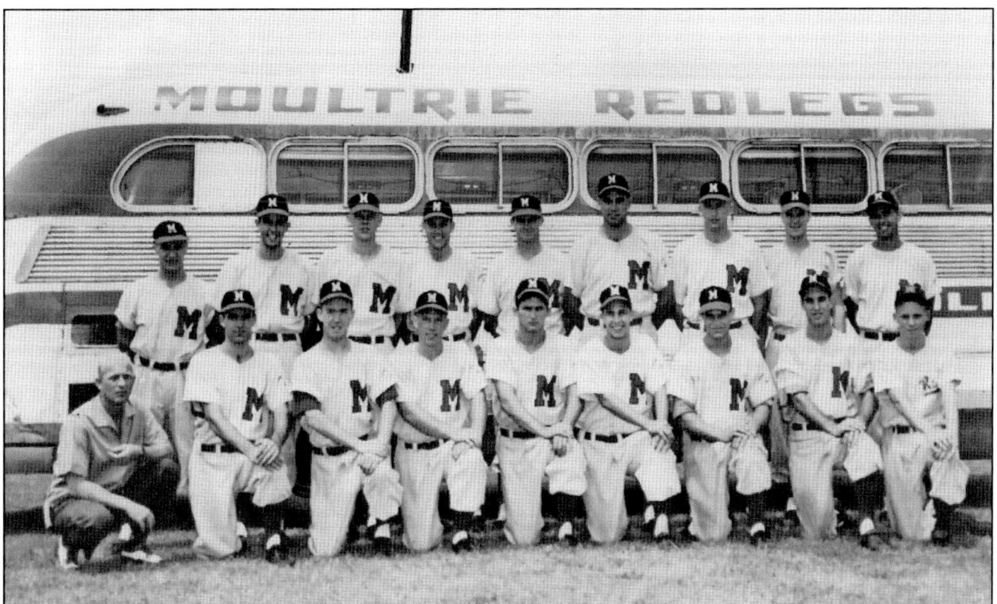

In 1955 and 1956, the professional baseball team that played in Moultrie was named the Moultrie Redlegs. This team picture shows the Redlegs in 1955. (CTC.)

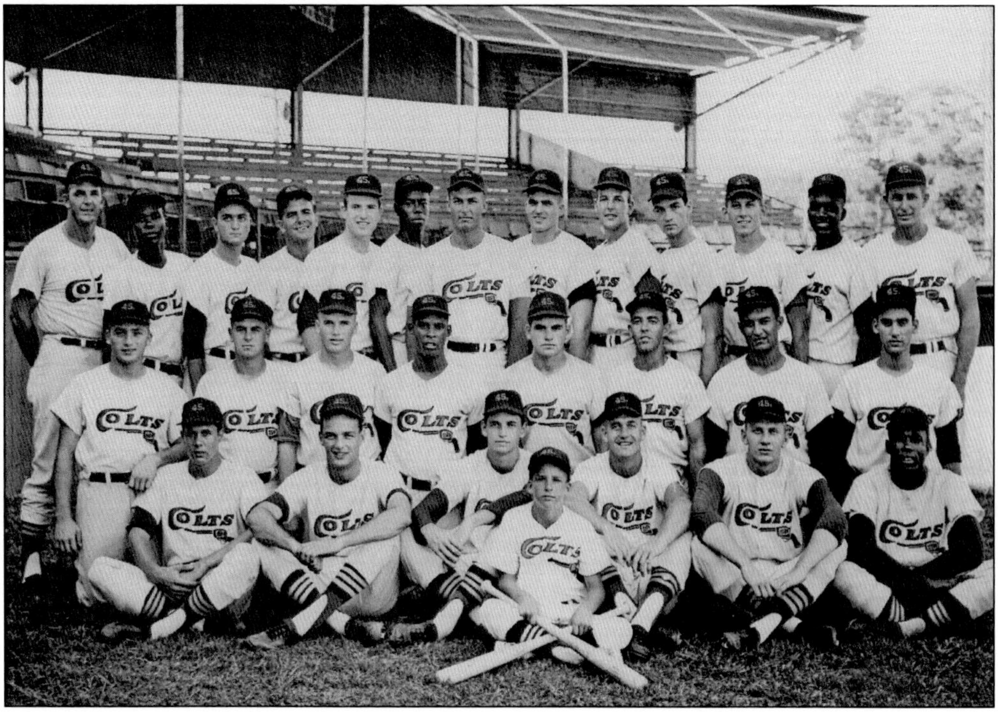

This team photograph shows the 1963 Colt .45s professional team. The stadium in this picture was built in the area where the Colquitt County High School is located today, on Veteran's Parkway South. When professional baseball was no longer played in Moultrie, the stadium was abandoned and eventually was moved to Douglas, Georgia, where it is in use today. Players are, from left to right, (first row) Bill Palko, unidentified, Vince Goodlett, unidentified bat boy, Bob Walenczyk, Frank Thomas, and Ivan Murrell; (second row) Jay Dahl, Ray Ferrand, Dennis Willet, Sparky Sparks, Jim Green, Jerry Ellis, Jim Murillo, and Al Goldfield; (third row) Chuck Churn (pitching coach), Ramon DeLaCruz, unidentified, Joe Panella, unidentified, Sammy Robinson, Kent Thaxton, Tommy Tucker, Chuck Warden, Larry Howard, Bob Rombach, Charlie Murray, and Jim Walton (manager). (CTC.)

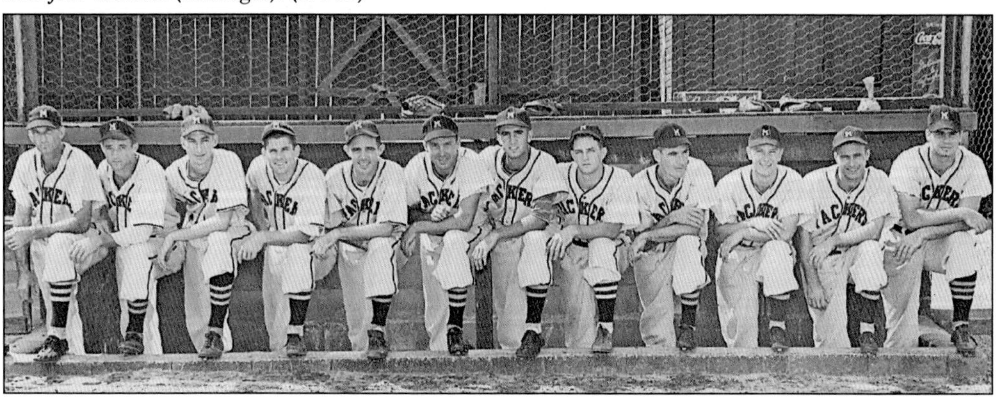

The professional team that represented Moultrie in the Georgia-Florida League from 1936 to 1942 and again from 1946 to 1947 was named the Packers. Team members in this undated photograph are, from left to right, Catfish Gowan, Steve Nukas, Paul Langemier, Milton Wrenn, Walter Lentz, John Herbik, Clyde Wilson, Harold Bryant, Pete Colombatto, Ray Sowins, Chick Lauman, and Bill LaFrance. (MCCL.)

Seven

RAILROADS

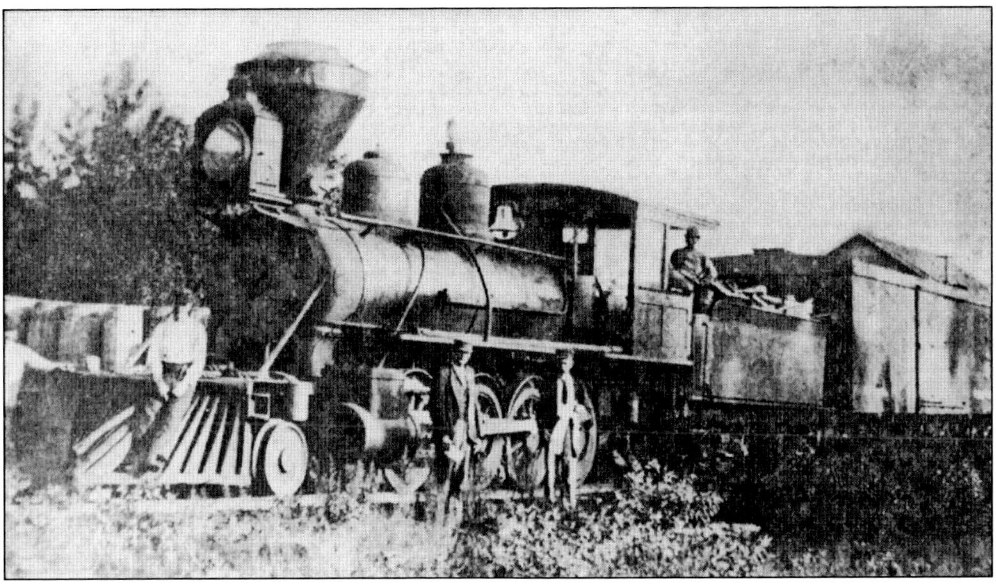

For 37 years after the creation of Colquitt County, the area was without major means of transportation and thus remained pastoral. On February 26, 1893, the first locomotive chugged into Moultrie, opening the territory to a great naval stores and lumber operation that started growth that has never diminished. That train was part of the Boston and Albany Railroad, which the following year became the Georgia Northern Railroad. The road, which is still most active in the territory, at that time extended from Pidcock in Brooks County to Moultrie. Here is the first Georgia Northern (B&A) locomotive, freight cars, and crew of the train that arrived over the freshly laid tracks with C. W. Pidcock Sr. at the throttle. The crew consisted of William G. Henderson, conductor, who died in 1895; J. C. Pope, engineer, who was killed in railroad service in 1911; and Rev. E. H. Bryan, the first agent of the road at Moultrie and a well-known preacher and church organizer, who died in 1899. (APP.)

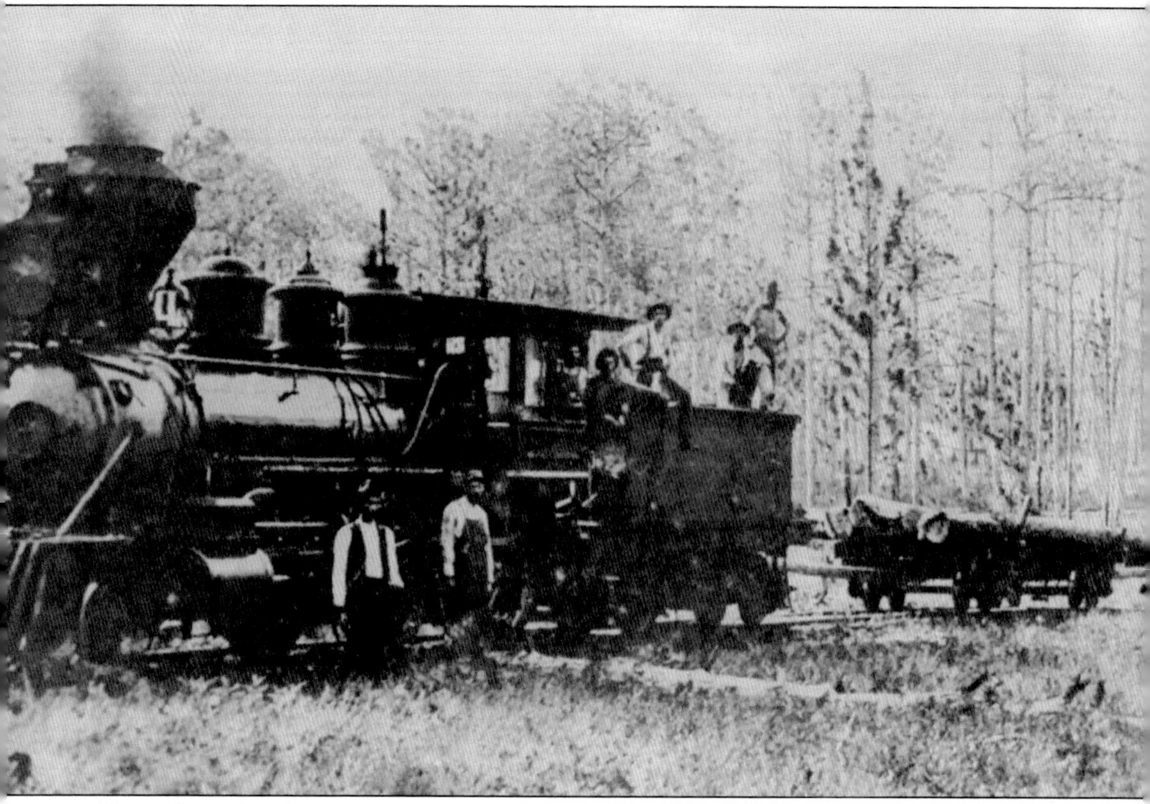

Once the railroads began penetrating Colquitt County in 1893, it was just a matter of years until the great stand of virgin pines was mostly removed, opening the land to agriculture and other uses. This tram road, one of several that extended deep into forest lands, paralleled the more recent Camilla Highway for some 15 miles west of Moultrie towards Meigs in 1903. These particular logs were cut from the John Morrison farm and were headed for the Sumner and Pounds sawmill. (APP.)

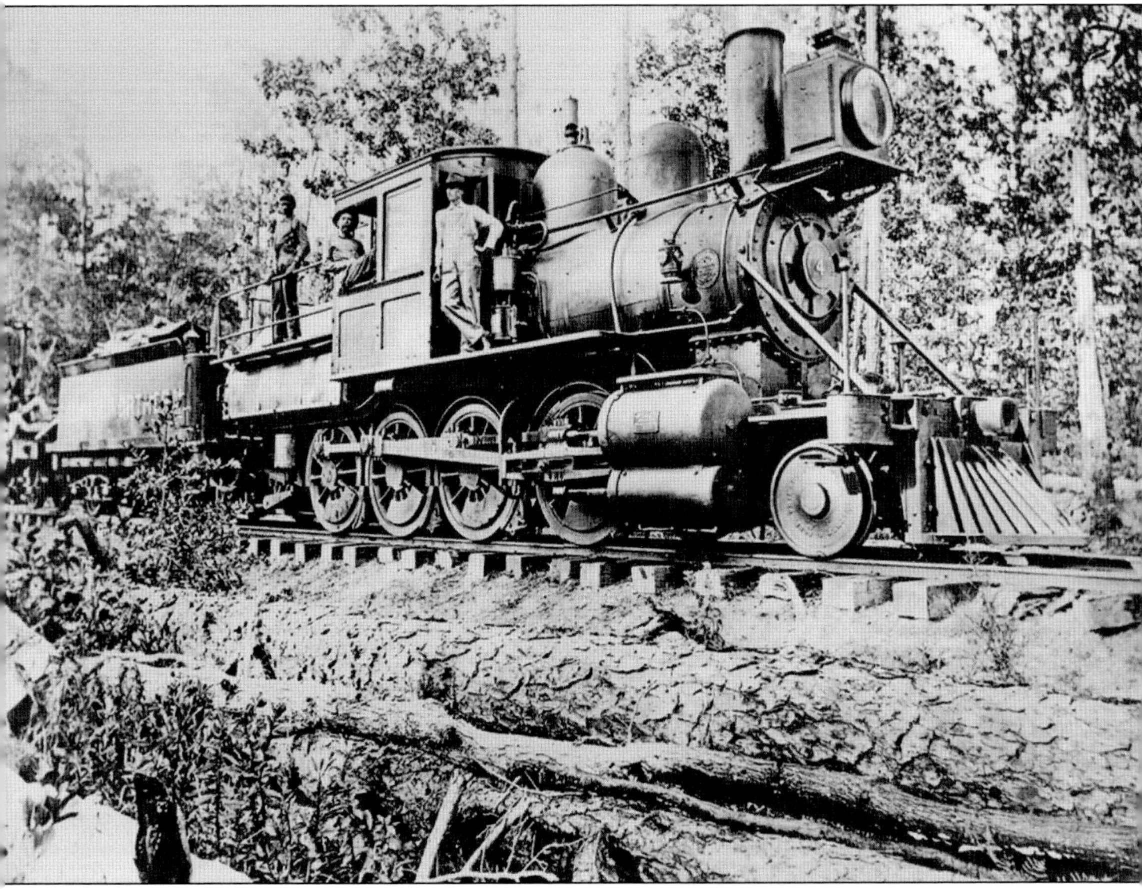

Engine No. 4, pictured in the late 1890s, came from the Rockaway Valley in New Jersey. It had originally been bought by the Rockaway to haul coal up heavy grades. Unfortunately it caused nothing but trouble once it arrived because of the poor track construction. When J. N. Pidcock and his sons formed the Georgia Northern Railway, this engine was driven from New Jersey to Georgia. (APP.)

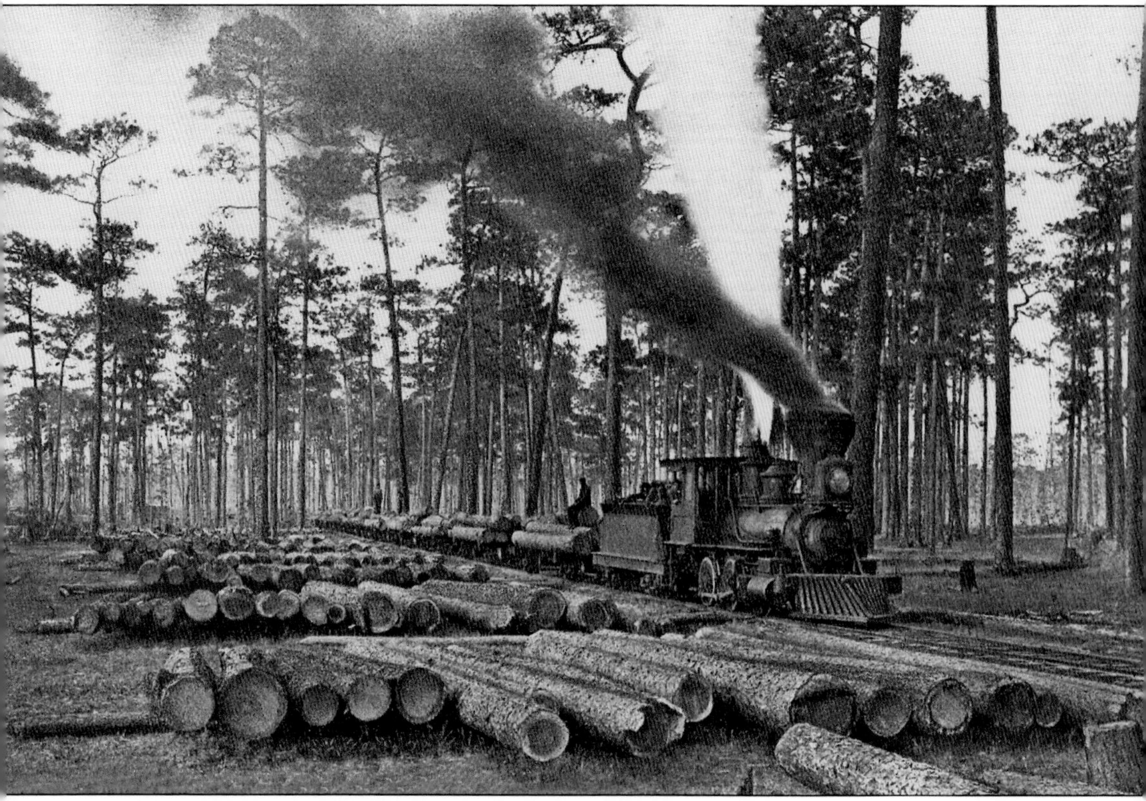

In the early days of the logging and naval stores industry in South Georgia, trains such as the one pictured here were used to haul trees and turpentine out of the virgin pine forests. In this late-1800s photograph, huge logs can be seen lined up on rollers ready to be loaded onto the train. (APP.)

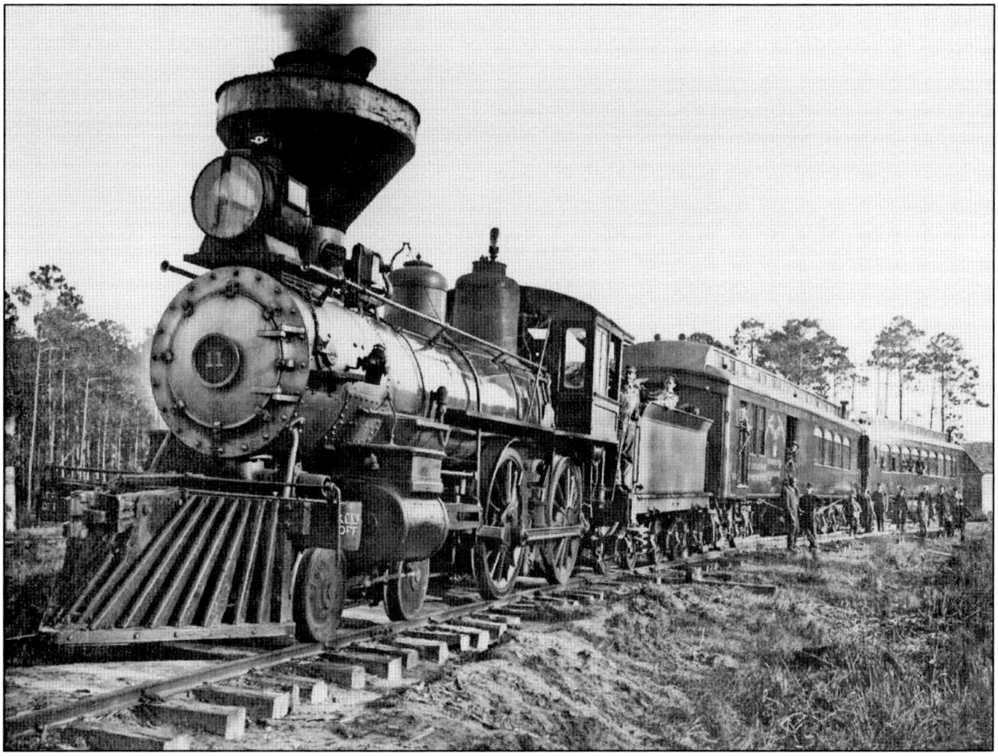

The Georgia Northern Railway train, shown in this 1911 photograph taken in Moultrie, featured a 4-4-0 steam locomotive, tender, and two passenger cars. This train provided daily passenger service between Albany and Boston, Georgia, with a stop in Moultrie. (APP.)

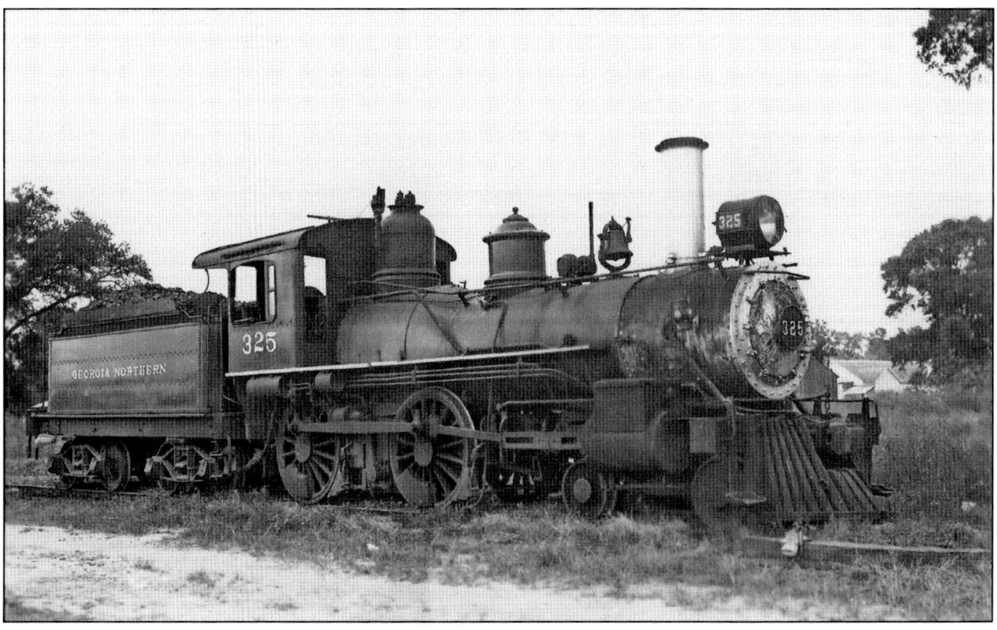

During the 1940s, Georgia Northern Railway was still operating steam locomotives. (APP.)

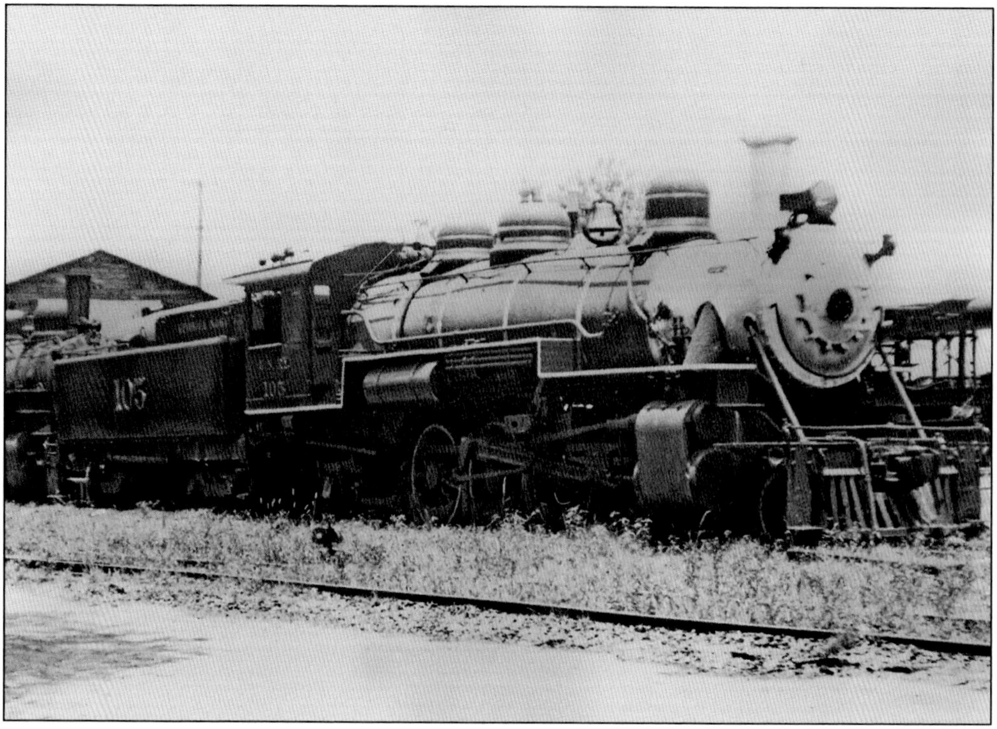

Pictured above, Georgia Northern Railway No. 105, a 2-8-2 steam locomotive built by Baldwin in 1929, is on outdoor display at 400 First Avenue SE in Moultrie, Georgia. Georgia Northern Railway donated the locomotive to the community in 1963 to mark the 70th anniversary of the arrival of the first train in the city. Steam locomotives gave way to the more modern diesel locomotives, such as the one pictured below, Georgia Northern No. 801. (Both, APP.)

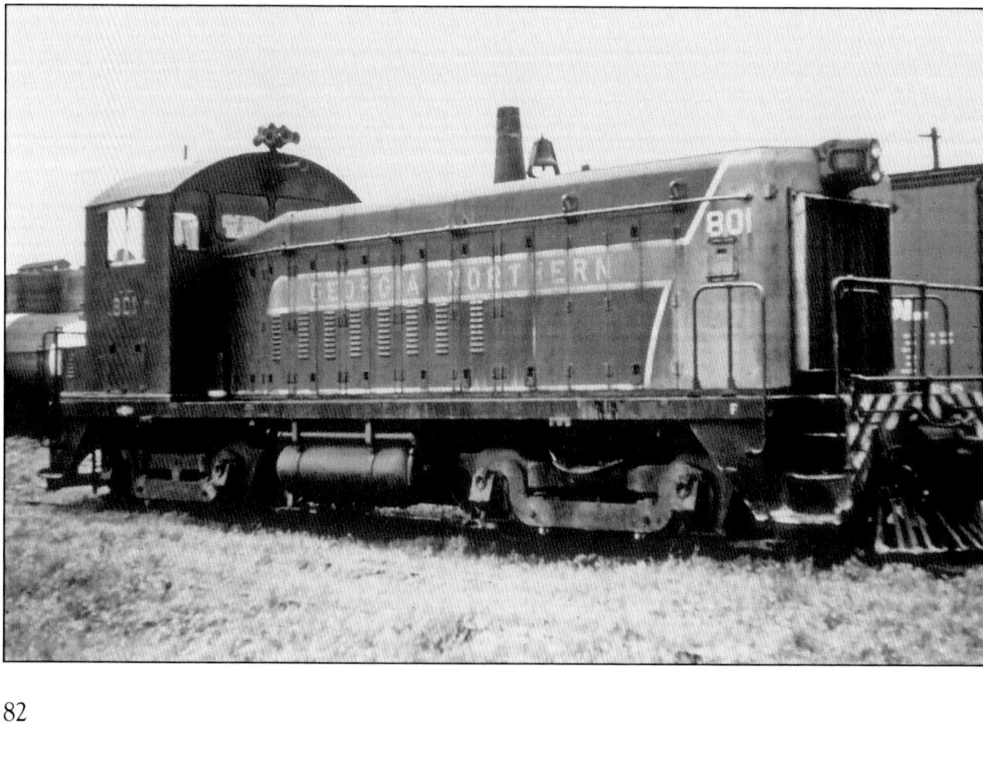

Eight

Agriculture

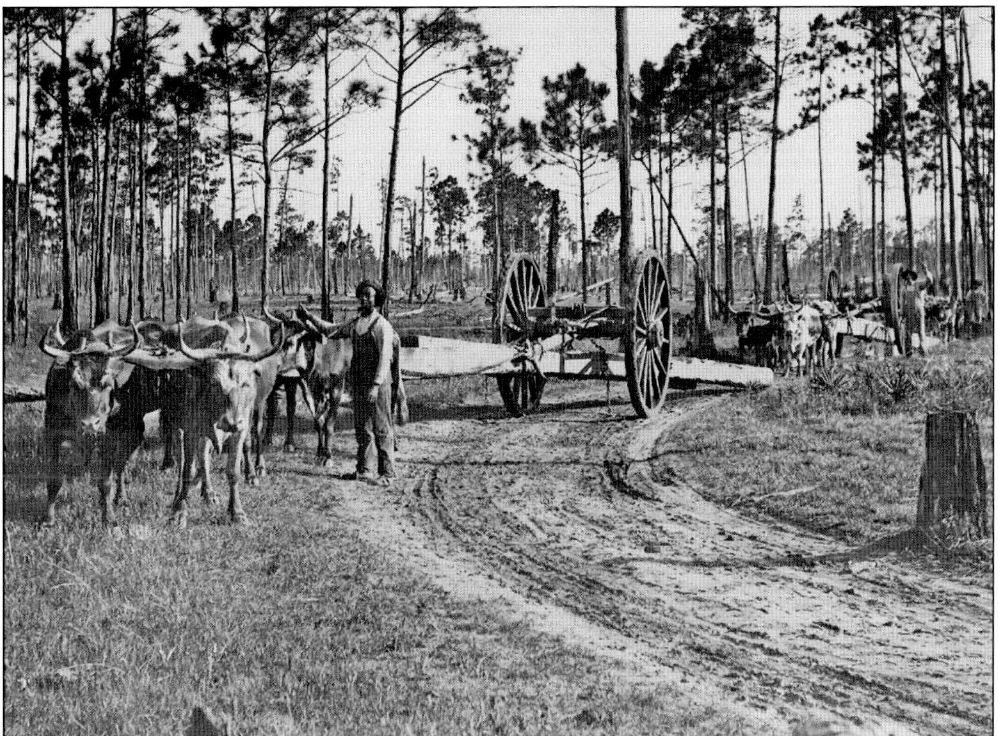

Colquitt County was part of an area of South Georgia called the Pine Barrens. This term came from the fact that the virgin pine trees that covered the land were so thick that they almost blocked the sun from the forest floor, not allowing vegetation to grow. However, these same pine trees would be the catalyst that changed Colquitt County. The longleaf yellow pines were as wide as 42 inches in diameter and over 60 feet in height. Teams of oxen, like the one seen in this photograph, were used to haul the cut trees out of the forest in the early years of the logging industry. (APP.)

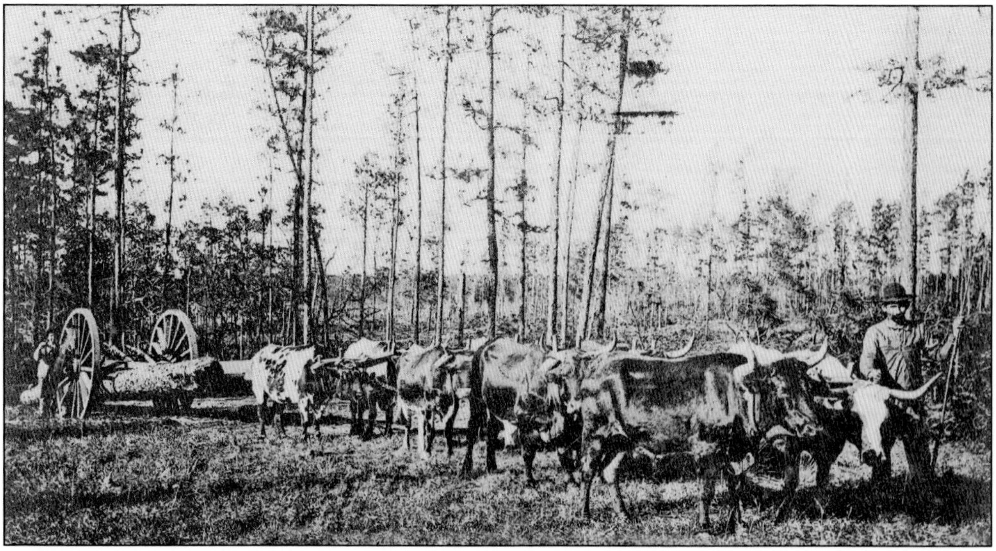

In the late 1880s, Colquitt County's pine trees attracted timber men from North Carolina. They had heard of the virgin pine forests in South Georgia and came to make their fortunes. Unfortunately, because Colquitt County had no railroads, harvesting pine trees was a slow process involving teams of oxen, such as the ones in these two photographs, dragging out logs one by one. Dragging a log attached to the axle of two giant wheels resulted in the back end of the log dragging the ground. This left deep gorges in the roads, making them more unusable in rainy weather. Because of this, temporary sawmills were built near where the timber was being harvested. As an area was cleared of trees, the sawmills were moved to the next site for clearing. (Both, APP.)

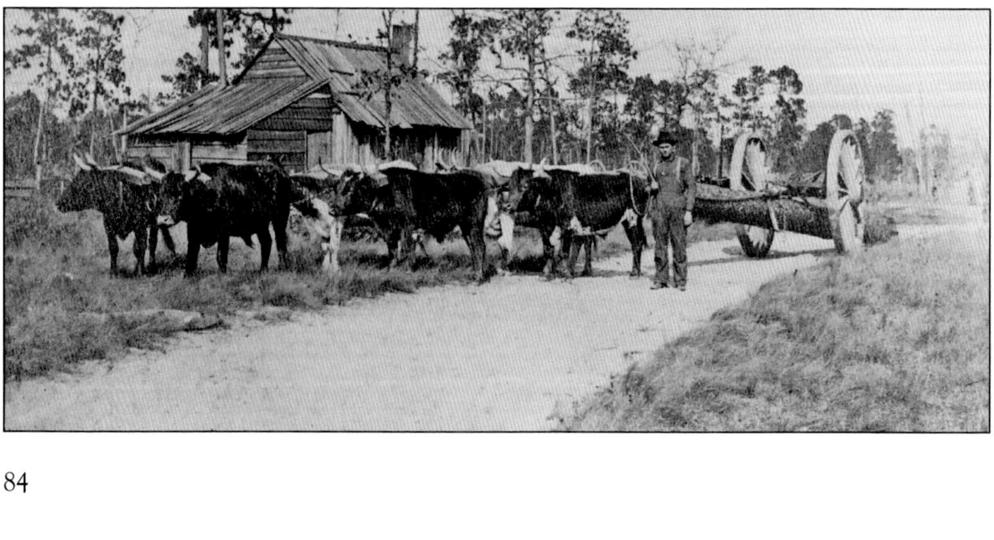

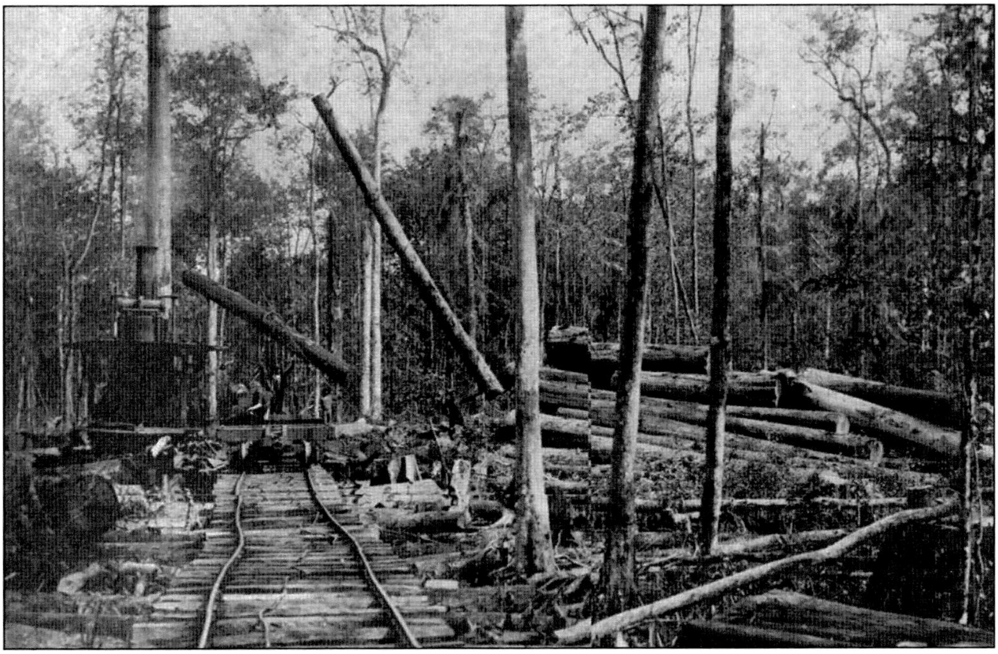

By the 1890s, more permanent sawmills were becoming possible. This was because timber companies began building temporary railroad trams, like the one pictured here, to the areas being harvested. One successful logging entrepreneur was James N. Pidcock, who had moved to Moultrie from New Jersey in the late 1880s. His Quitman Lumbering Company harvested timber just south of Moultrie in Brooks County. (APP.)

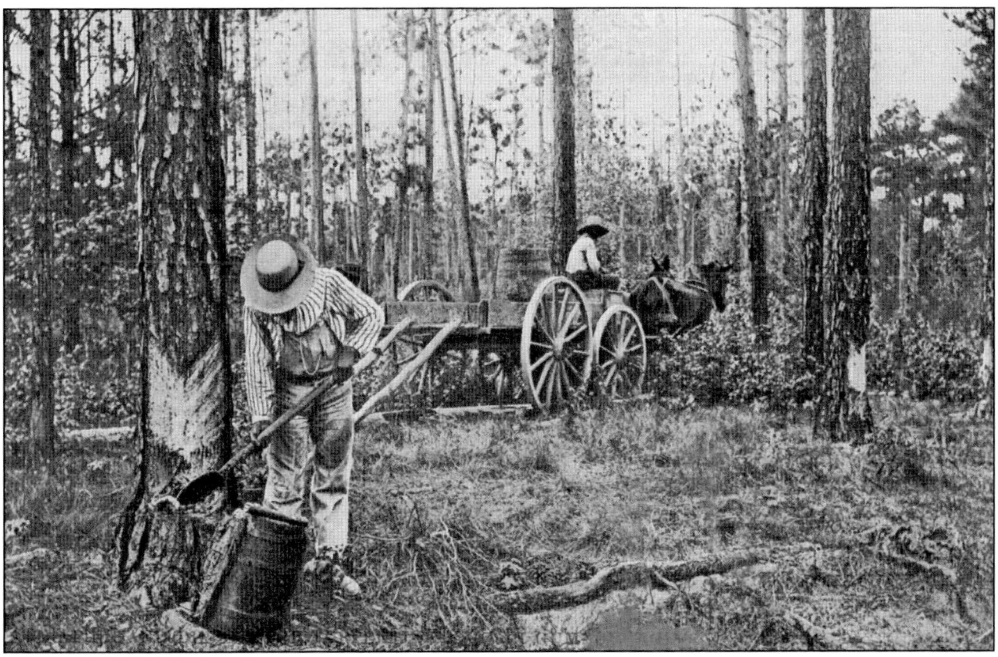

The second industry that grew from the longleaf yellow pine trees was naval stores. First cuts were made near the base of the pine trees, as shown in this undated photograph. These cuts drain pinesap into metal collecting trays. (APP.)

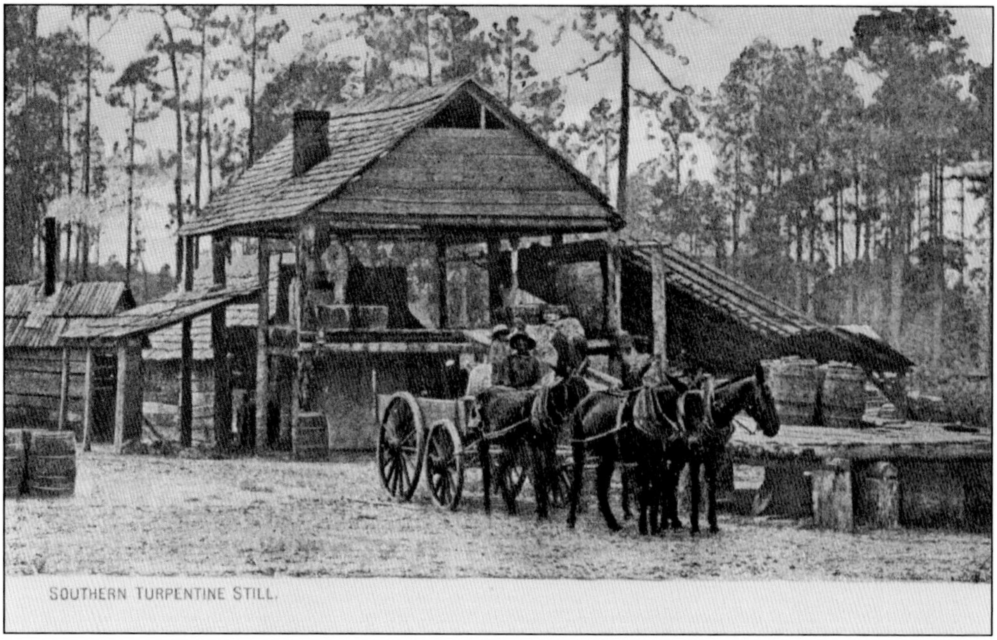

The collected sap was poured into barrels and loaded onto wagons to be taken to a nearby still for distillation. In these photographs from the beginning of the 20th century, teams of mules can be seen pulling wagons loaded with pinesap. (Both, APP.)

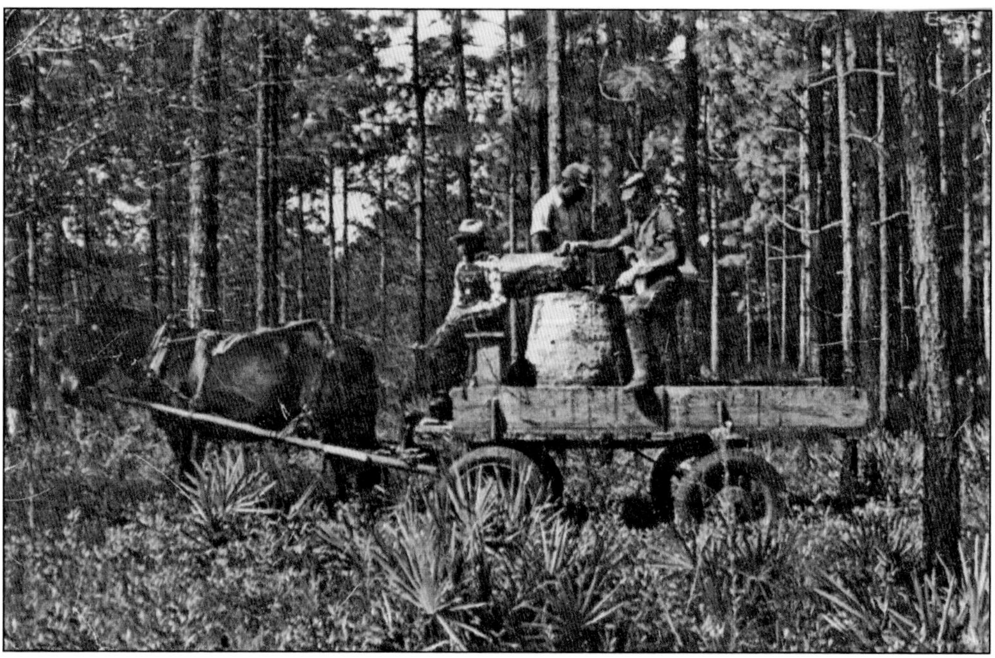

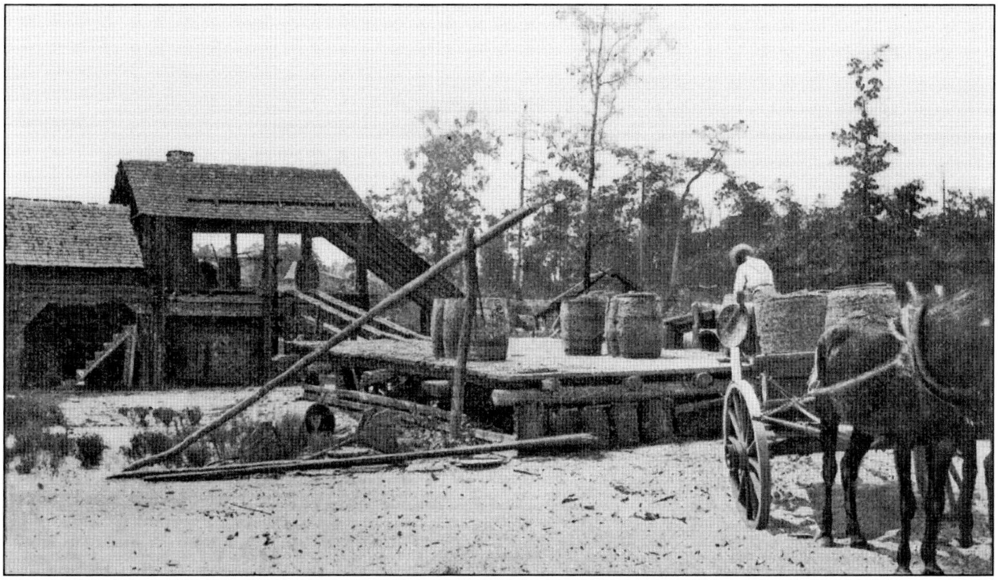

In the 1890s, there were over 20 turpentine stills, like the ones pictured here, located in Colquitt County. The barrels of pinesap were very heavy, and in these isolated areas, there were no pieces of automated equipment to aid in unloading the wagons. In the photograph above, the long pole in the center foreground was used as a fulcrum and lever to lift heavy objects. The photograph below shows the distillation process in action. (Both, APP.)

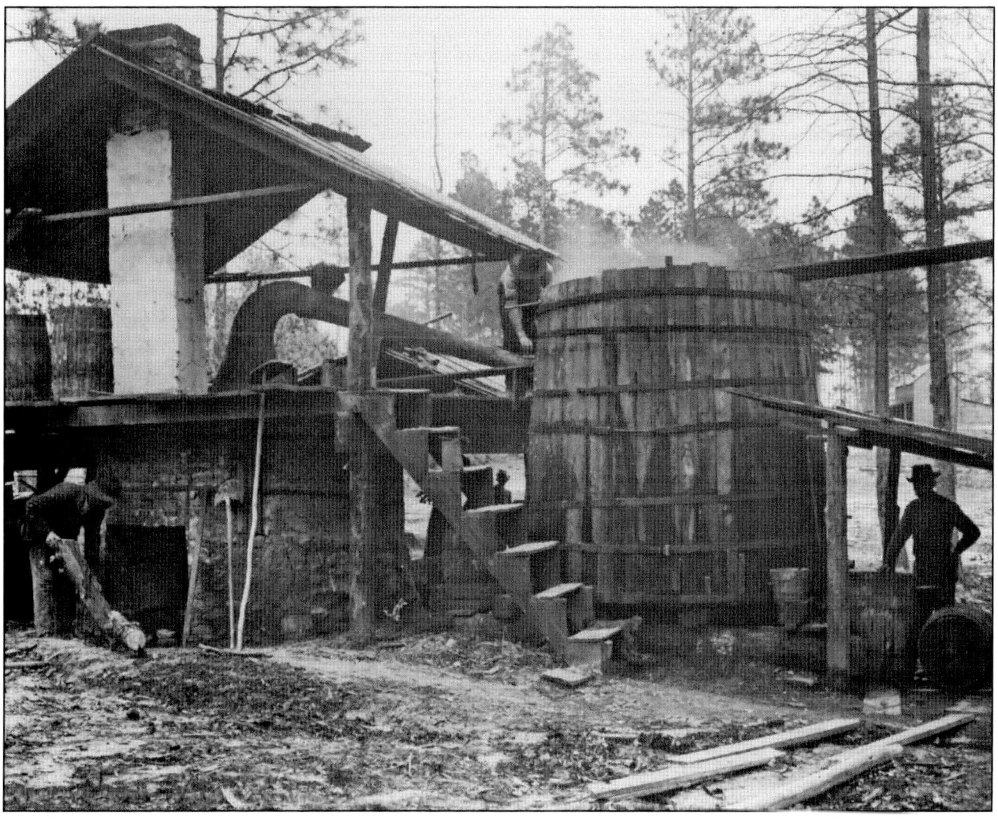

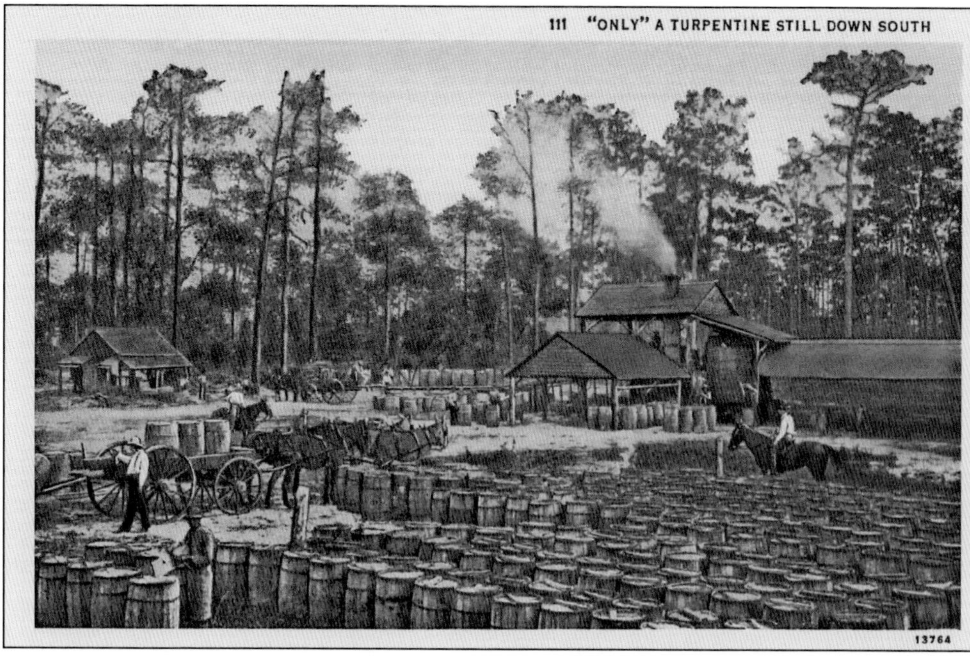

This postcard shows a typical South Georgia turpentine still. Barrels of turpentine and rosin can be seen waiting to be loaded onto a wagon and carried to the nearest railroad. They were carried by rail to Savannah and Brunswick, where they were sent aboard ships to the north and destinations around the world. (APP.)

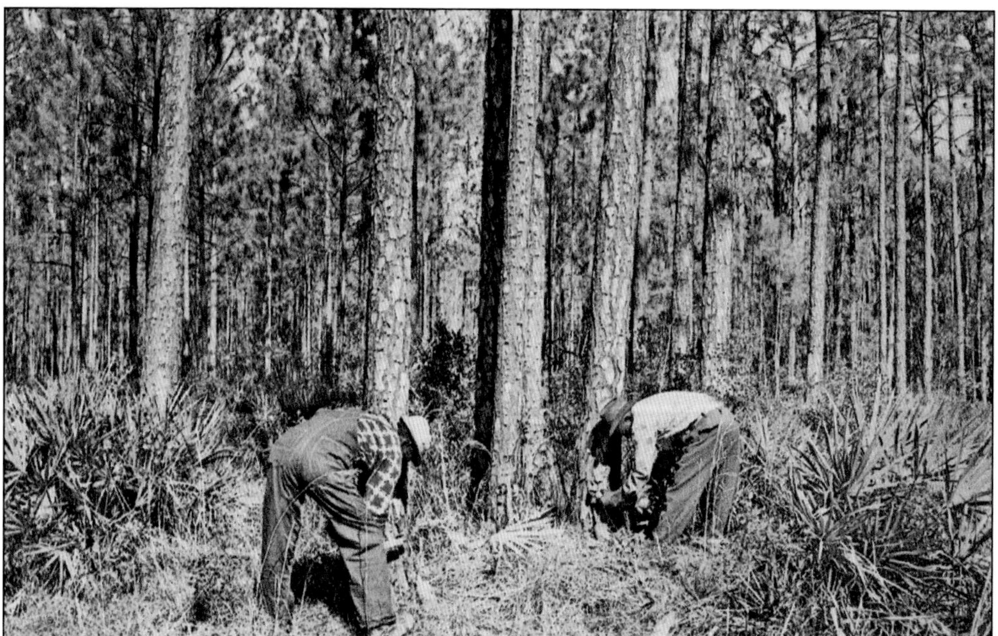

Although the process of distilling and transporting the rosin and turpentine changed over the years with the advent of more modern equipment, the process of harvesting the pinesap from the trees changed very little. These workers can be seen "chipping" the trees. (APP.)

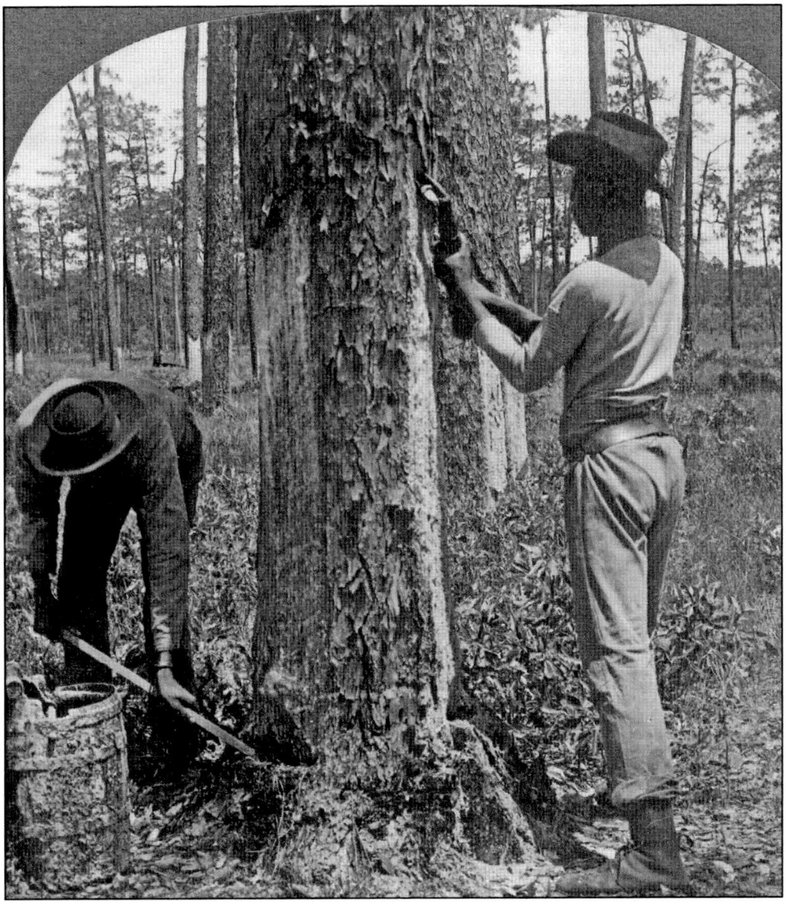

These workers, shown during the 1950s, are "chipping" pine trees in a long, diagonal pattern. The pattern resembled a chevron on a military uniform. The sap drained from the trees through these open areas and was collected in various containers. The pattern on these trees is marked by a shelf-like cut at the bottom. A round container was hung in this shelf and collected the sap. (Both, APP.)

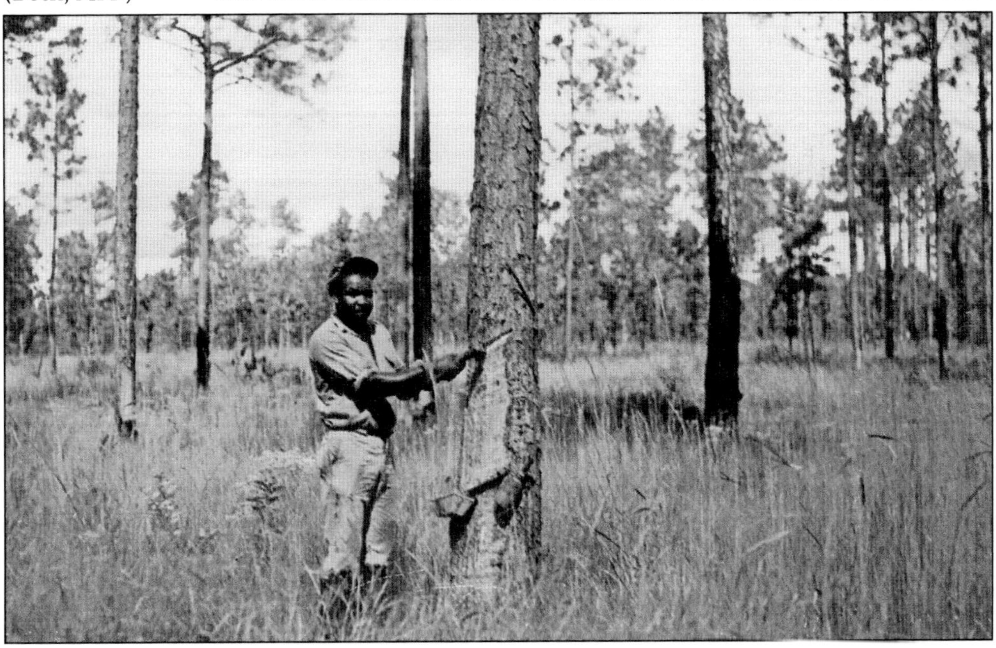

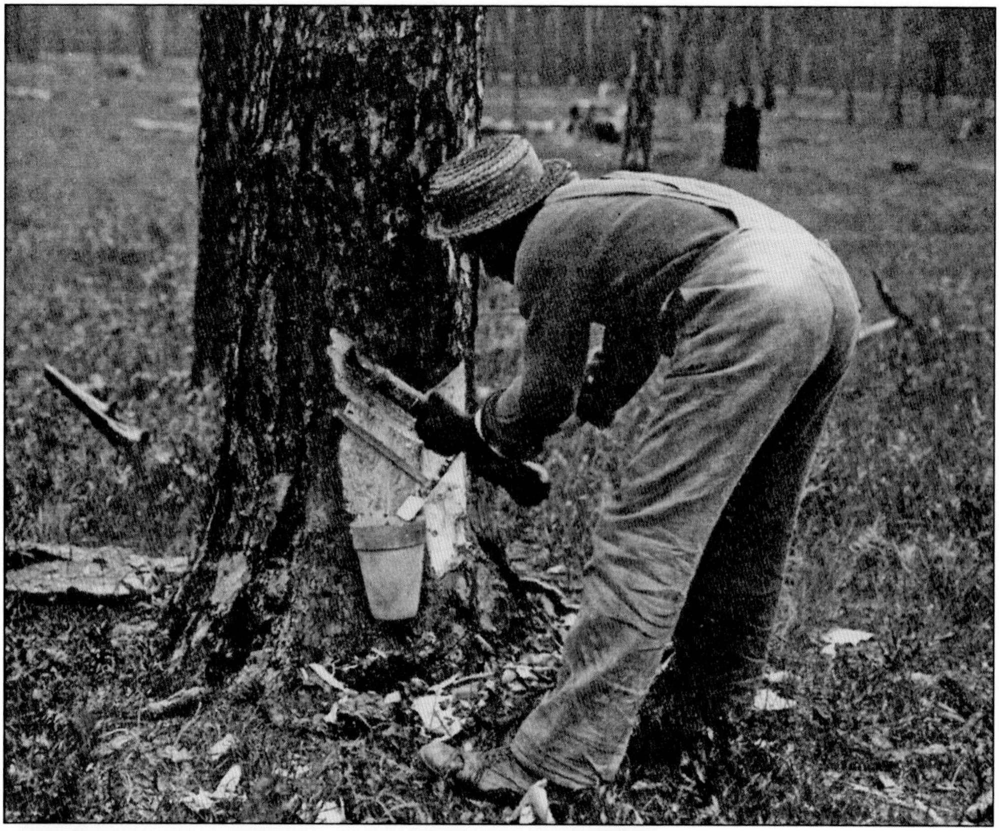

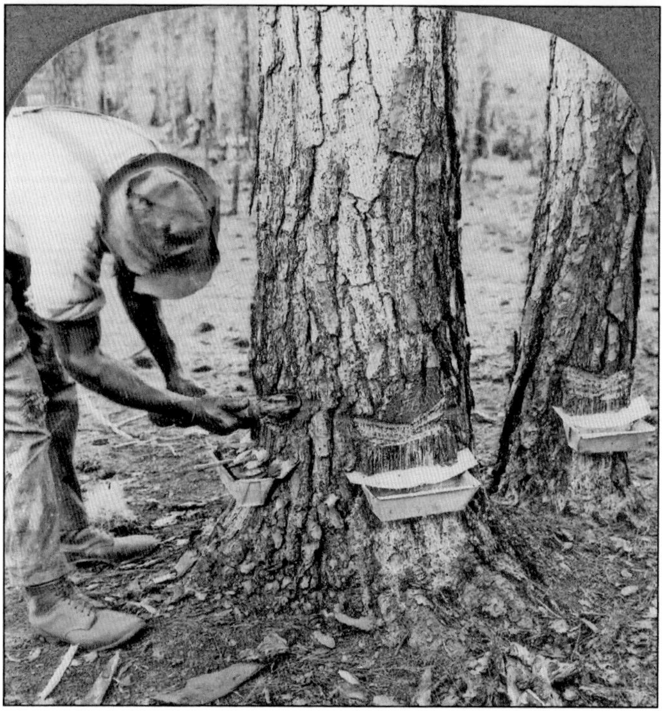

These close-up photographs of the chipping process and the containers used to collect the sap were taken in the 1940s. The photograph above shows the chevron-shaped chipping pattern and the collection container. The photograph at left shows a wider and narrower chipping pattern with an elongated collection tray. The worker has placed a narrow piece of metal into the slit to direct the sap into the pan. (Both, APP.)

Gasoline-powered trucks replaced the mule wagons as the method to transport the sap from the tree to the still, as shown in the photograph at right, taken in the early 1940s. However, the collection of the sap still held to the old-fashioned method. In the photograph below, the worker can be seen emptying the sap into a barrel for transport. This is an example of a new industry that was spawned by the successful naval stores industry. In 1895, a barrel-making factory opened in Colquitt County. It was the county's first manufacturing plant. A second barrel factory followed the next year. (Both, APP.)

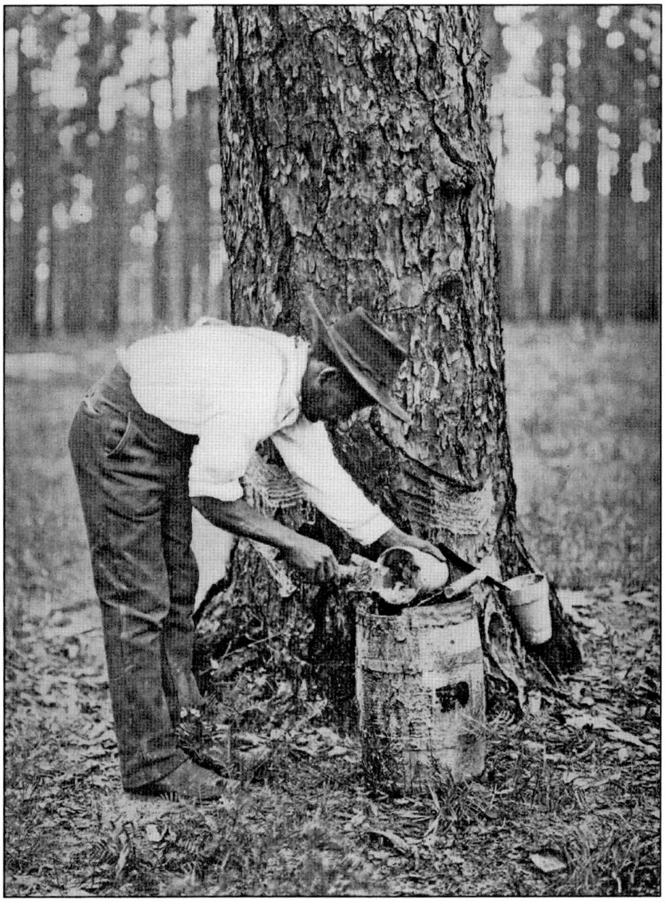

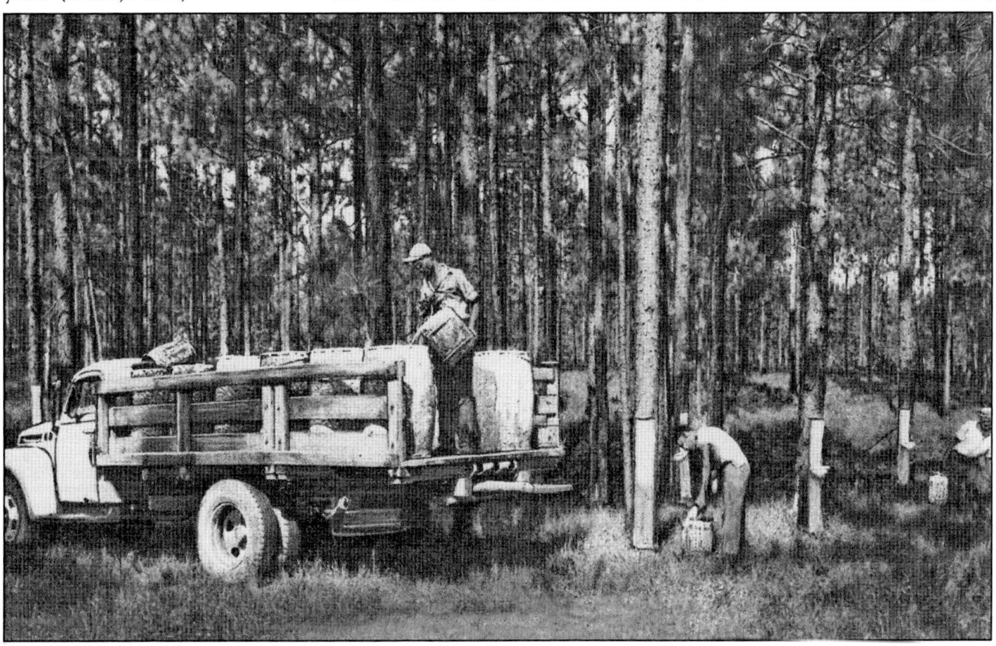

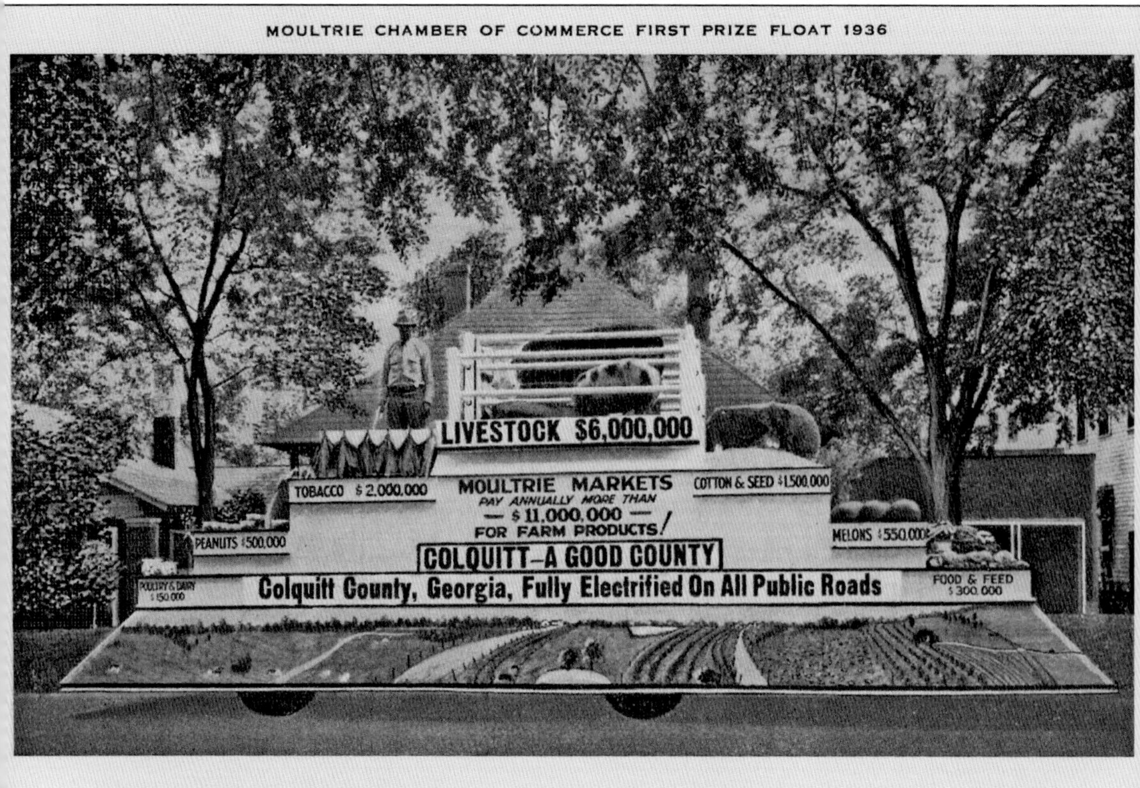

The committee of businessmen who developed the agricultural diversification plan in the early 1900s had the best interests of the citizens of Colquitt County at heart. They realized that reliance on one crop or product could not promise sustained growth and economic stability. In this 1936 photograph of the chamber of commerce's winning entry in a parade, the evidence of their wisdom can be seen. Touting that agricultural products added more than $11 million to the local economy, the float highlighted the many farm products that made up the total—poultry, dairy products, peanuts, tobacco, livestock, cotton, melons, food, and feed. (APP.)

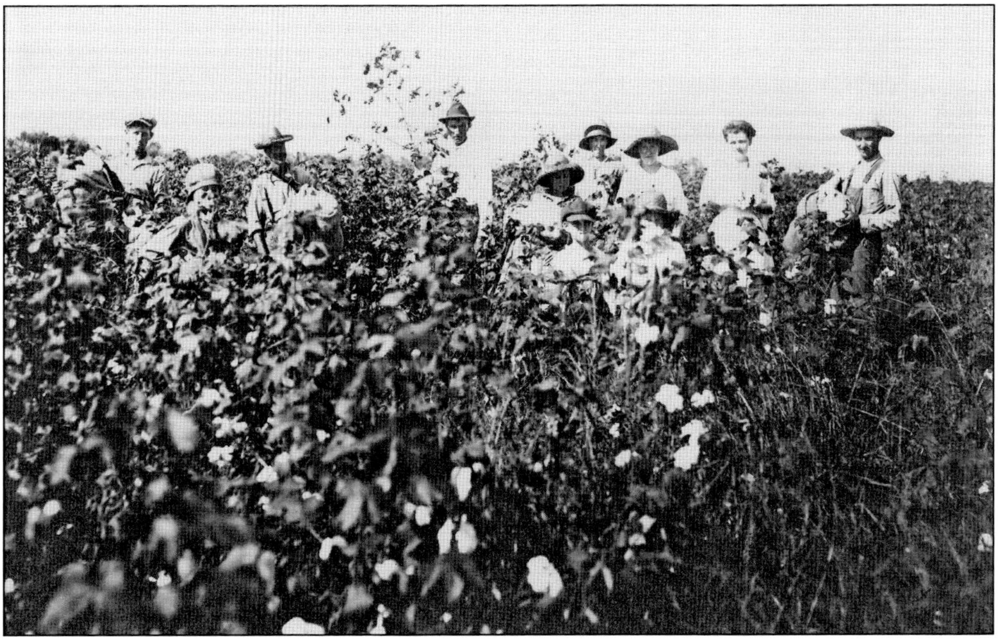

After the naval stores and lumber industries had cleared most of the virgin forests in South Georgia, the next logical step for land use was farming. Cotton was one of the first crops produced. No mechanized equipment was available, so the cotton had to be picked by hand. The families in these two photographs can be seen harvesting a cotton crop. The entire family worked to bring in the crop in these early 1900s photographs. (APP.)

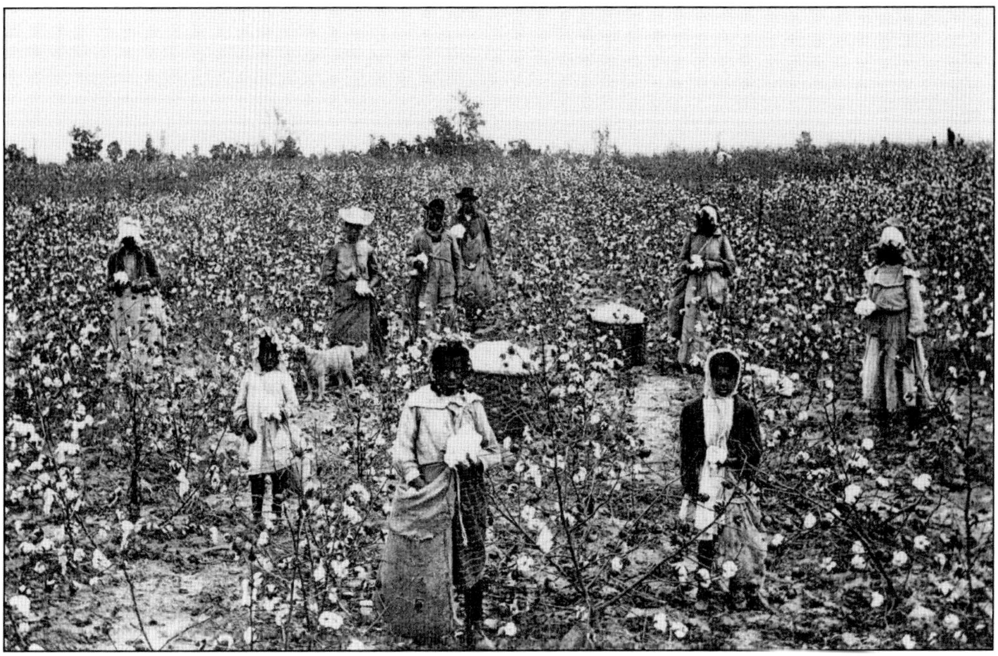

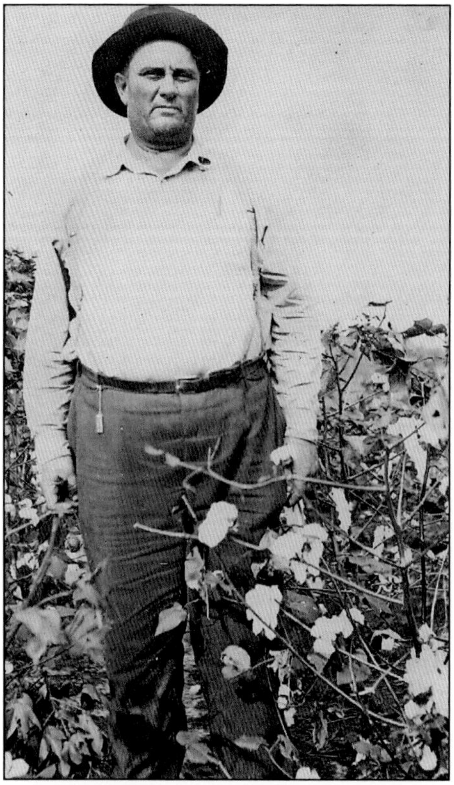

Colquitt County farmer Cliff Jenkins stands in his cotton field in this undated photograph. Jenkins's family had moved to Colquitt County from North Georgia before the beginning of the 20th century to engage in the lumber industry. Cliff's father, Davis Jenkins, and Cliff's brothers opened a sawmill in northeast Moultrie in 1913. Cotton had been important to the economy of Colquitt County, but the arrival of the boll weevil forced farmers to turn to other crops. (MO.)

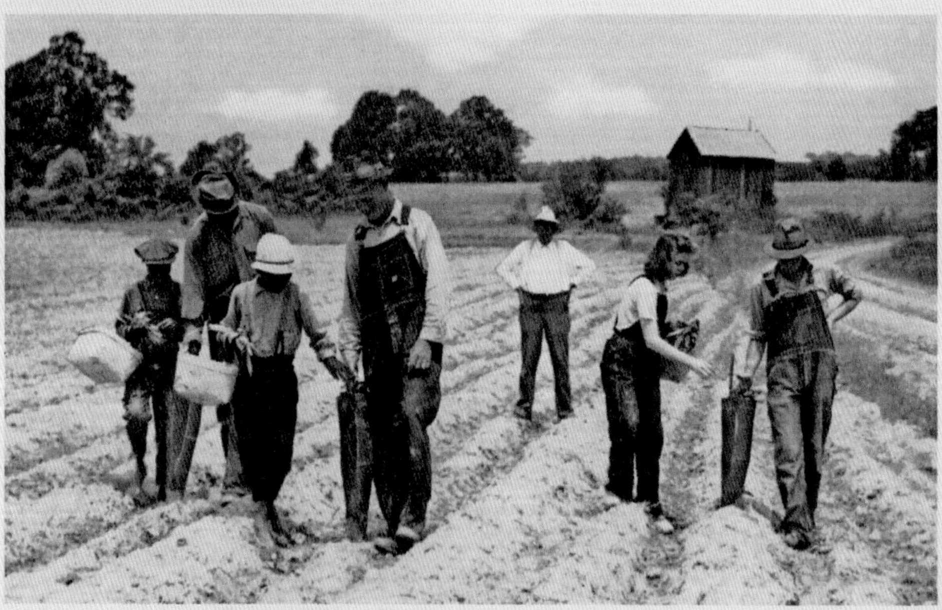

Tobacco Planting Time in Georgia

The first tobacco crop in Colquitt County was grown in 1900, but it was the arrival of the boll weevil a decade later that led more and more cotton farmers to turn to tobacco. In this 1930s photograph, a Colquitt County family plants tobacco before the process was mechanized. (APP.)

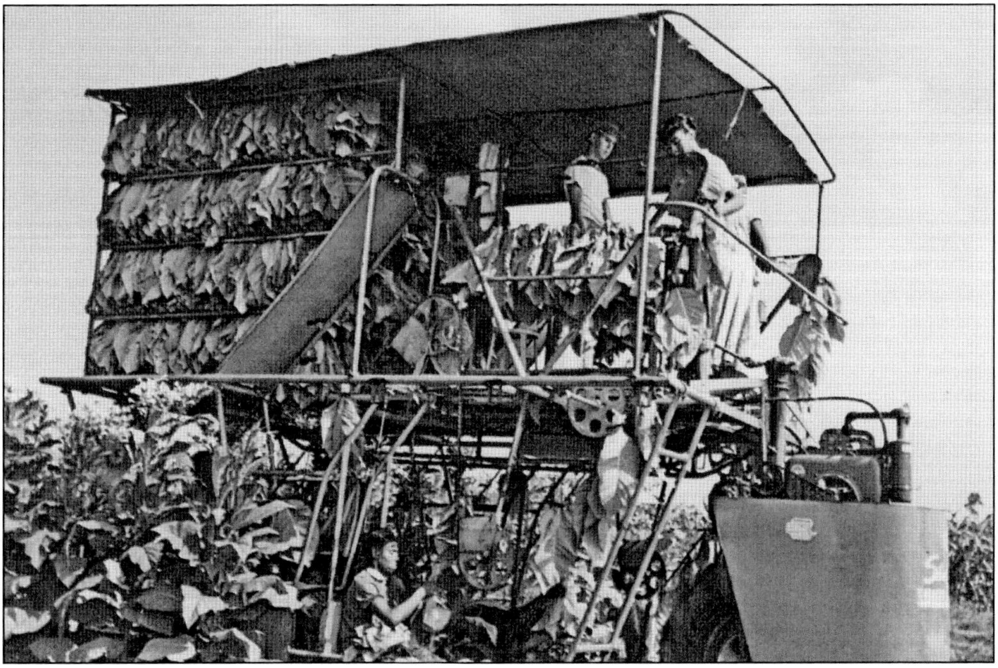

With the advent of mechanical planting and harvesting machines, the work of the tobacco farm became somewhat easier and much faster. Both processes could be accomplished using fewer workers. The harvesting machines shown in these two photographs were typical of the ones used by many local farmers in the 1950s and 1960s. (Both, APP.)

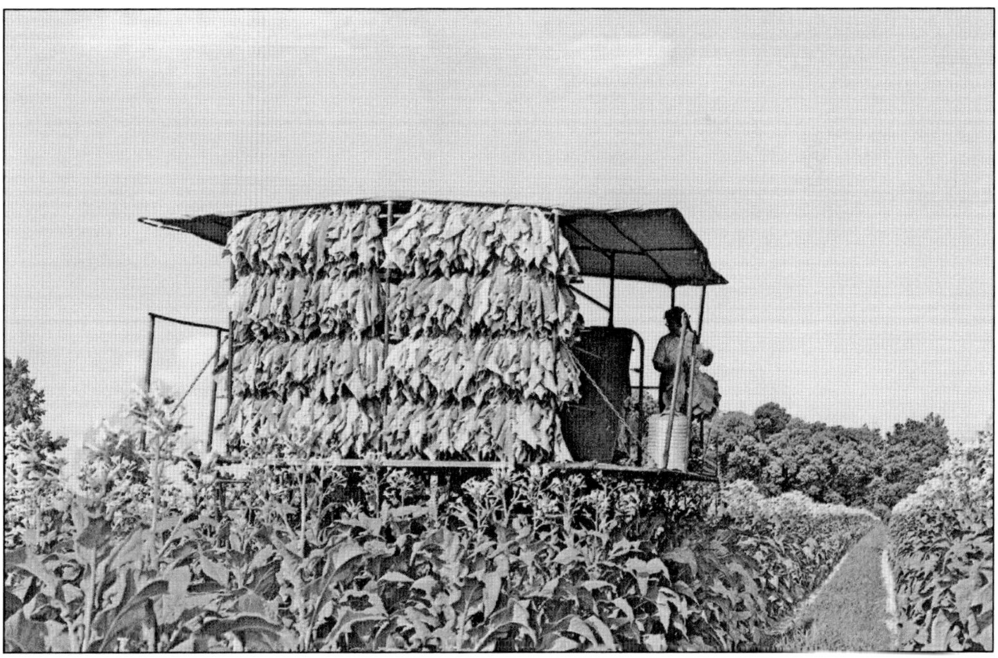

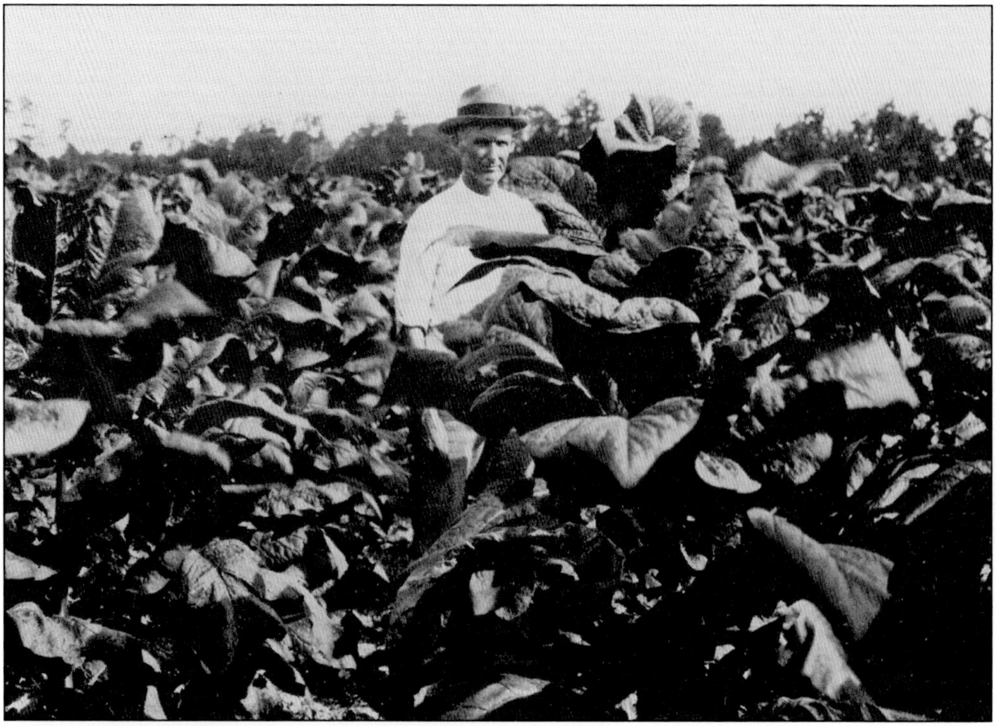

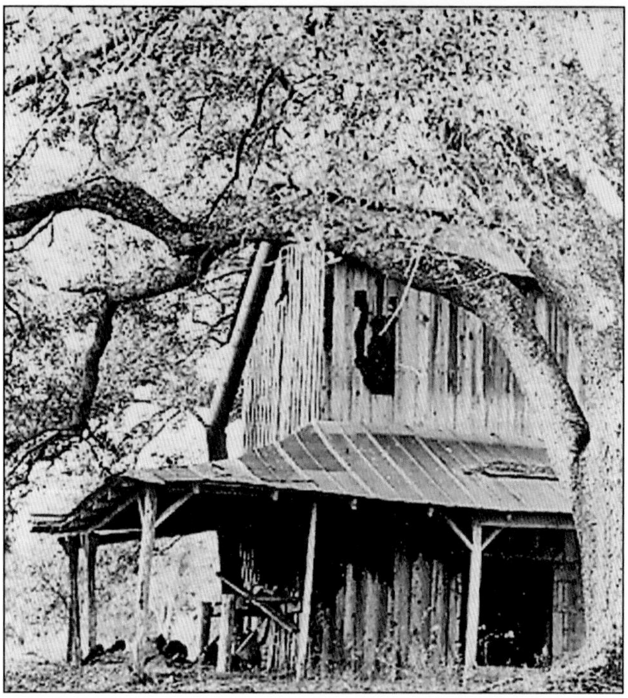

The unidentified man above stands in a field of tobacco that is ready for harvest. At the time this photograph was taken in the 1950s, tobacco was gathered and hung in barns, such as the one at left, to dry. These tobacco barns were noted for their two-story construction and the wide canopy porches that encircled them. The workers could stand under the porch as they removed the tobacco from wagons and prepared it to be hung in the barn. The covering protected them from the intense heat of the summer sun and was used in the winter months to protect farm equipment from the weather. This method was known as flue-cured and would later be replaced by curing the tobacco in bulk barns using heat. (Above, APP; left, MO.)

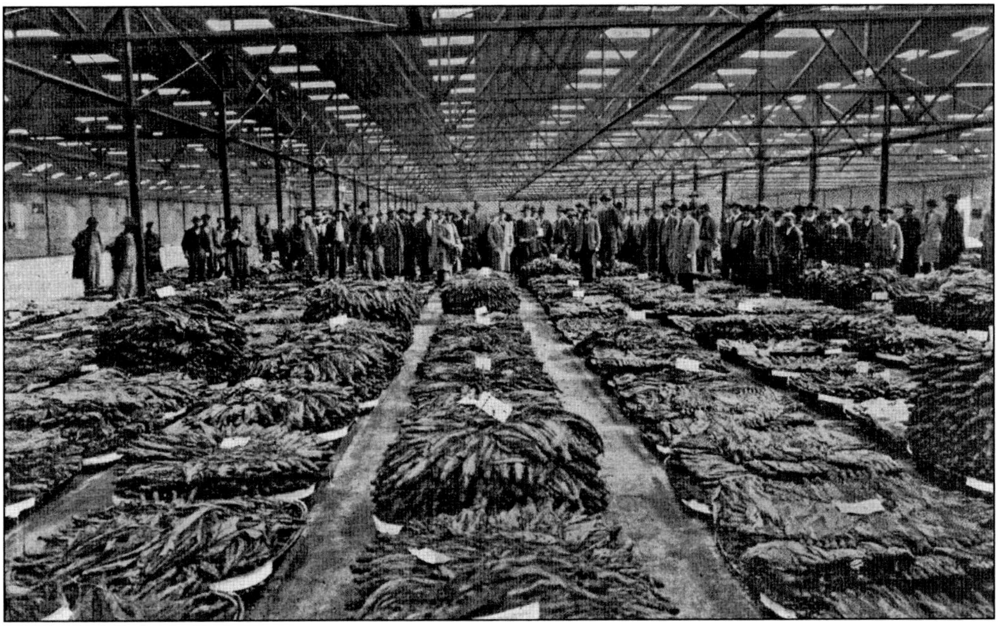

After the tobacco was cured, the farmers would bring it to the markets in Moultrie. After years of attempting to secure approval from the U.S. Tobacco Association, a tobacco market was finally opened in Moultrie in 1925. This allowed county farmers to sell their crops locally. In these photographs of the tobacco markets of the late 1920s, farmers and buyers can be seen in the background behind stacks of cured tobacco. (Both, APP.)

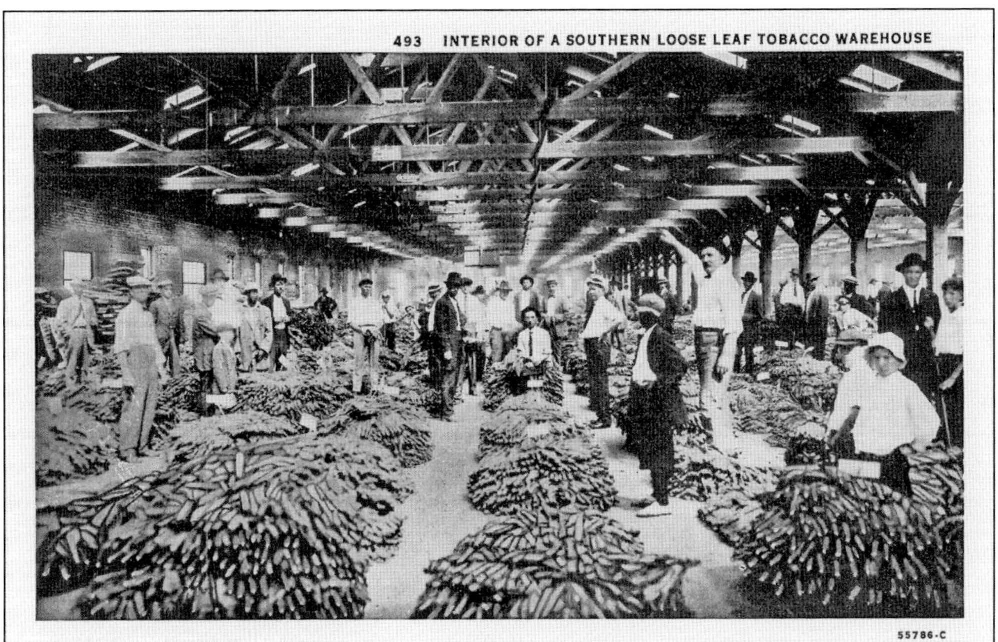

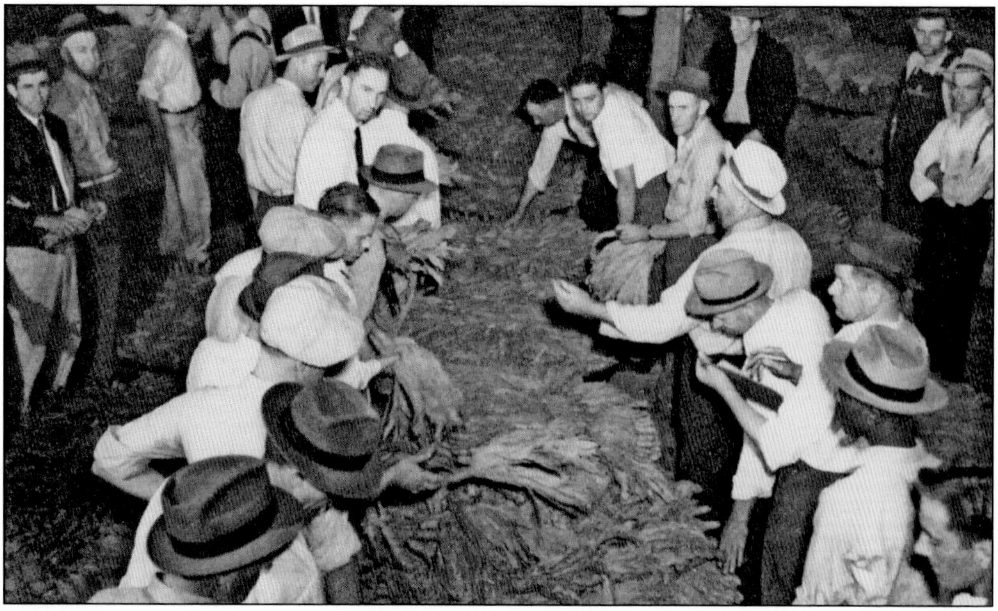

In later years, the tobacco markets became very active. Buyers came to Moultrie from all over the country representing the large tobacco companies. The market season lasted from mid-summer until early fall. Auctions were held daily in warehouses that dotted the downtown area. A typical sale day is seen in these two photographs from the 1950s. Above, buyers and warehousemen follow the auctioneer down each row of tobacco as he calls out the current bid. As each pile of tobacco was sold, it would be marked and prepared for shipment. Below, warehouse workers can be seen in the foreground collecting the tickets on each pile and keeping track of selling prices and buyers. (Above, APP; below, MO.)

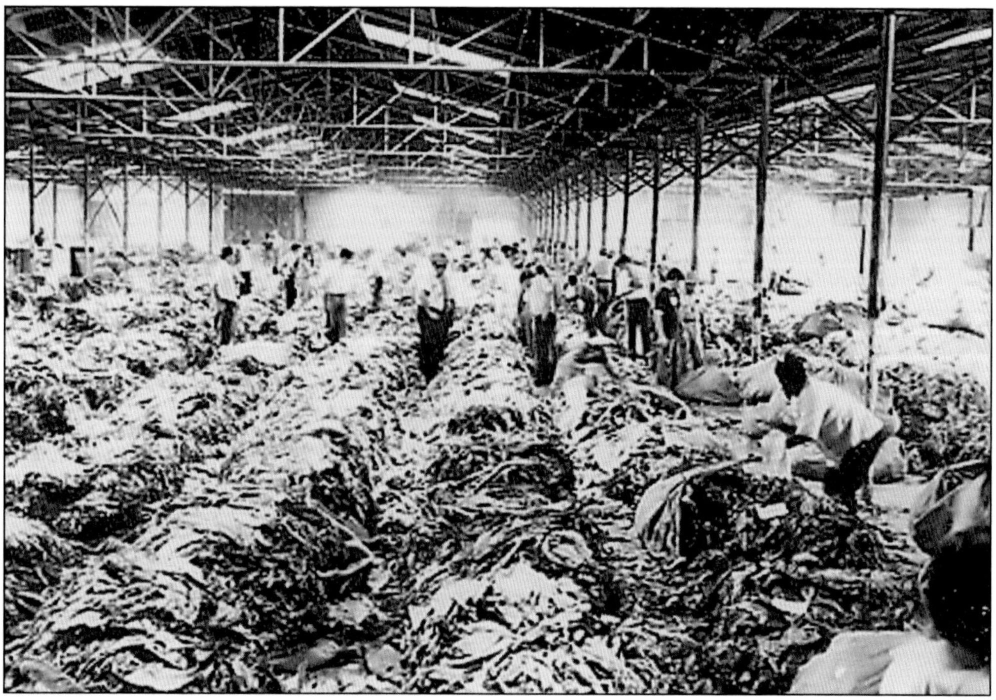

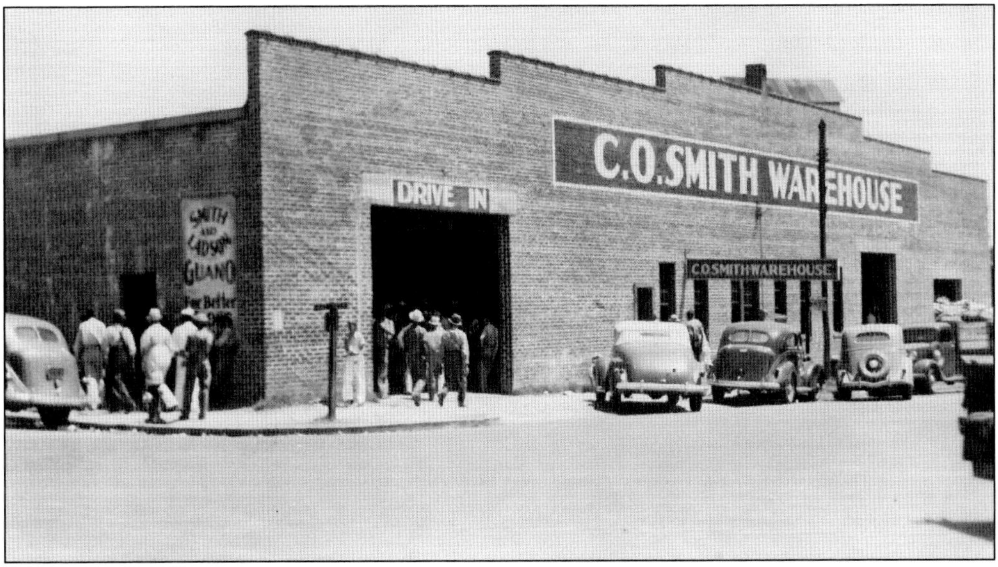

These exterior photographs show two of the many tobacco warehouses scattered throughout Moultrie. These photographs of the C. O. Smith Warehouse and the Peoples Warehouse were taken in the late 1930s or early 1940s. Each warehouse had a large door on each side to accommodate the large farm trucks that carried the tobacco from farm to market. The flat roof had openings that provided illumination for the sale. The smaller doors on the side were opened during the day to allow the breeze to cool the warehouse. When the doors were opened each morning, the smell of tobacco would fill the air. (MSP.)

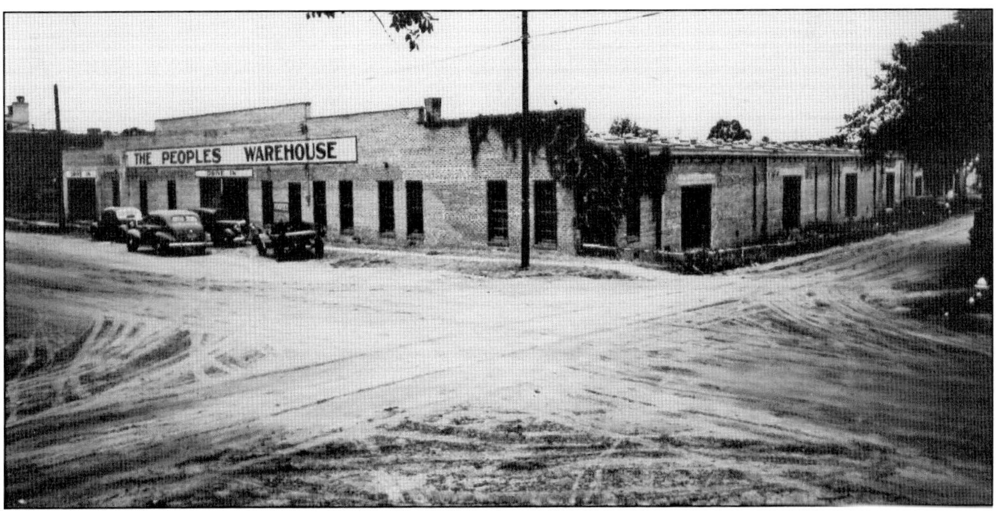

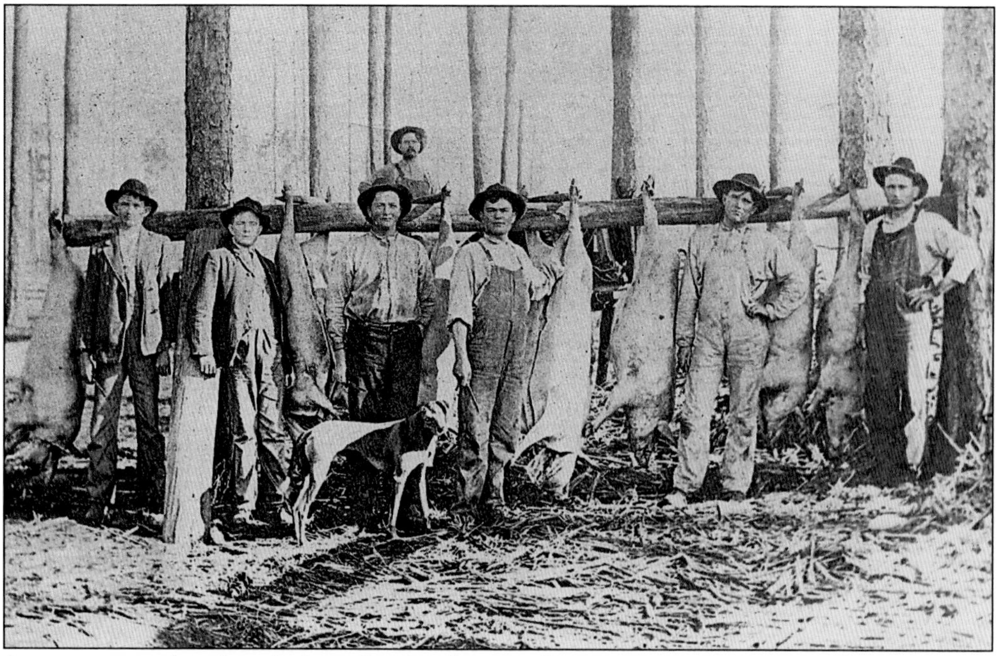

A community of unidentified men butcher hogs in the 1940s. Most farmers raised enough hogs, chickens, and cattle to supply the needs of their families. After butchering, the meat was usually stored in smokehouses to preserve it before the invention of modern refrigeration. (MO.)

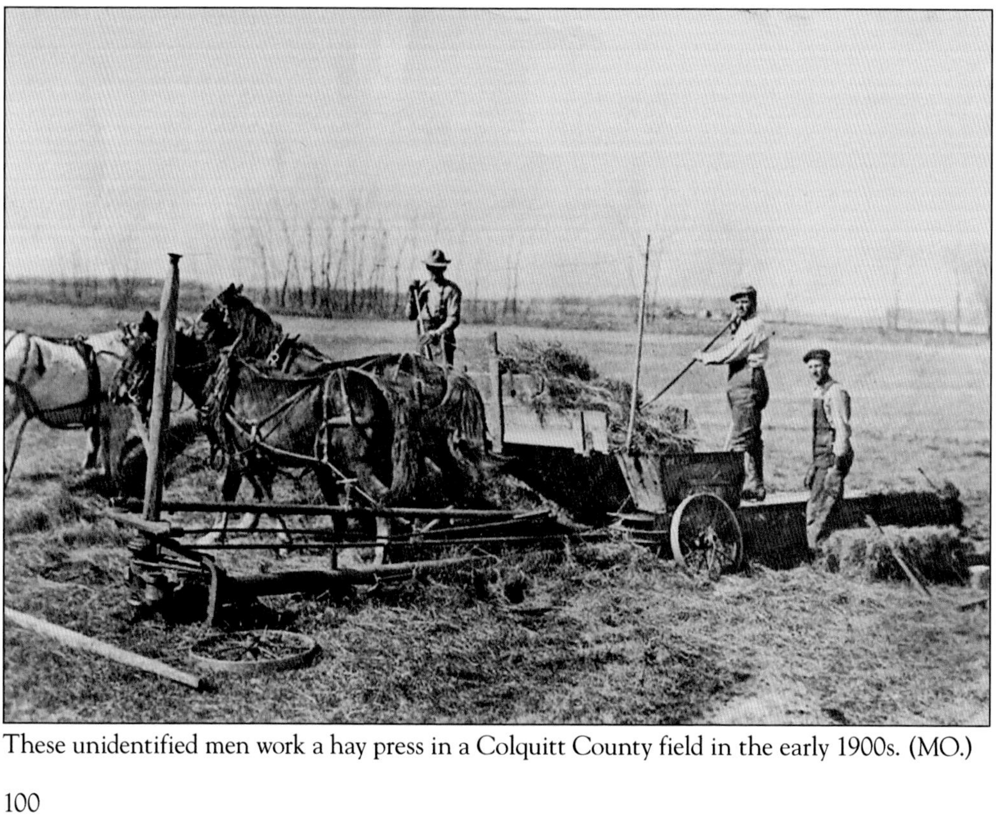

These unidentified men work a hay press in a Colquitt County field in the early 1900s. (MO.)

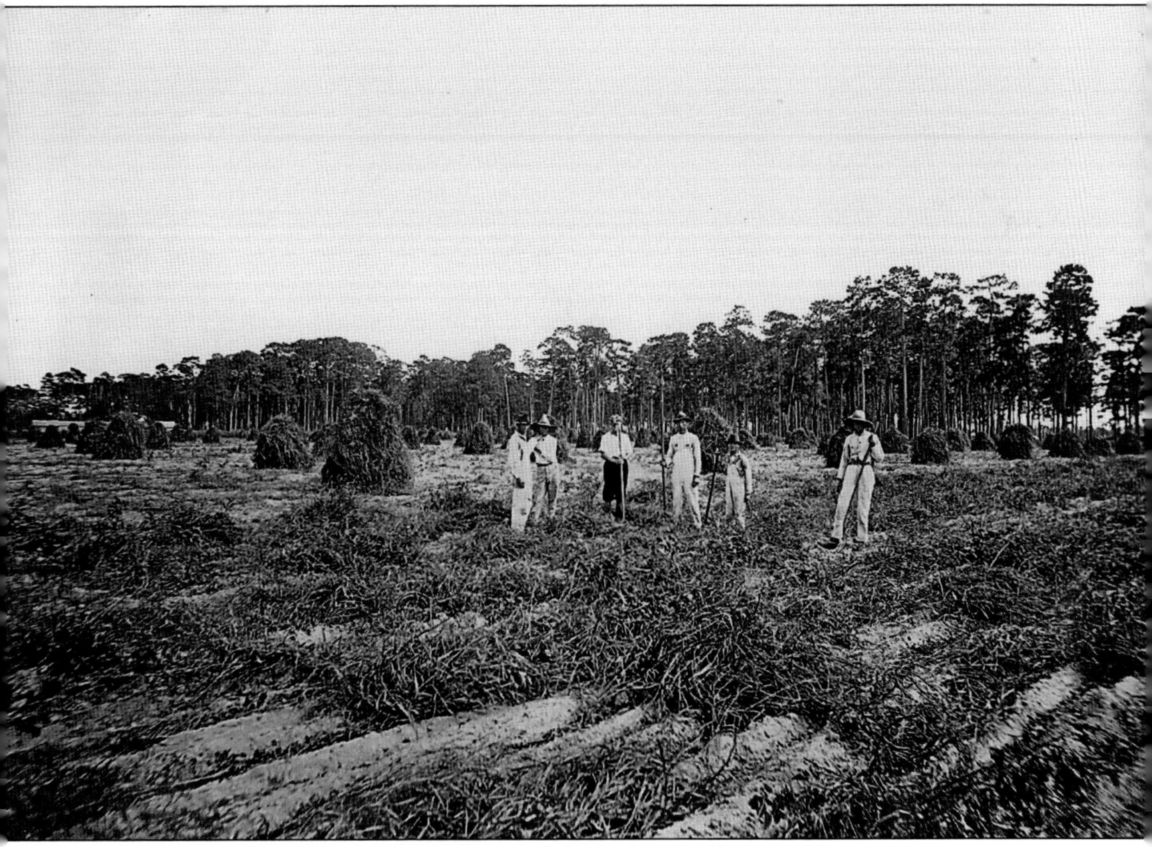

Peanuts were another very important crop for Colquitt County farmers. The nuts were important as a food crop, but oil was also extracted from the nuts. The oil was excellent for frying and was very popular because of its higher boiling point, which kept it from burning when frying. The unidentified workers above are making stacks of the peanut hay after the peanuts have been harvested. (MO.)

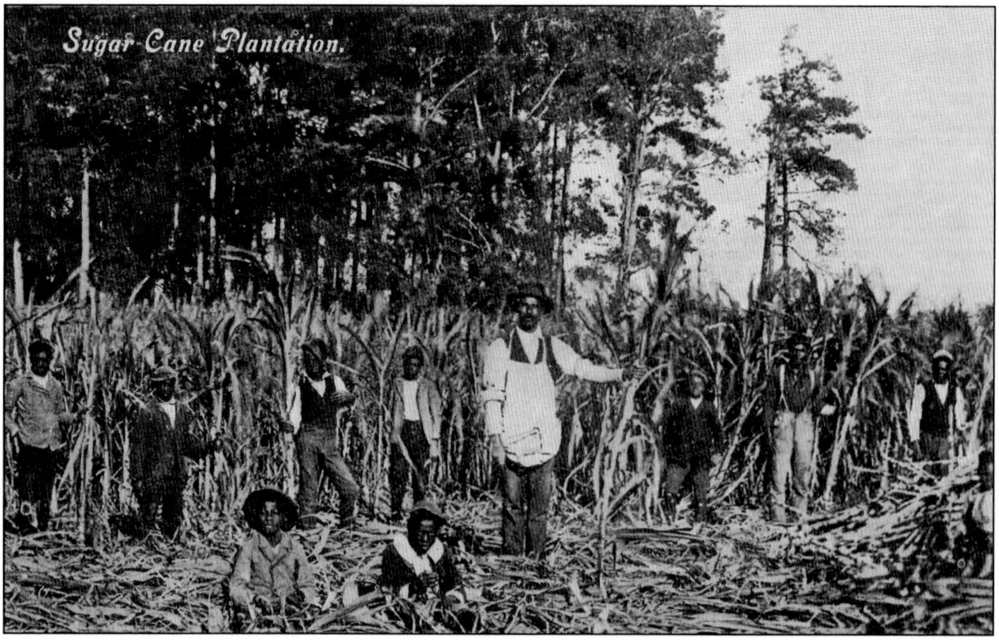

Sugar cane was another important crop in Colquitt County and the South. Once the cane was harvested, as seen in the photograph above, it was taken to the grinding mill, shown below. Before mechanization, the cane was harvested by hand, loaded on horse or mule-drawn wagons, and taken to the mill. The mill was powered by a horse that walked in a circle around the mill, turning a large pole attached to the wheel. (APP.)

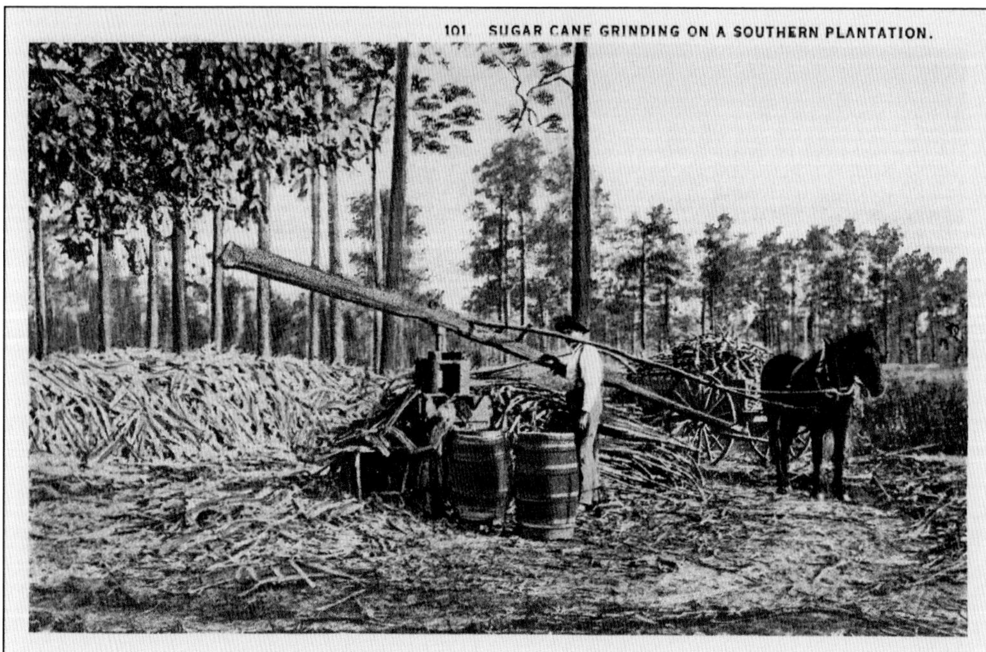

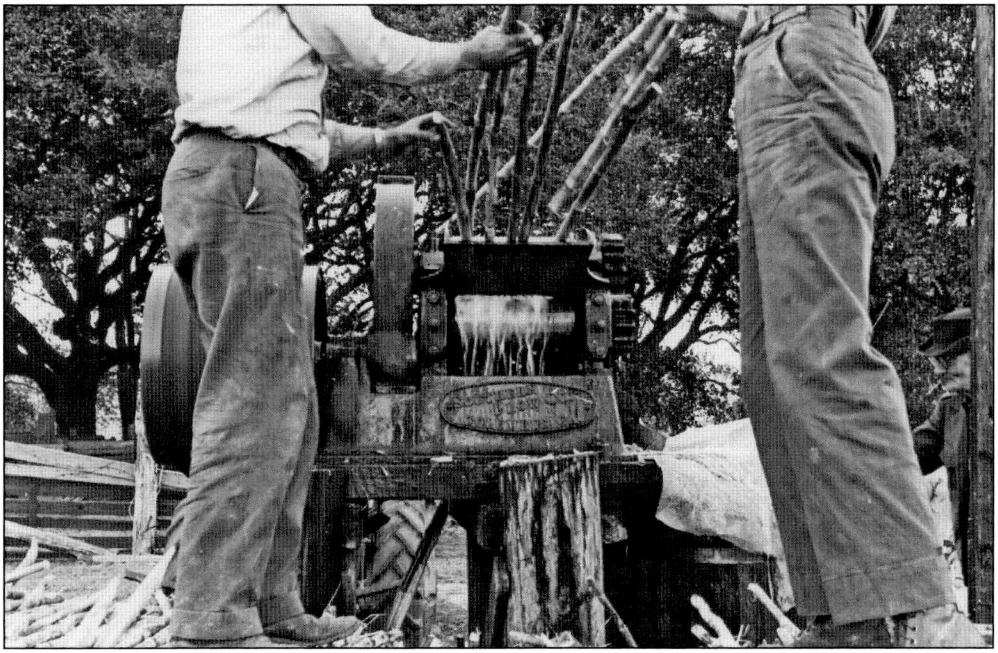

This 1930s close-up view of a cane-grinding mill shows how the workers fed the harvested cane into the mill. As it was pulled between two rollers, the juice was extracted, much the same way that clothes were wrung out using an old-fashioned wringer washing machine. The cane juice could be drunk as a beverage or boiled until it formed a thick, sweet syrup that was used to sweeten cakes and cookies or sop biscuits. (MO.)

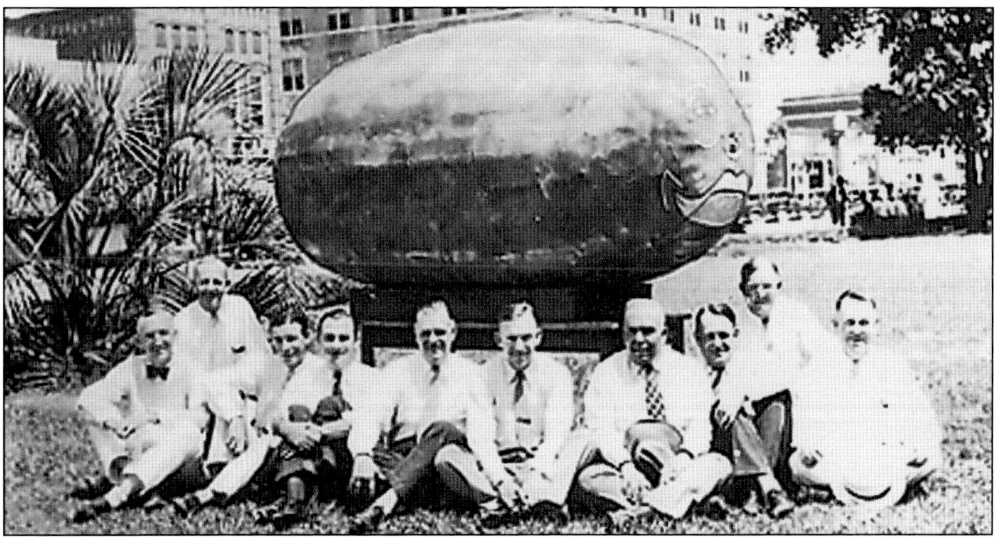

In the 1930s, Moultrie was recognized as the "watermelon center of the world." Richard Aycock and his father, W. E. Aycock, organized the Watermelon Festival of 1932 to celebrate the event. Richard and W. E. Aycock built a talking watermelon. Smith A. Harris spoke over a microphone concealed in the watermelon so that it appeared the huge melon was talking. Gathered around the watermelon are members of the chamber planning committee. From left to right are P. Q. Bynum, Homer Stark, John Parker, David Cohn, Horace McDowell, Alex Hall, Joe Horne, Oscar Kincaid, Jeff Austin, and Smith A. Harris. (MO.)

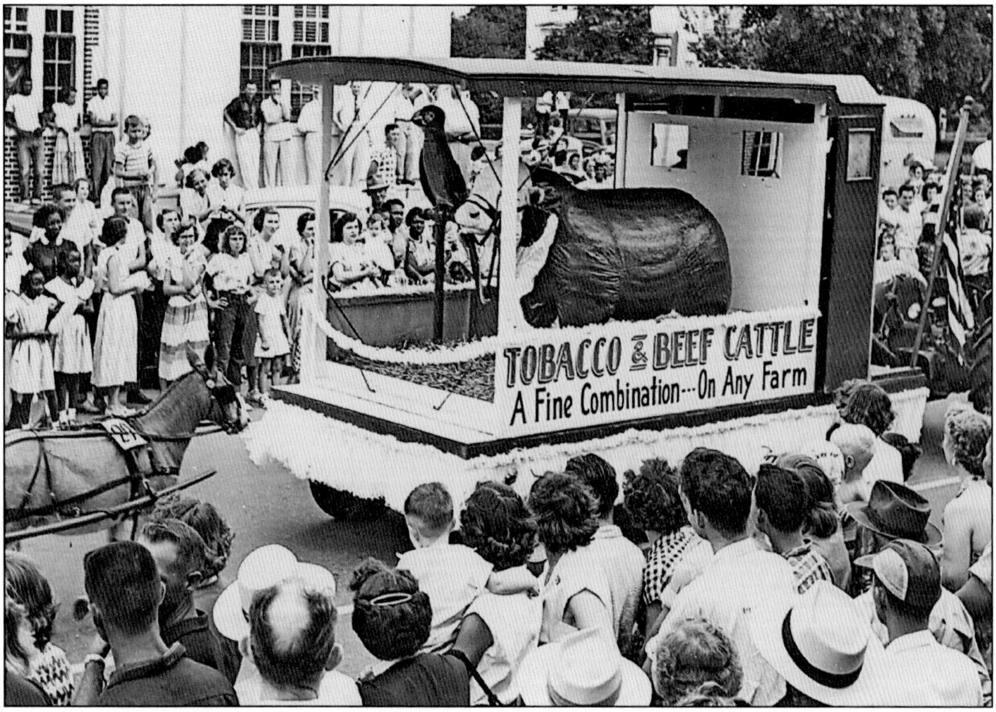

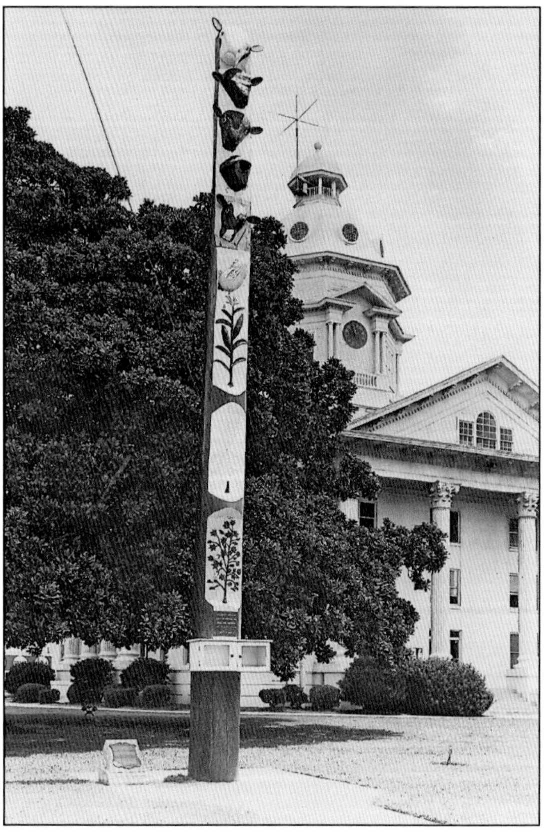

Agriculture was the dominant theme of parades through Moultrie during the 1930s and 1940s. W. E. Aycock is shown on this parade float with his talking bull and talking parrot. Aycock was always promoting Moultrie and Colquitt County products. Like the talking watermelon of the 1932 Watermelon Festival, the bull and the parrot touted the agricultural products raised in Colquitt County. (MO.)

This "Agricultural Totem Pole" was carved in 1963 by W. E. Aycock, an 88-year-old pioneer and civic leader. The pole was dedicated to the farmers of Colquitt County, the number-one agricultural county in Georgia. The pole measured 32.5 feet tall and was carved from a red cypress log that Aycock had found several years earlier in the Ochlocknee River. He carved for four months to complete the tribute, which showed all phases of the county's farm income. The totem pole stood on the courthouse lawn for many years until it fell victim to weather and insects. (MO.)

Nine

Police and Fire Departments

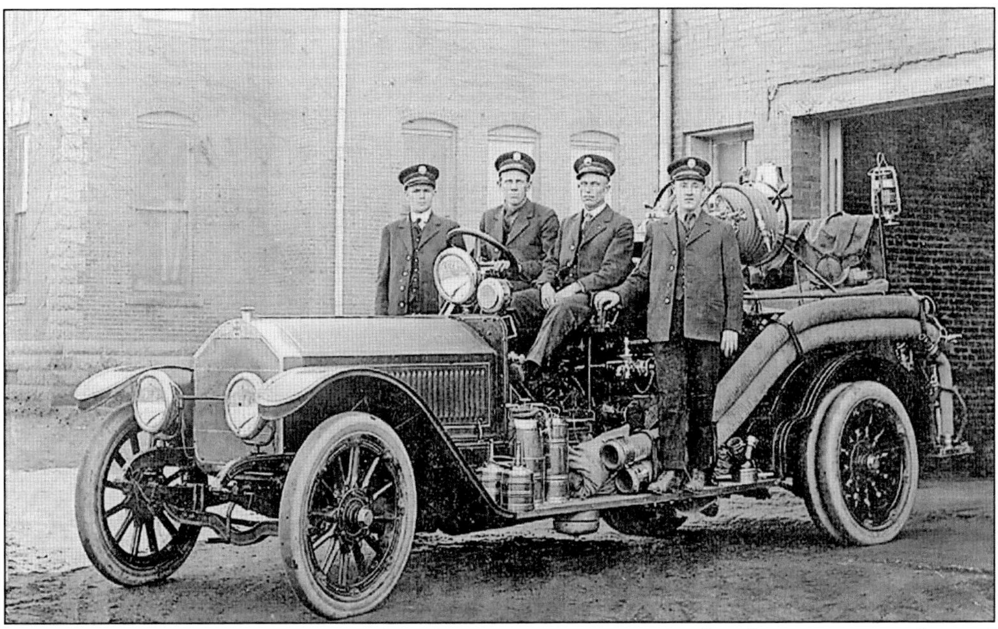

Four Moultrie firefighters pose on their fire engine in 1920. The fire department was located in the rear of the municipal building that stood at the corner of First Street and First Avenue NE. Pictured are, from left to right, two unidentified, fire chief George B. Hunt, and David Marlin Foster. (MCCL.)

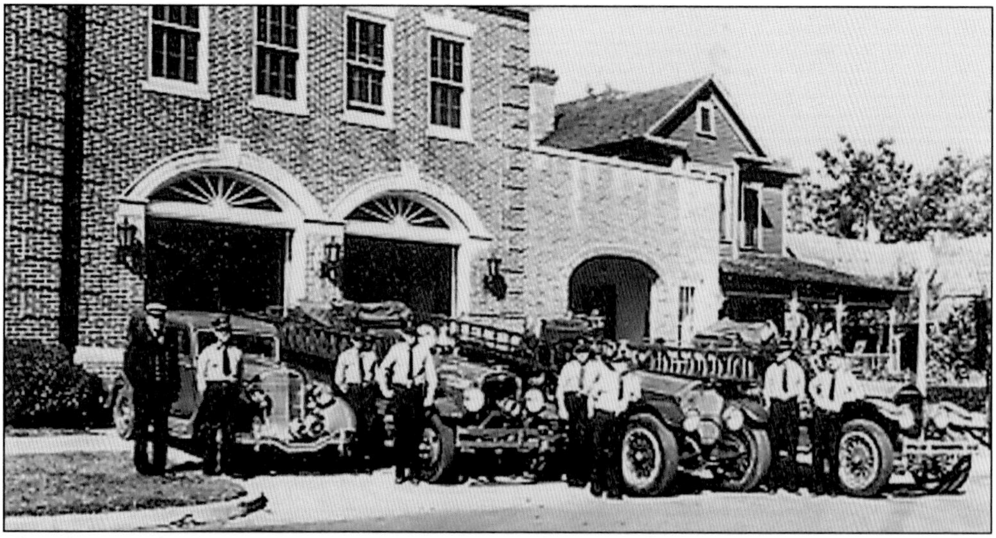

The photograph above, taken in 1939, shows a well-equipped Moultrie Fire Department. The firefighters are, from left to right, Chief George B. Hunt, Herman DeLaughter, Lester Norman, Ivey Castleberry, Charles Rhodes, Oscar Ricks, Kermit Hunnicutt, and Homer Price. Homer Price later became the fire chief. The building below served as the home of the Moultrie Fire Department for many years. It was located on First Avenue NW, directly behind the Carnegie Library. The building was razed in 1966. (Both, MO.)

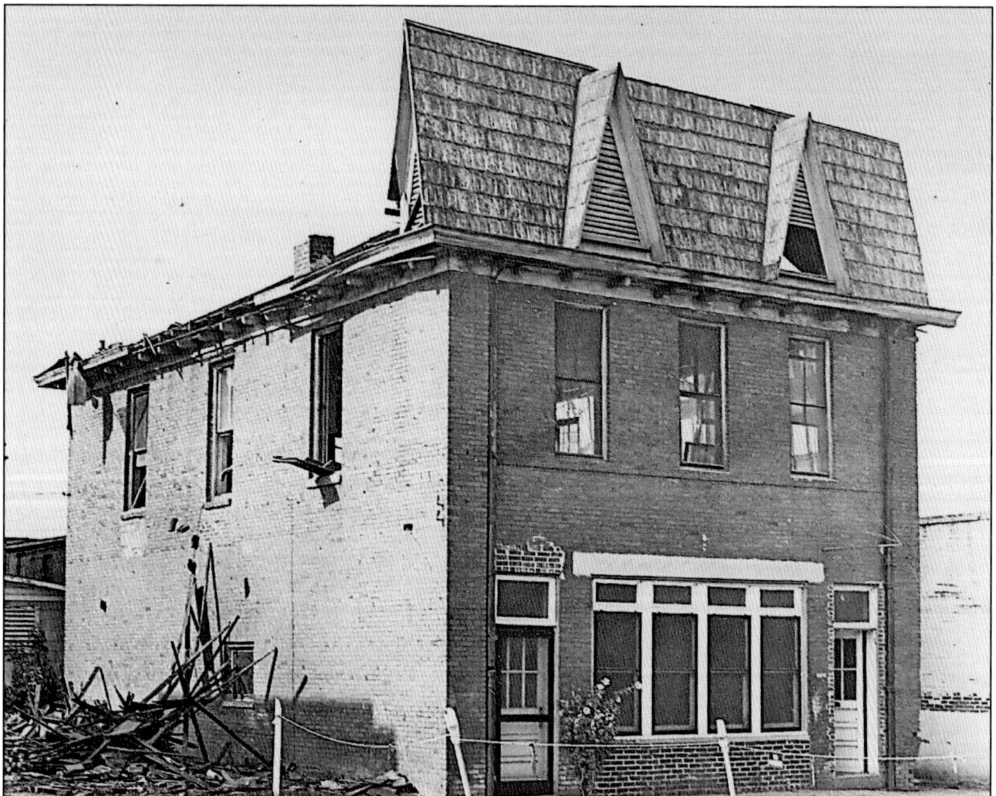

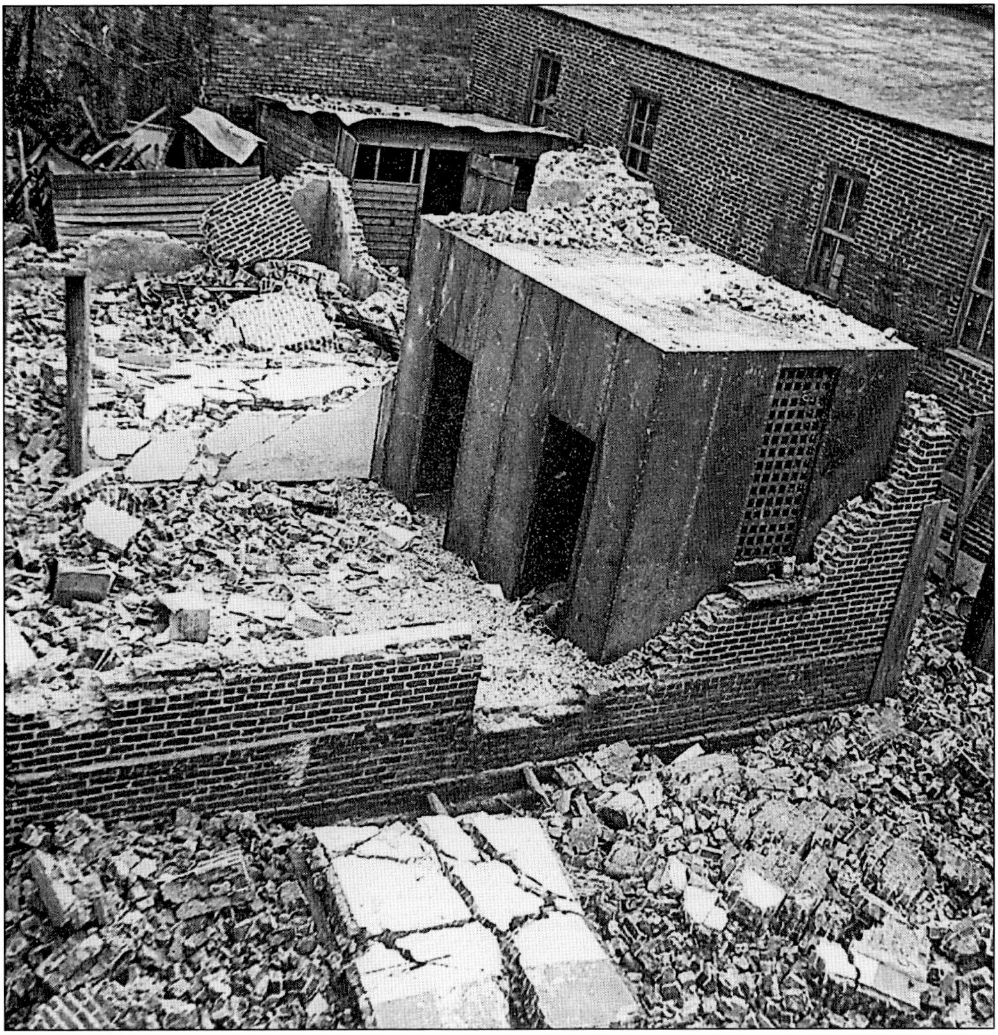

The old Moultrie jail, razed in 1953 to make way for the Colquitt Agricultural Building on First Street and Second Avenue SE, was said to one of the oldest brick structures in the county. It was second in age only to Greenfield Church, located near Autreyville, which was used as a hospital during the Civil War. This photograph was taken during the demolition and shows the maximum-security cells of the jail. (MO.)

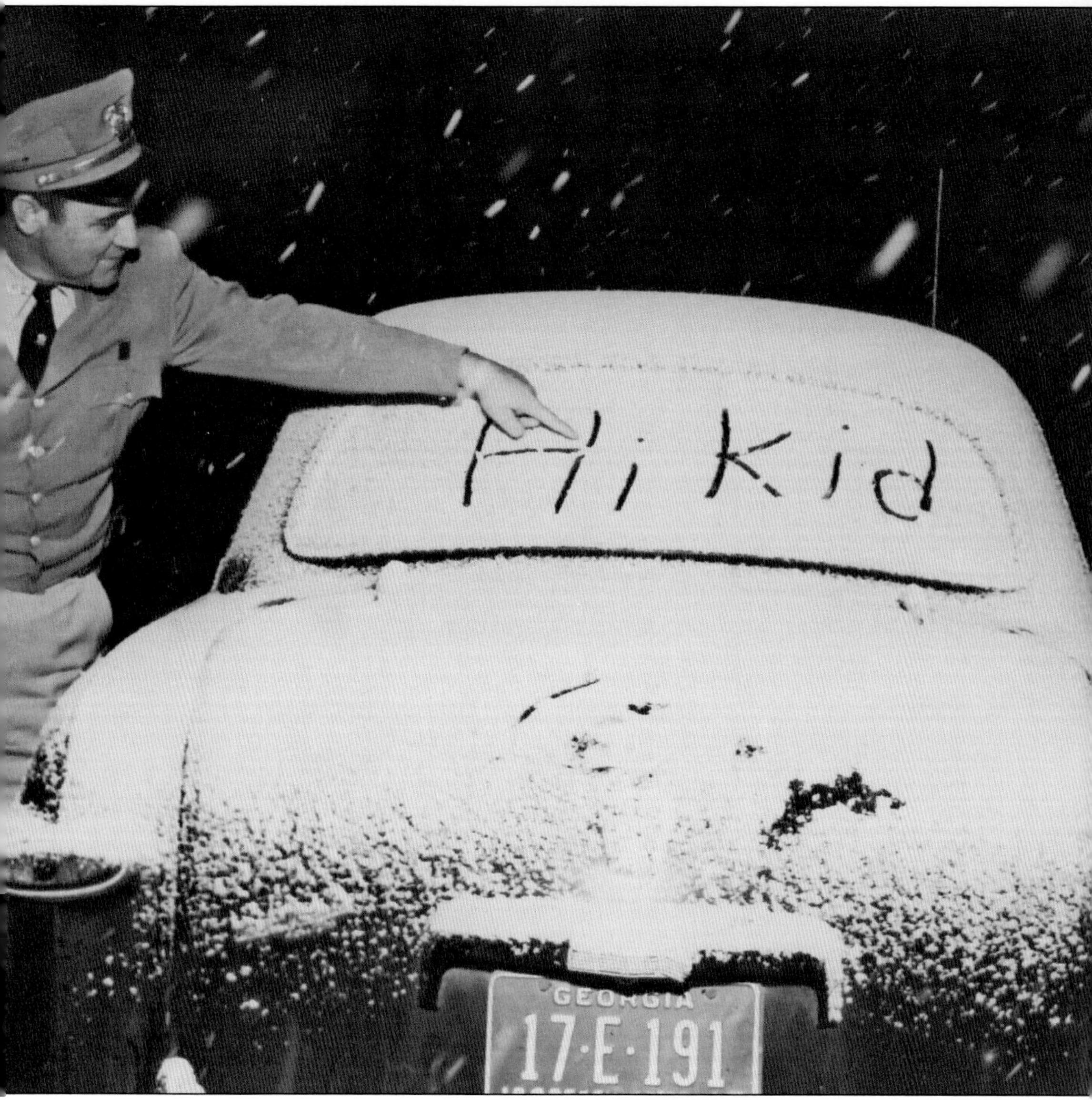

The temperature rarely drops below freezing in Moultrie long enough for it to snow, but this 1957 photograph gives evidence that is has happened occasionally. The unidentified police officer in this photograph cannot restrain himself from acting like a child and scrawling a message on his car. (MO.)

Ten

This and That

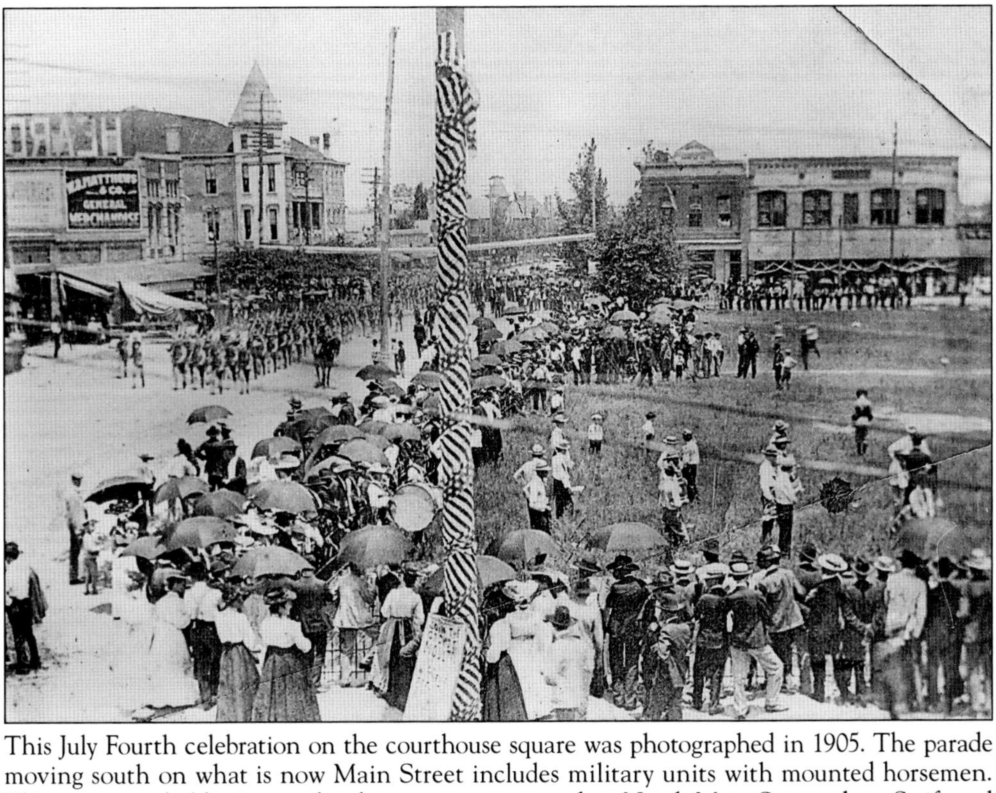

This July Fourth celebration on the courthouse square was photographed in 1905. The parade moving south on what is now Main Street includes military units with mounted horsemen. This event was held prior to a battle reenactment staged on North Main Street where Swift and Company was located. The original Hotel Colquitt, with its distinctive tower, can be seen to the left of the bunting-covered pole. (MO.)

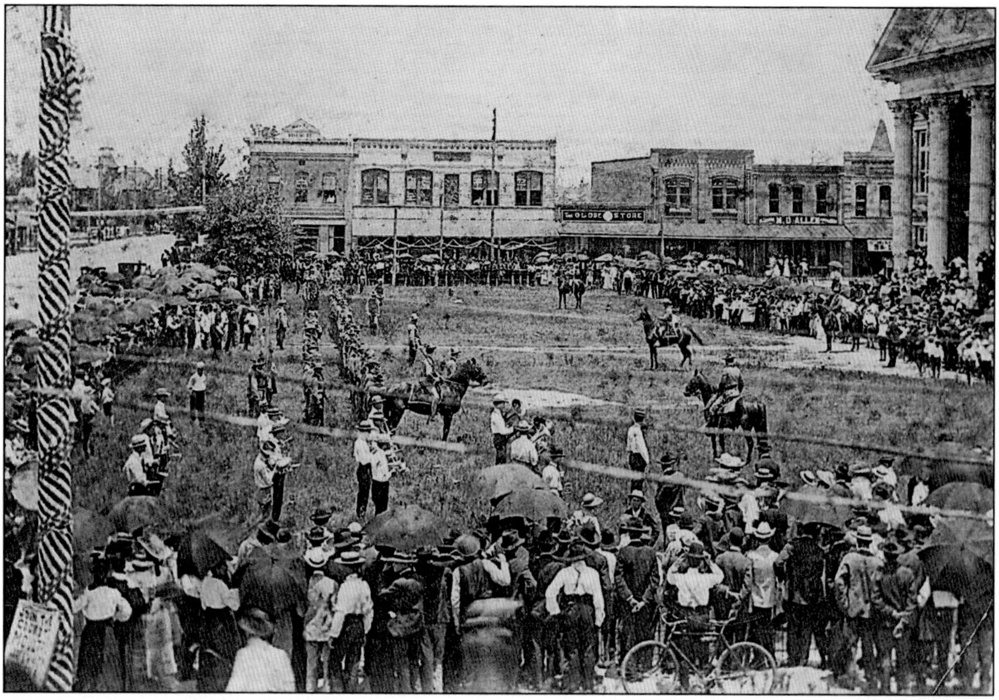

A military unit stands in formation on the west lawn of the courthouse square in this photograph of the July 4, 1905, celebration. A band plays in the foreground, and Moultrie residents in their Sunday-best outfits surround the performance. Notice the ladies with parasols to shield them from the sun and the men wearing skimmer straw hats. One man near the center foreground has dismounted from his bicycle to watch the event. (MO.)

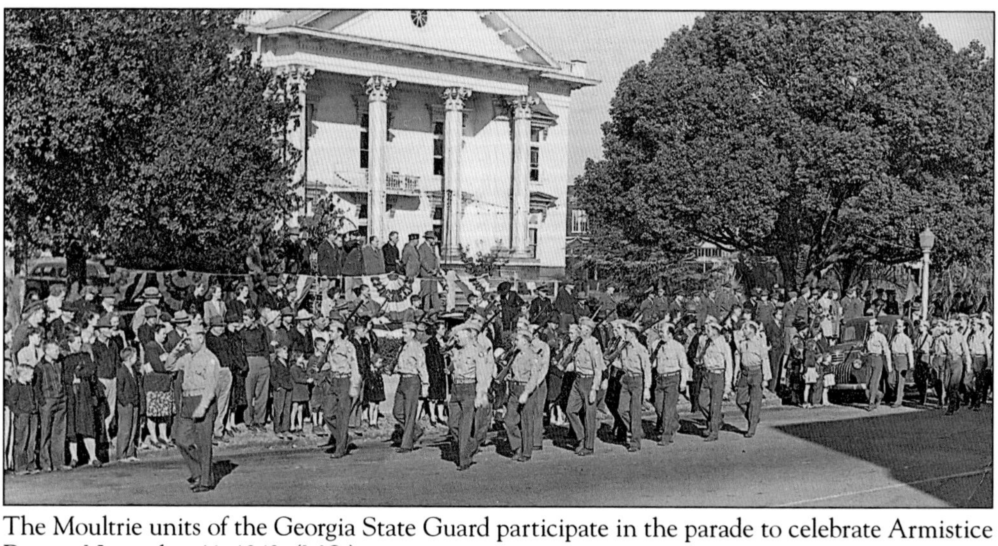

The Moultrie units of the Georgia State Guard participate in the parade to celebrate Armistice Day on November 11, 1942. (MO.)

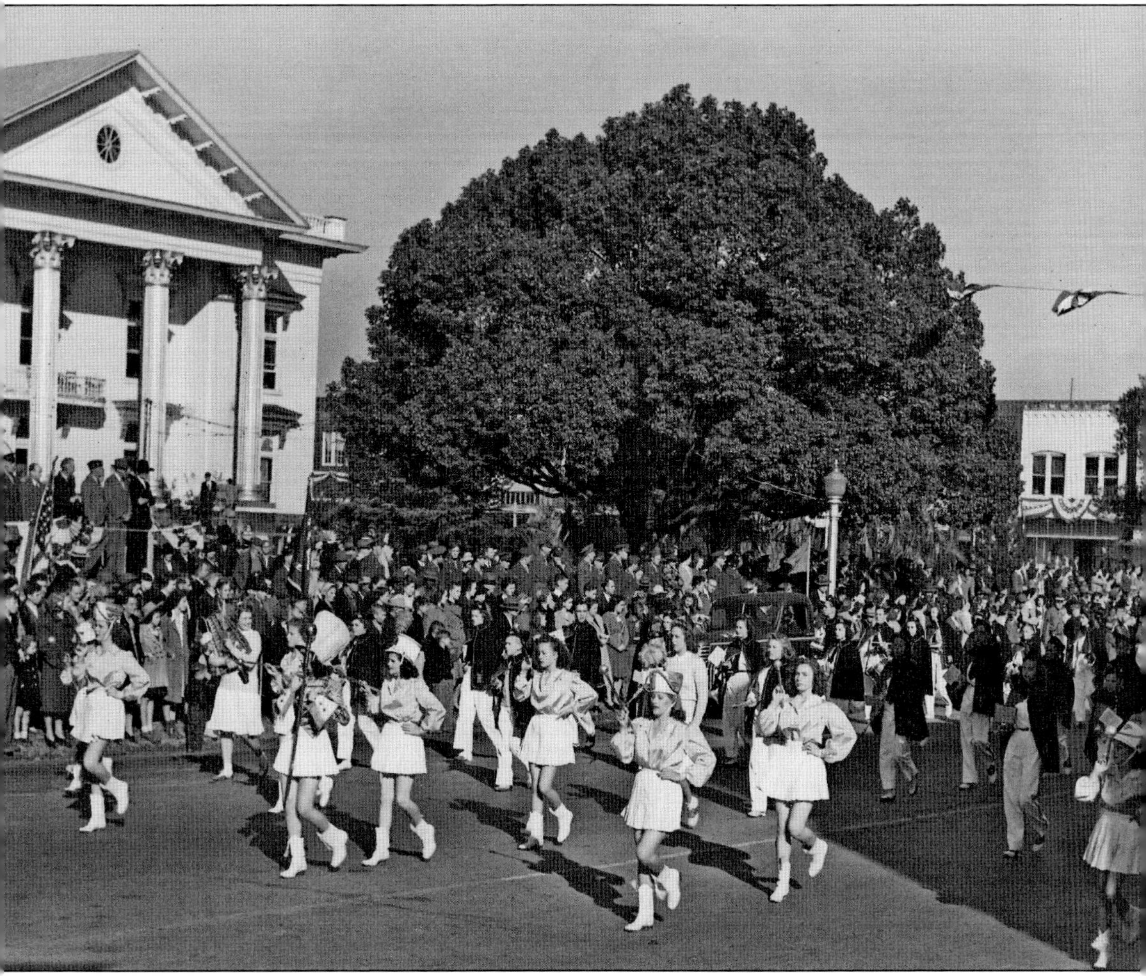

In this post–World War II parade, majorettes and a band march north on Main Street on the west side of the courthouse. This is believed to be an Armistice Day parade in November because of the patriotic decorations and the coats worn by spectators. The band was always a favorite in any parade, because the noise of the instruments encouraged residents to come out on the street to see what was happening. (APP.)

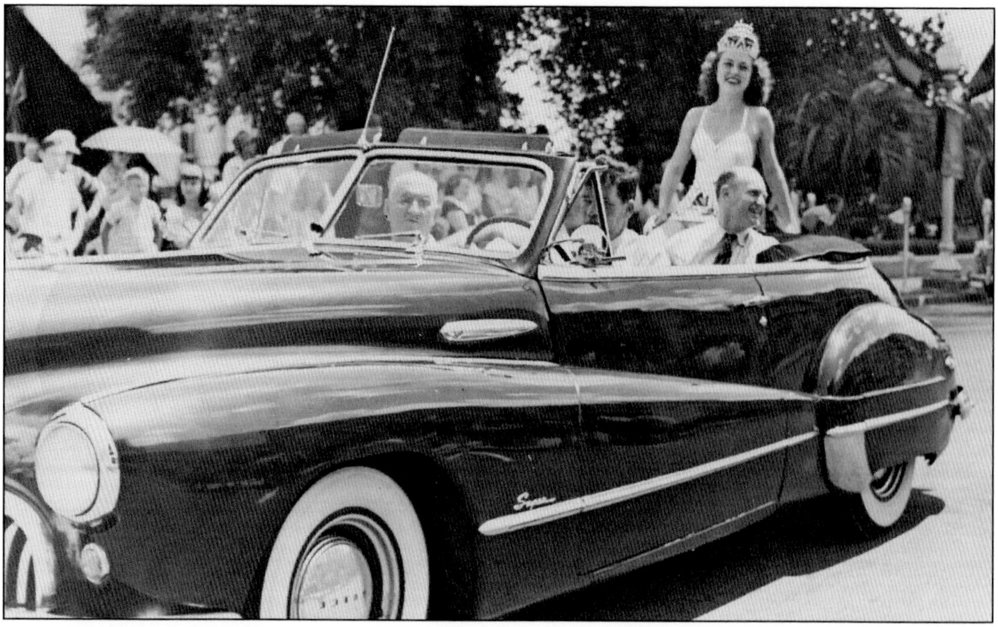

An unidentified queen of a Tobaccoland Parade in the 1950s rides atop the back seat of an eye-catching convertible. Homer Ray Sr. sits in the front passenger seat, and Bill Ladson drives the car. Riding in the back seat behind the driver is longtime Moultrie mayor Willie B. Withers. (MCCL.)

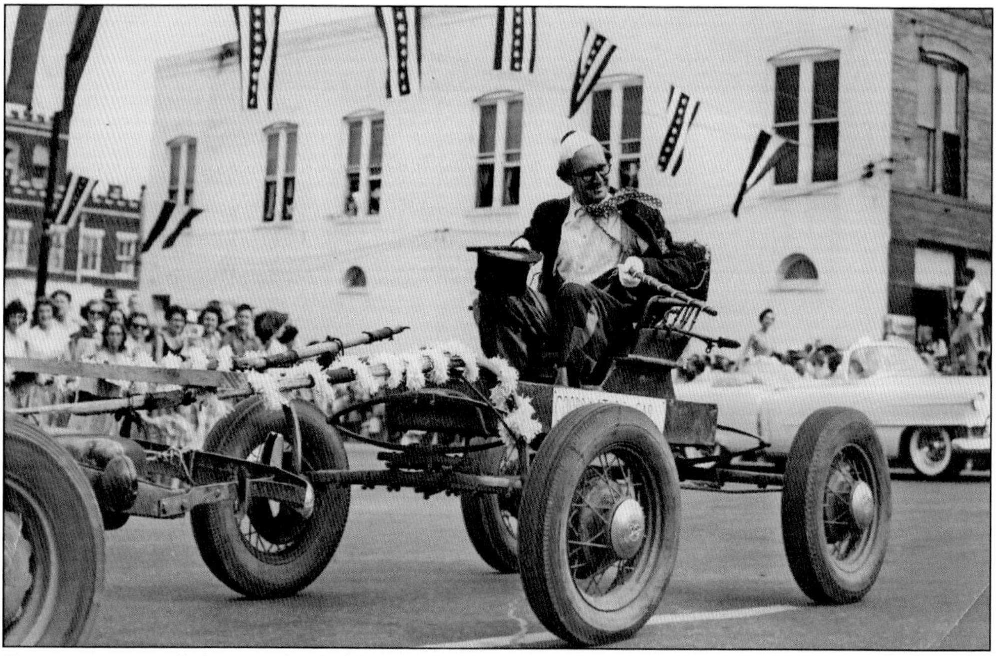

Everyone enjoyed the parades held on the streets of Moultrie. In this 1950s photograph of the Tobaccoland Parade, the clown in the "Coronation Car" is enjoying the attention he receives from spectators. His enjoyment will be short-lived, because the queen's car can been seen rounding the corner behind him. In the background, the Colquitt County Jail can be seen on the left, and Lazarus Department Store can be seen behind the clown. (MCCL.)

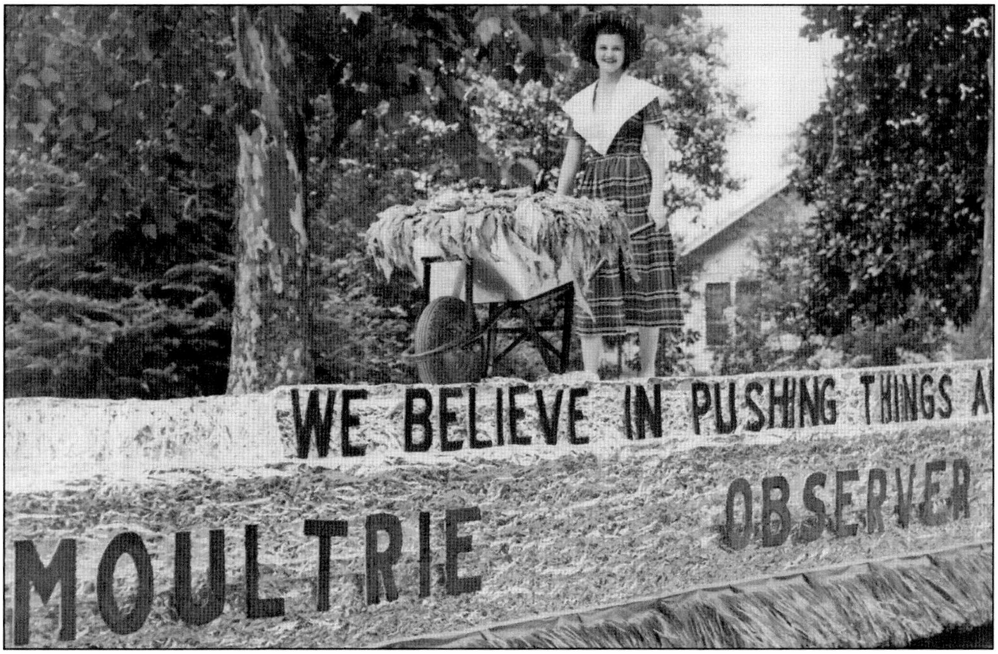

When the Tobaccoland Parade was held, everyone joined in the fun. Businesses, organizations, and churches constructed elaborate floats to participate. This unidentified young lady rides atop the *Moultrie Observer* float while holding a wheelbarrow filled with tobacco. The motto emblazoned on the side conveys that the newspaper believes in pushing things along. (MSP.)

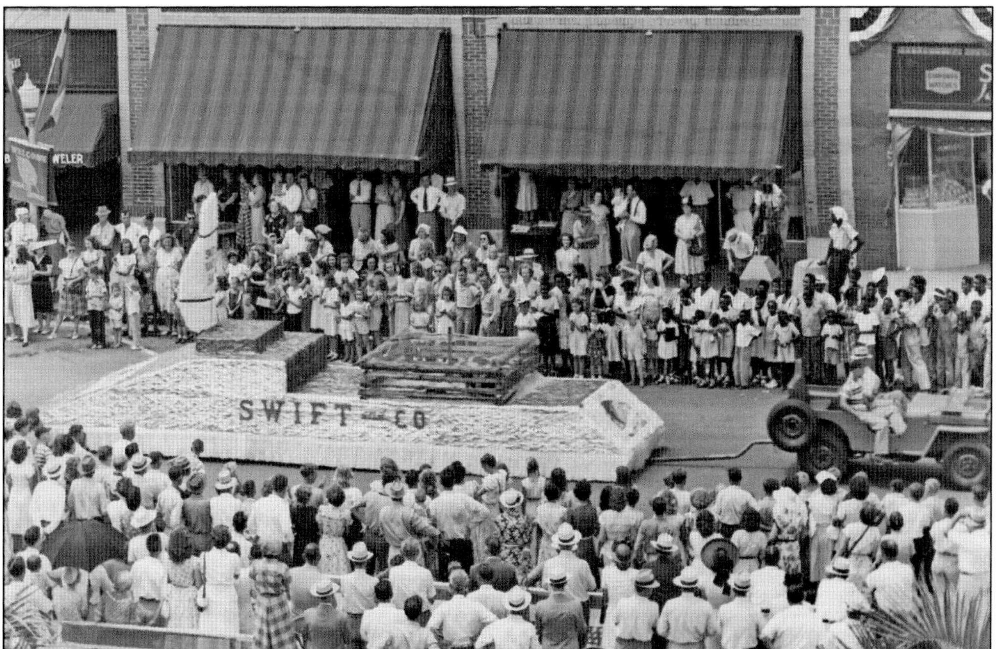

This entry in the parade was provided by the Swift and Company packing plant on North Main Street. The float was passing the judging stand, located on the west side of the courthouse square, as the photograph was taken. (MCCL.)

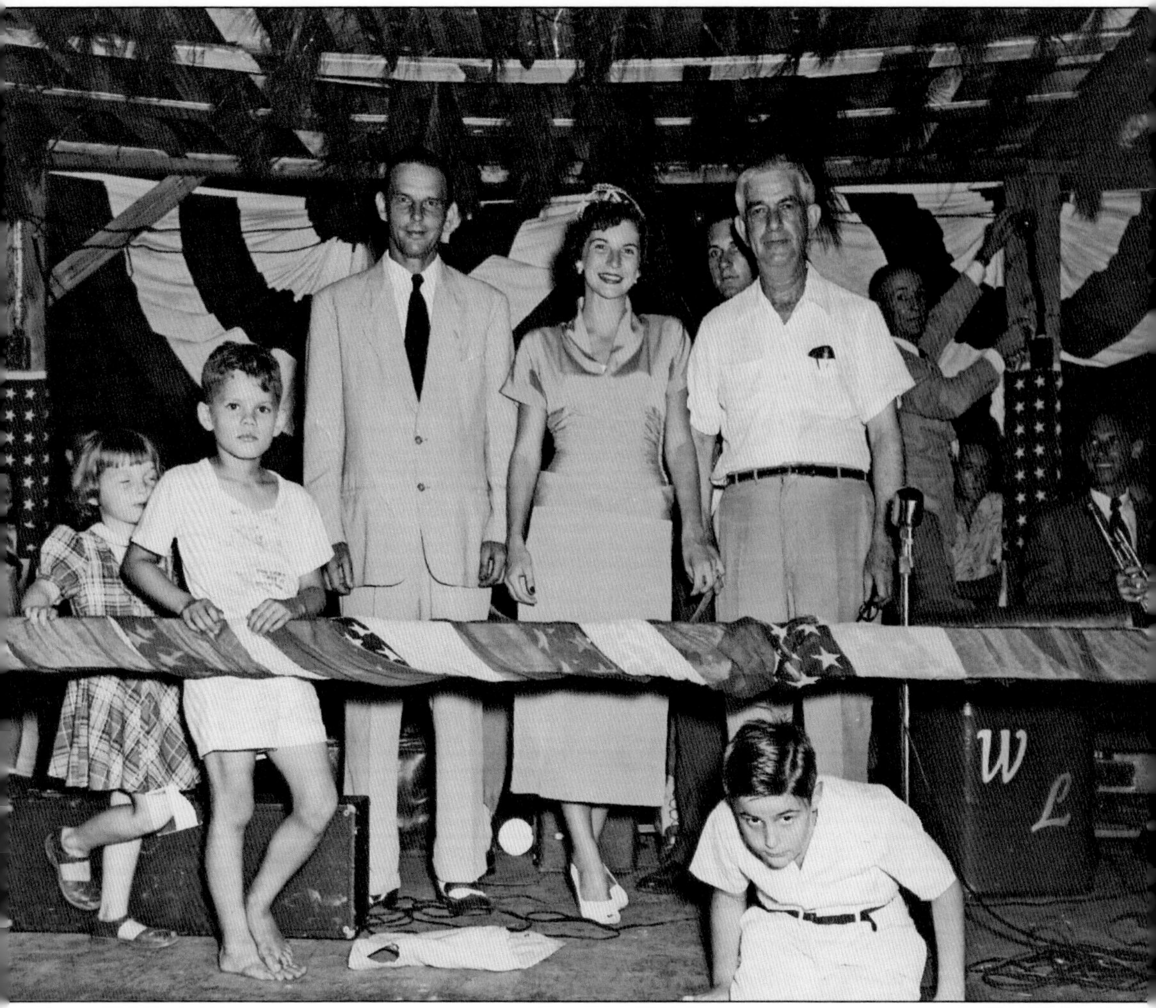

After the festivities and parade during the day in downtown Moultrie, the Tobaccoland celebration moved inside one of the tobacco warehouses for an evening of dancing. The children in this photograph are unidentified. Standing at the bunting-wrapped rail in the center of the scene are, from left to right, Welby Brantley, the unidentified queen of the festival, and Henry Cohen. (MCCL.)

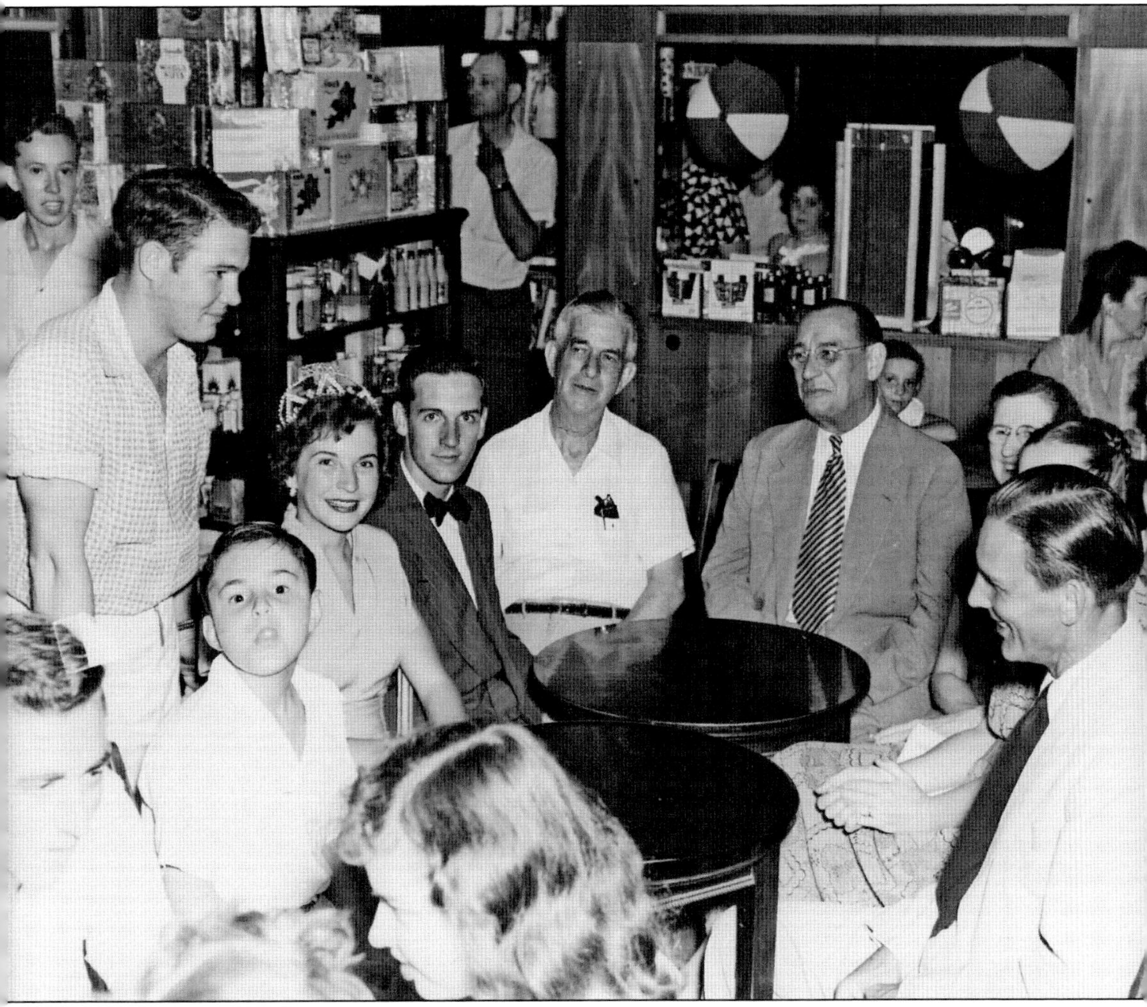

During a break in the activities, the Tobaccoland queen rests for a moment at a table. Standing behind her is Herbert Chastain. Henry Cohen is seen in the center wearing a white shirt. In the foreground on the right is Welby Brantley. The young lady in the center foreground is Claire Mobley. (MCCL.)

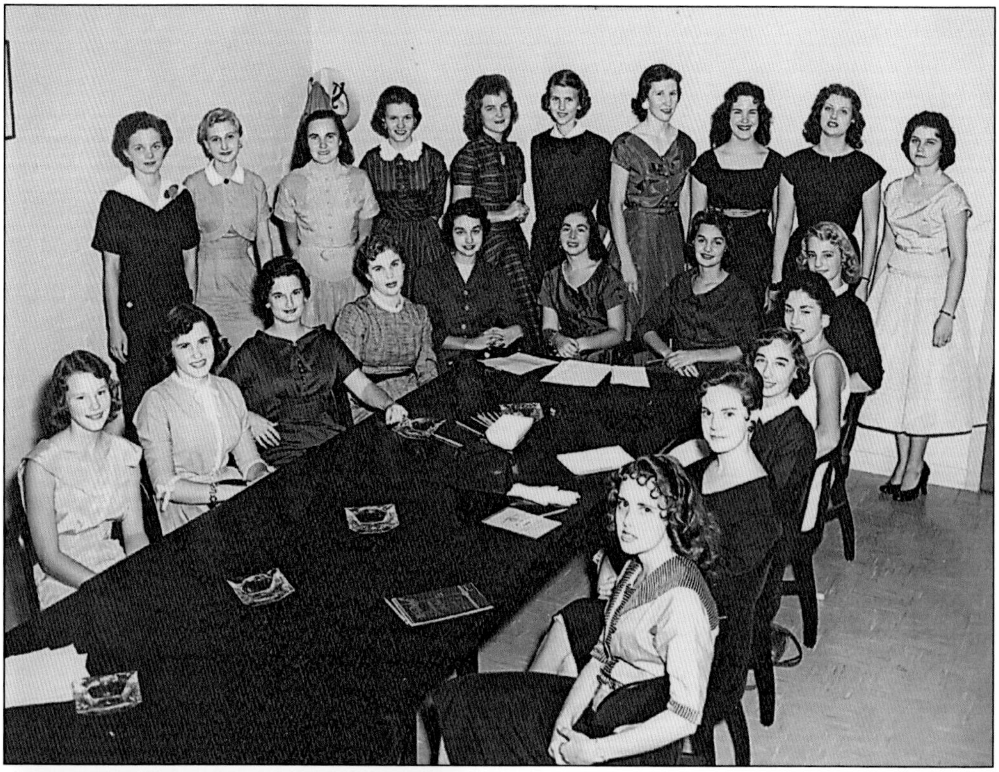

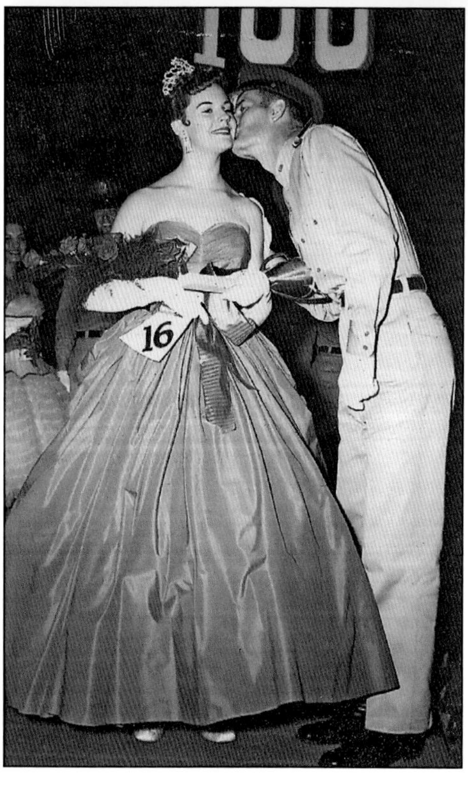

Moultrie and Colquitt County staged a mammoth weeklong celebration observing the county's 100th birthday in 1956. Part of that celebration included the Miss Century pageant. Above, the unidentified young ladies vying for the title pose for a publicity photograph. At left, Jean O'Neal accepts a congratulatory kiss from a young cadet as she is crowned Miss Century. (Both, MO.)

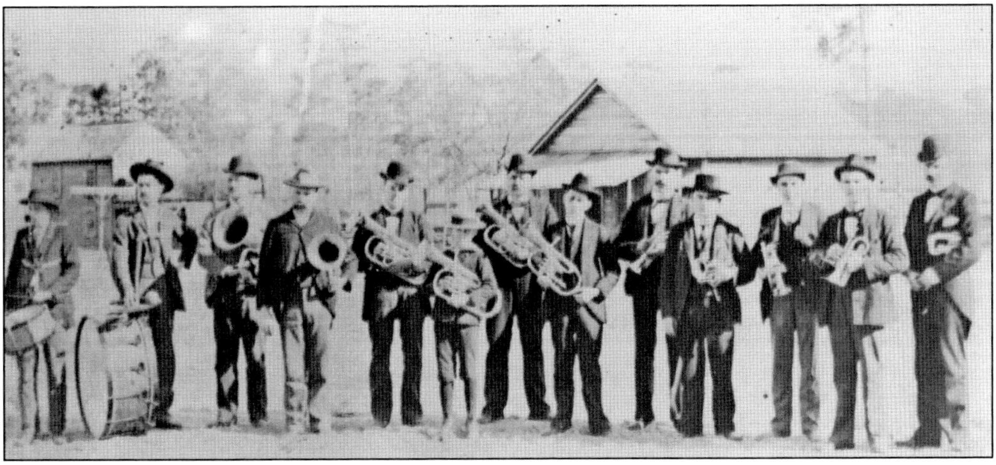

Moultrie's citizens must have been musically inclined, because there are many mentions in the *Moultrie Observer* of bands being formed and performances being given. Early pictures of the courthouse square show a bandstand located on the southeast corner, where the bands probably performed. The unidentified men in the band above are seen in 1893. The photograph below shows "Pop" Jennison's band. C. H. Jennison was the band teacher at the high school, and the group featured here was a popular addition to social events during the 1930s. (Above, MSP; below, MO.)

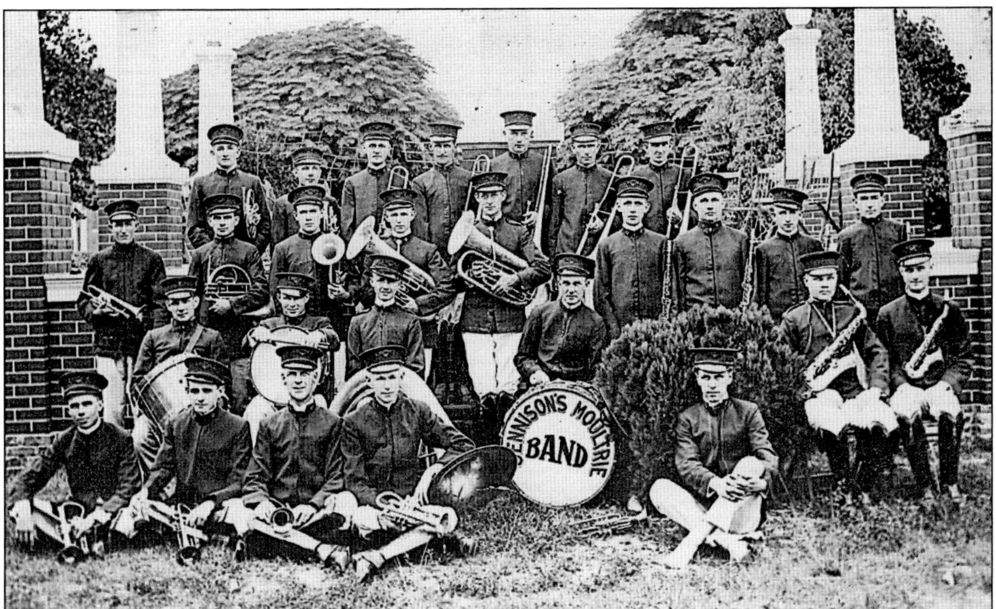

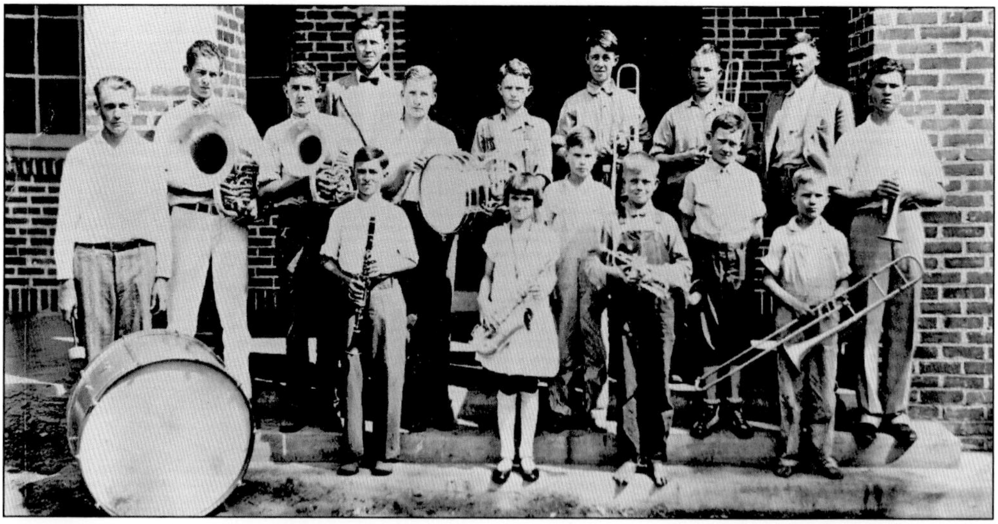

The unidentified members of the Okapilco School band pose at the main entrance to the school in this 1927 photograph. (MO.)

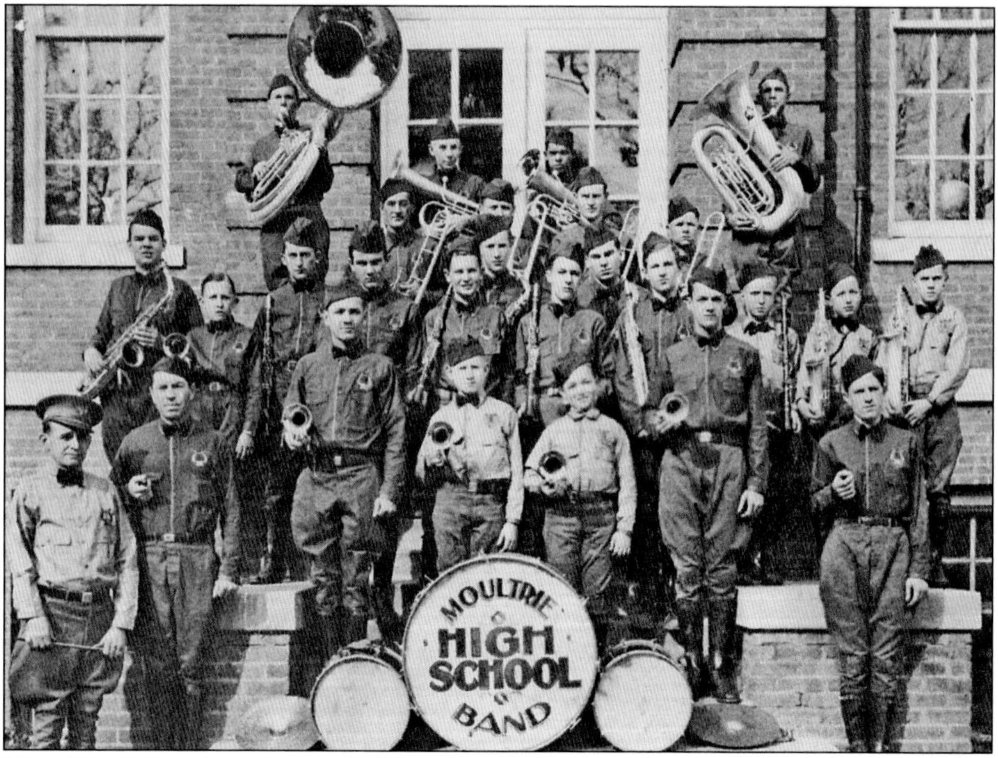

The 1928–1929 Packer marching band, under the direction of W. E. Hipsman, had seven listed sections and instruments. Members are, from left to right, (first row) W. E. Hipsman, Earl Holmes, Floyd Adams, William Latham, Irvin Friedlander, Robert West, and Tommy Moore; (second row) John Finch, Charles Knapp, Curtis Murphy, E. W. Rhoden Jr., Ivan Monk, Ben Van Dalsem Jr., Edward White, James Hicks, Malvin Friedlander, Hallman Trimble, Louis Moore, and Charles Goforth; (third row) Ruis West, Raymond Adams, Willie B. Withers, and Wallace Allen; (fourth row) Boozer Slocumb, Russell Rogers, Neal Love, and V. B. Fisher. (MO.)

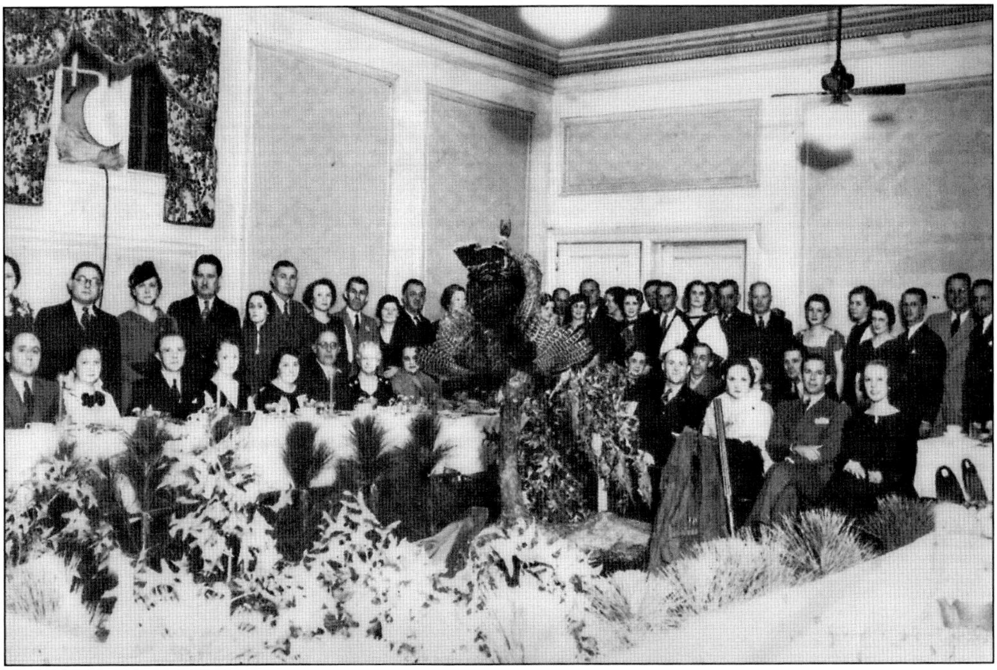

This 1934 photograph shows the Thanksgiving Ladies' Night, which was hosted by the Moultrie Kiwanis Club. The group is gathered in the banquet room of the Hotel Colquitt, which was located in the rear of the lobby. (MSP.)

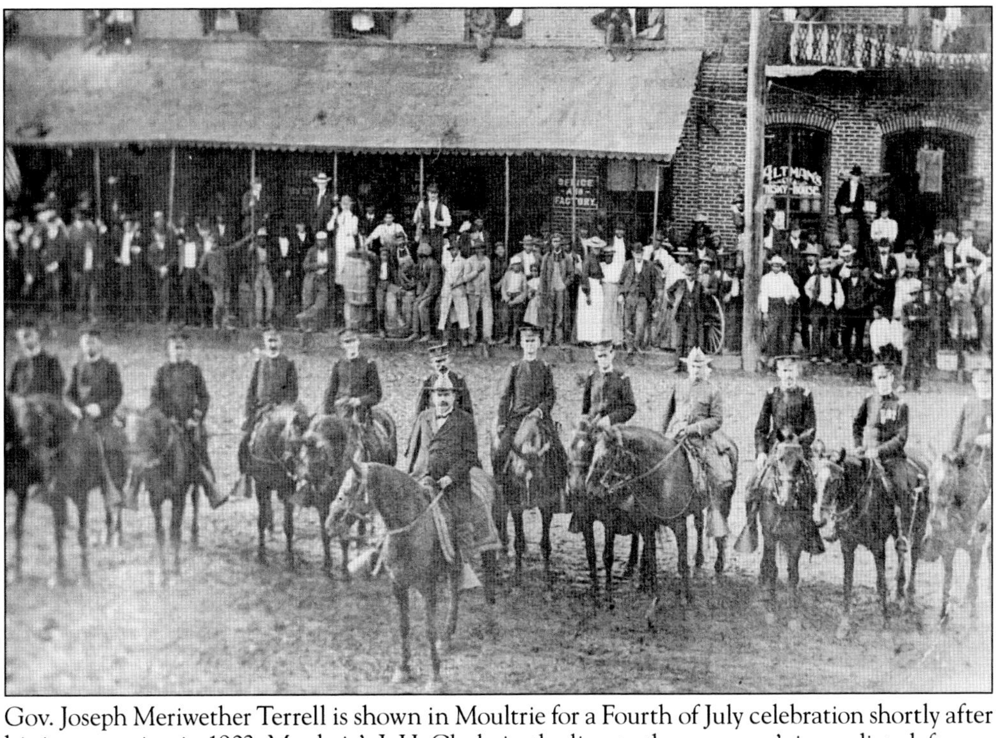

Gov. Joseph Meriwether Terrell is shown in Moultrie for a Fourth of July celebration shortly after his inauguration in 1902. Moultrie's J. H. Clark, in the line to the governor's immediate left, was a lieutenant colonel on Terrell's staff. (MO.)

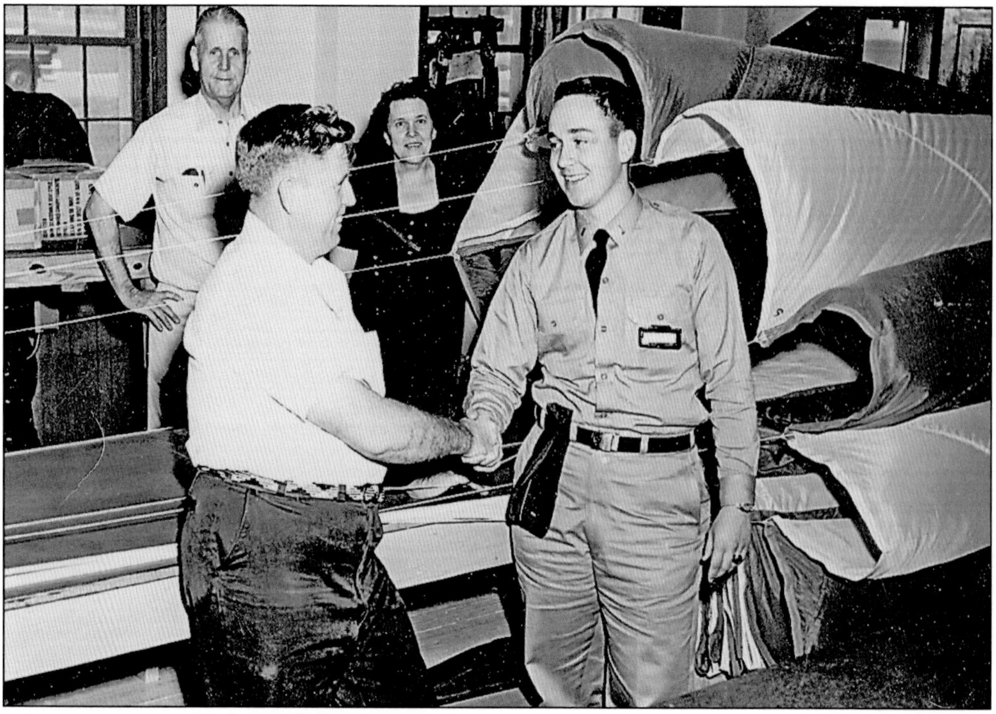

The Reverend Raymond McCorvey, front left, shakes the hand of an unidentified U.S. Air Force officer at the parachute department of Spence Field Air Base. The officer had completed a successful jump using a parachute that McCorvey had packed and requested to shake his hand. John G. McCorvey (back left), the head of the department, and Mildred Bass look on. (MO.)

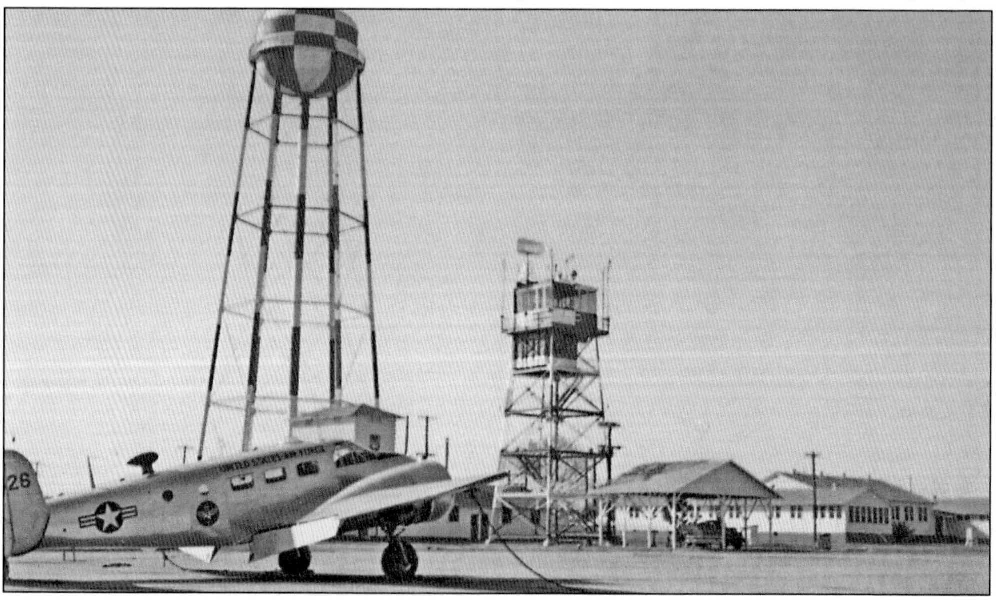

Spence Field Air Base was an important part of the county's economy from the beginning of World War II until it closed in the early 1960s. It was used first as a U.S. Army Air Corps training base, and after the war, Hawthorne School of Aeronautics, a private pilot school, was housed there. This photograph shows the base when it was in use by Hawthorne in the late 1950s. (APP.)

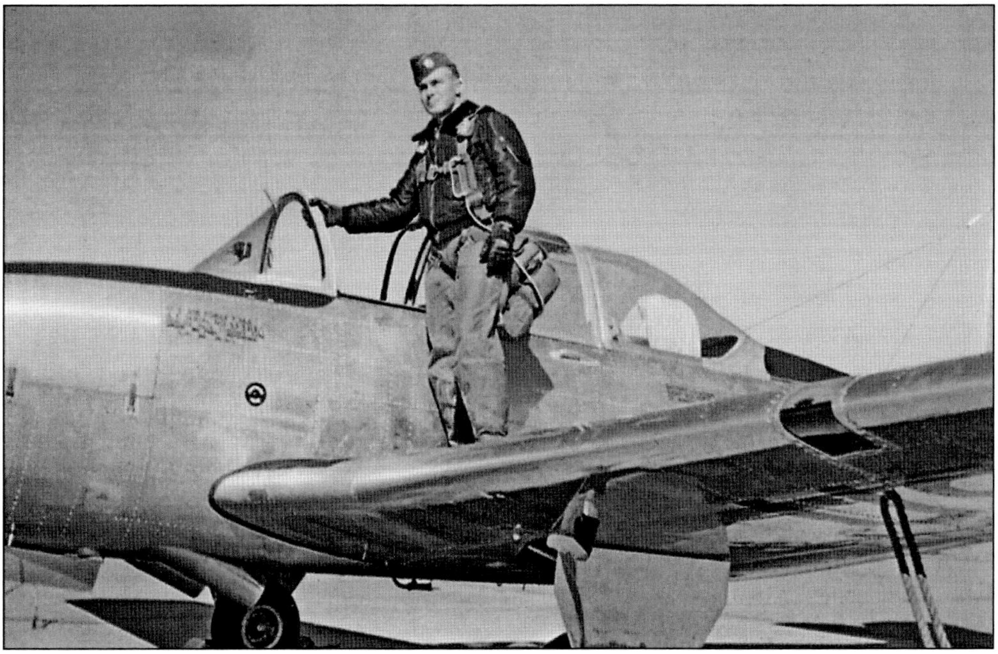

This unidentified young cadet was stationed at Spence Field during World War II. He was one of over 6,000 pilots trained at the facility before it closed in 1944. (APP.)

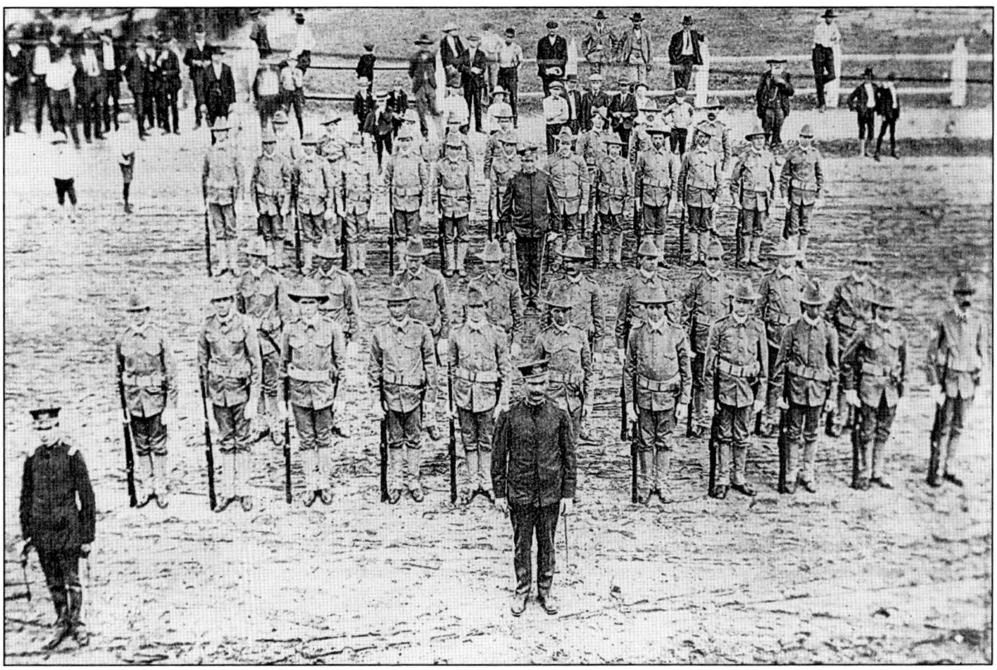

The Moultrie Rifles militia unit musters on the grounds of the courthouse in this early-1900s photograph. None of the members of the unit are identified. (MCCL.)

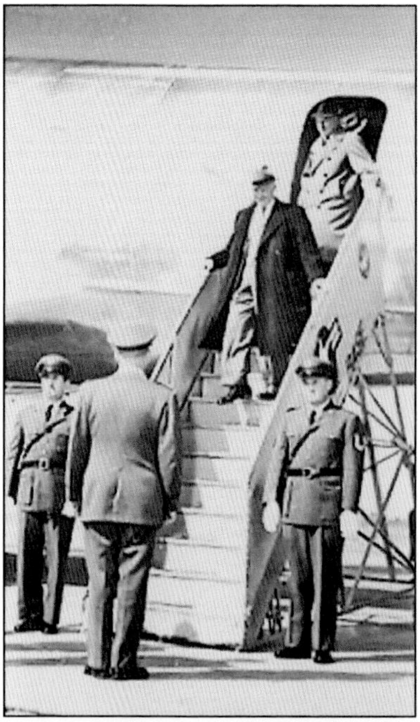

Pres. Dwight Eisenhower descends the stairs of his airplane upon his arrival in Moultrie during the mid-1950s. The president was an avid sportsman and came to South Georgia for several hunting trips on plantations and hunting preserves in the area during his presidency. (MCCL.)

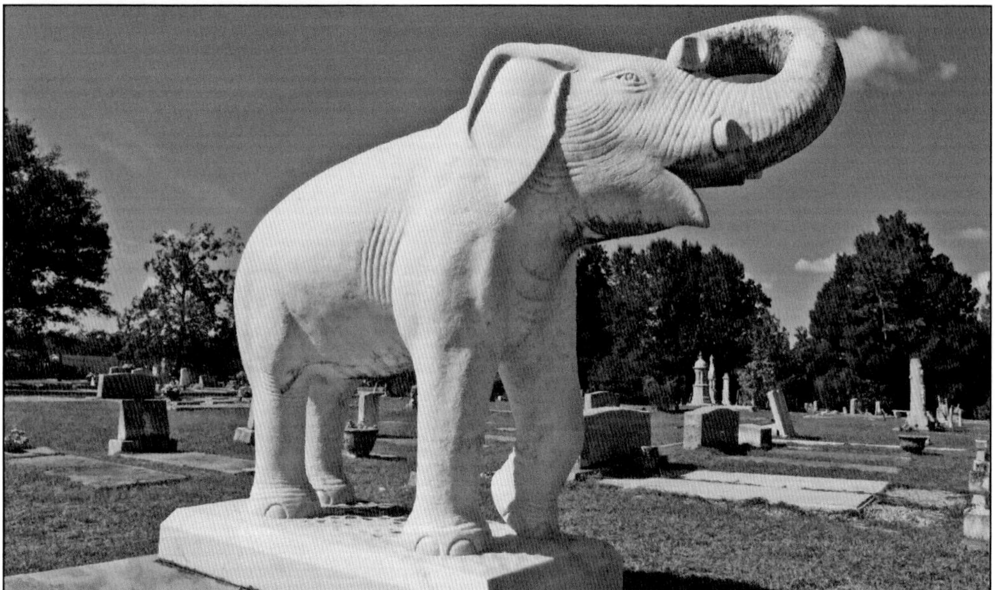

This white elephant statue stands in the cemetery of Pleasant Grove Church, located on the Adel Highway just a few miles east of Moultrie. The elephant marks the grave of William F. Duggan Sr. Duggan, who was orphaned at an early age, toured with circuses all of his life. When he died suddenly on December 22, 1950, he was buried in the Moultrie cemetery because a relative lived here. His friends and fellow circus workers felt that a life-sized sculpture of a baby elephant would be a fitting monument. It was carved from white Georgia Cherokee marble from Tate, Georgia, and weighs over eight tons. A 6-foot-deep foundation was poured around the gravesite to support the weight of the elephant. The slight tilt of the young elephant's head seems to suggest that he is listening for his master's voice. (MCCL.)

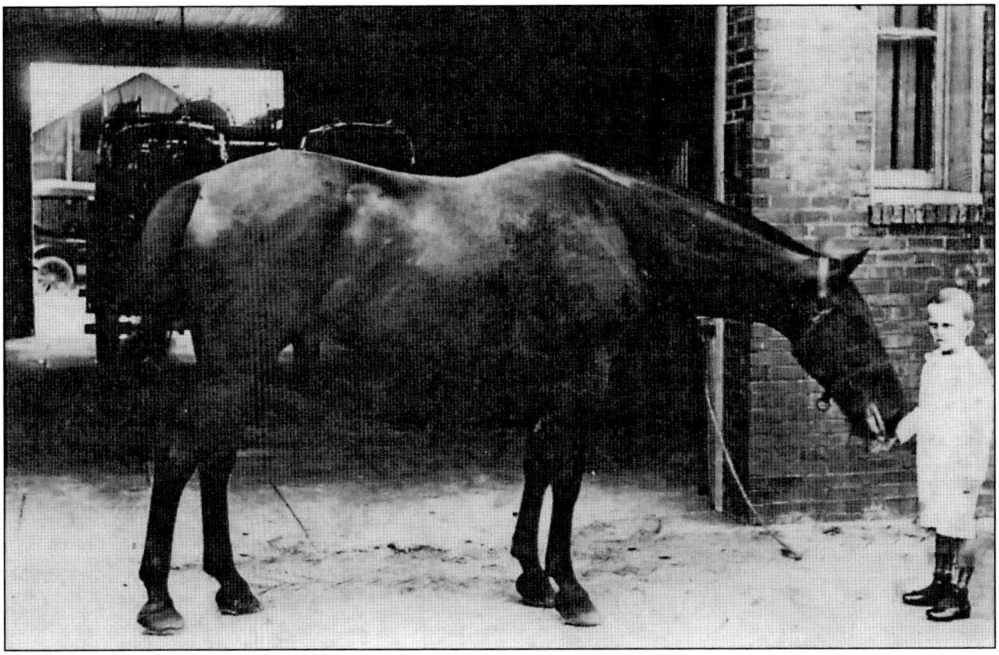

These two photographs share an interesting situation. The photograph above was taken at the beginning of the 20th century in the rear of the Moultrie Fire Department. At that time, fire wagons were pulled by horses, which were stabled at the fire department. The young boy feeding the fire wagon horse is Arthur B. "Sid" Hunt, son of Moultrie fire chief George B. Hunt. The photograph below shows the Moultrie High School Packer "M" Club in the 1920s. The only person identified on the back of the photograph is the young man seated second from the right on the front row, Sid Hunt. A close examination of the two photographs shows a definite resemblance, leading one to believe that it is the same person. (Both, MCCL.)

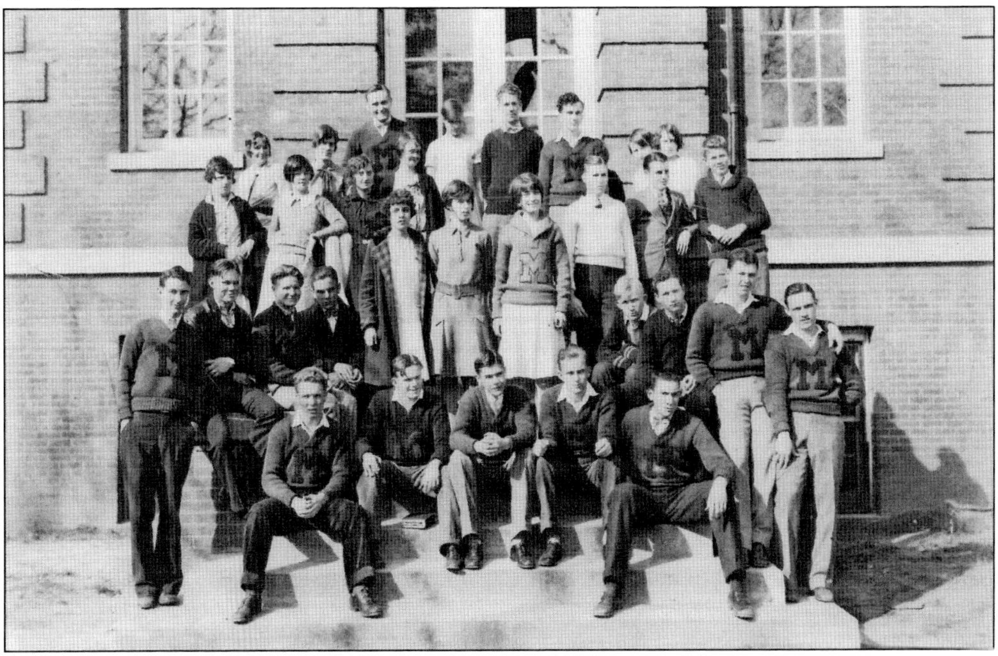

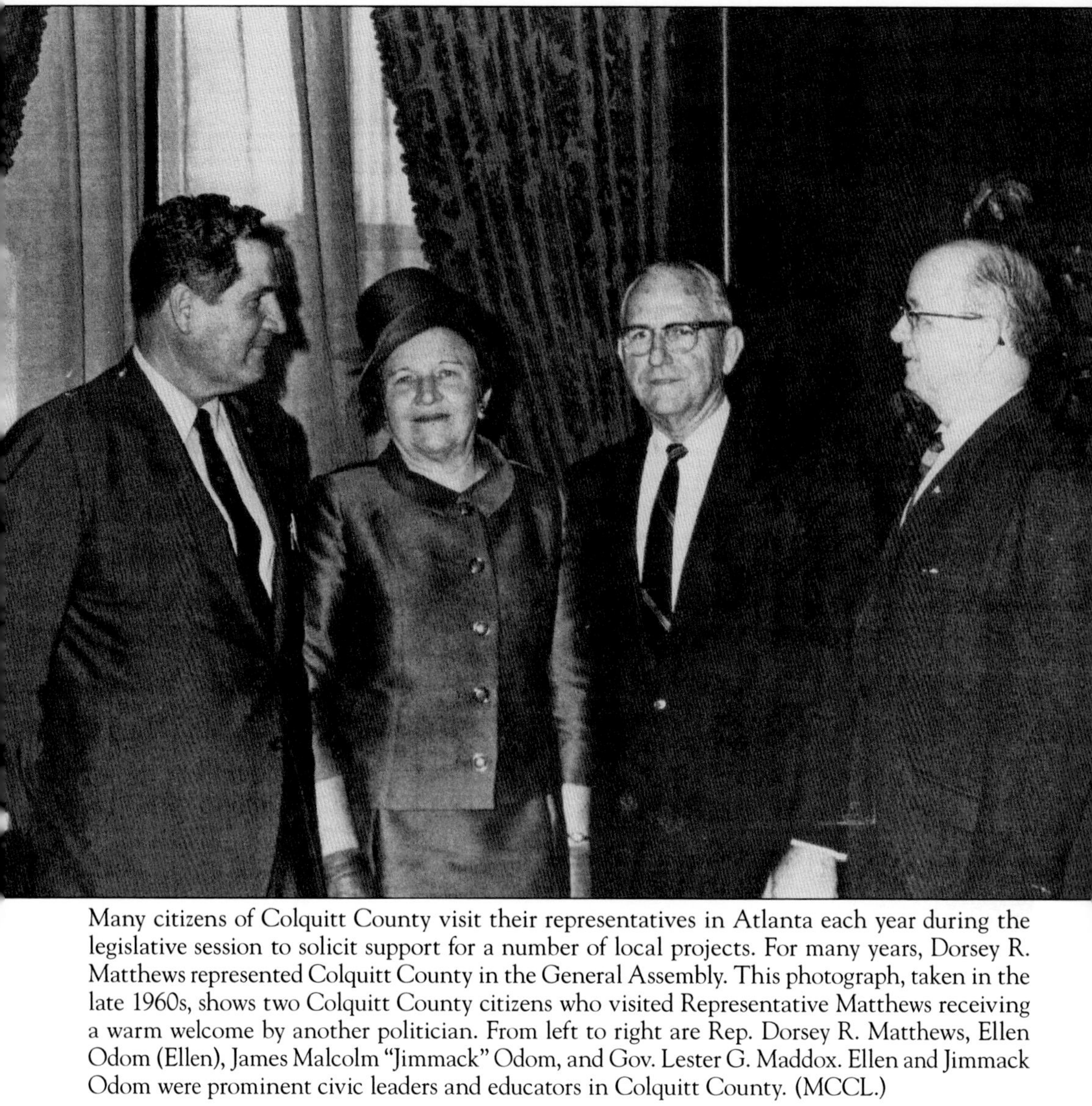

Many citizens of Colquitt County visit their representatives in Atlanta each year during the legislative session to solicit support for a number of local projects. For many years, Dorsey R. Matthews represented Colquitt County in the General Assembly. This photograph, taken in the late 1960s, shows two Colquitt County citizens who visited Representative Matthews receiving a warm welcome by another politician. From left to right are Rep. Dorsey R. Matthews, Ellen Odom (Ellen), James Malcolm "Jimmack" Odom, and Gov. Lester G. Maddox. Ellen and Jimmack Odom were prominent civic leaders and educators in Colquitt County. (MCCL.)

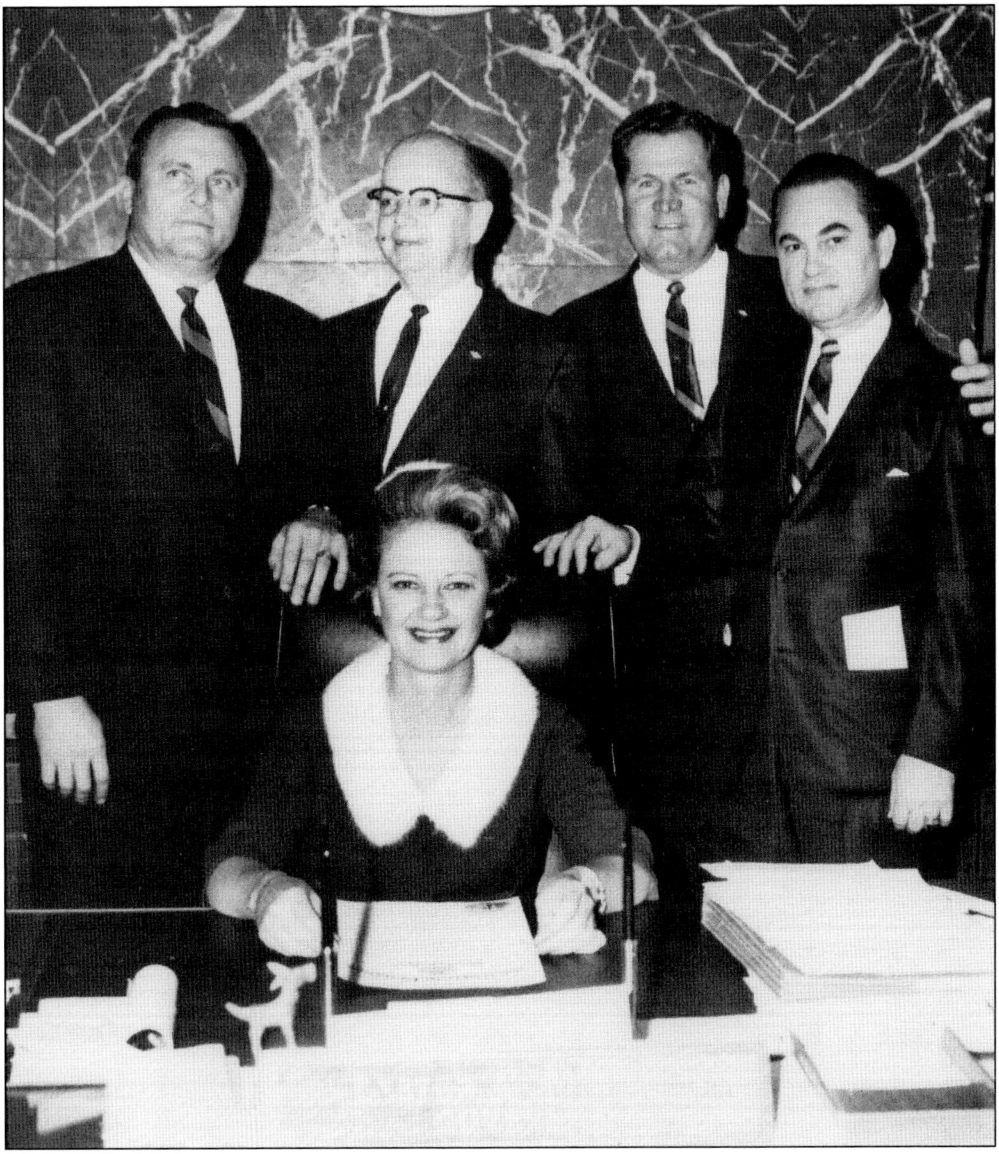

This late-1960s photograph shows Rep. Dorsey Matthews with several distinguished people. From left to right are unidentified, Gov. Lester G. Maddox, Rep. Dorsey Matthews, Gov. George Wallace of Alabama, and Lurleen Maddox (seated). (MCCL.)

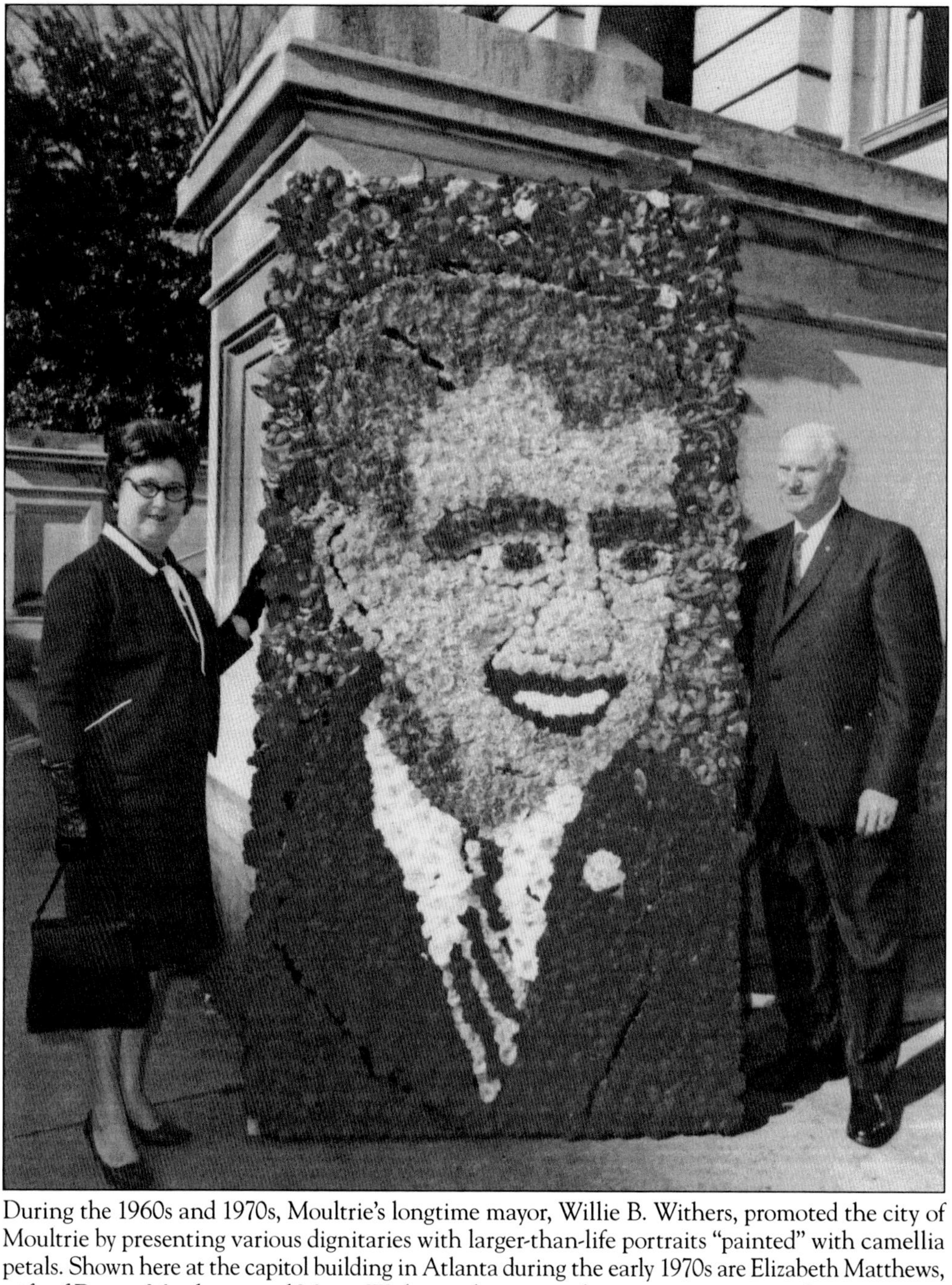

During the 1960s and 1970s, Moultrie's longtime mayor, Willie B. Withers, promoted the city of Moultrie by presenting various dignitaries with larger-than-life portraits "painted" with camellia petals. Shown here at the capitol building in Atlanta during the early 1970s are Elizabeth Matthews, wife of Dorsey Matthews, and Mayor Withers, who are on their way to present such a portrait to Gov. Jimmy Carter. (MCCL.)

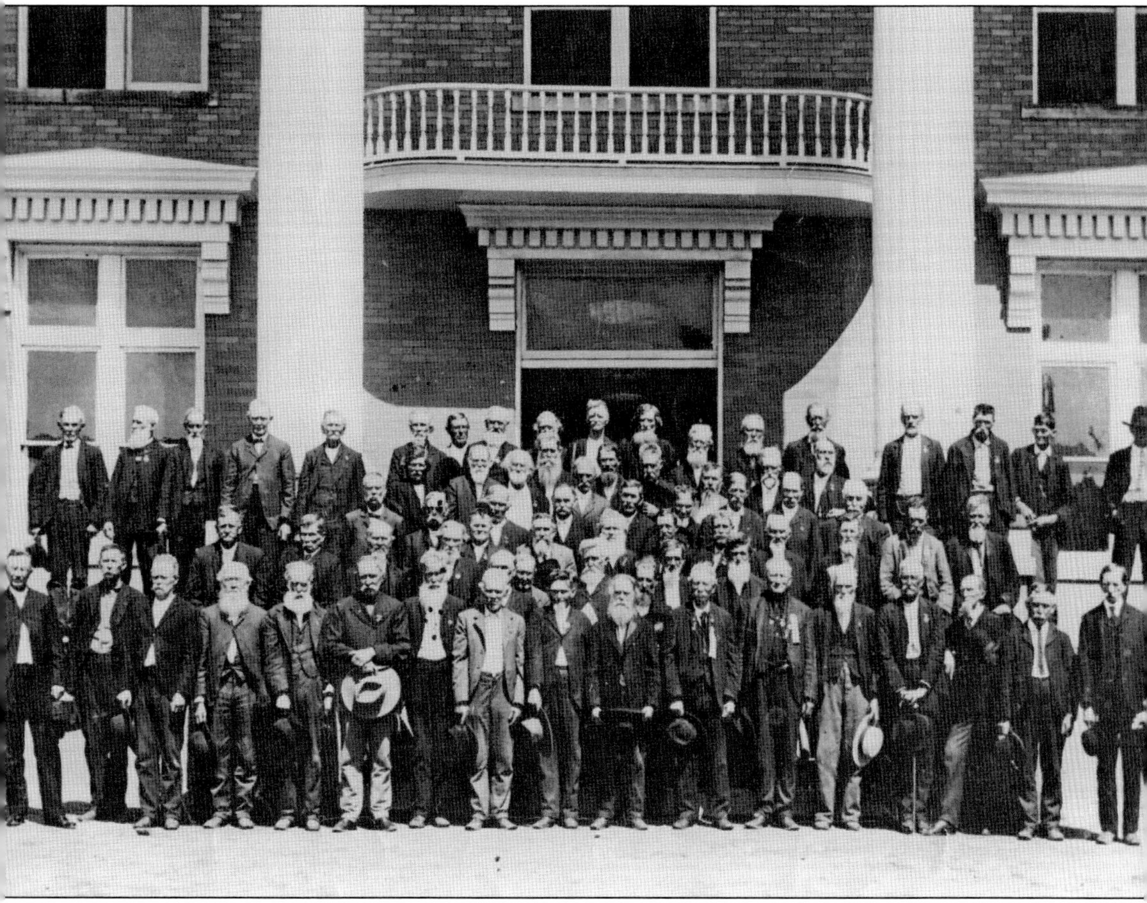

As late as 1903, there were nearly 100 men living in Colquitt County who were Confederate veterans. This 1903 photograph taken on the courthouse steps show 73 of them gathered to receive their Cross of Honor from the United Daughters of the Confederacy. An additional 22 men were awarded the medal later that year. (MCCL.)

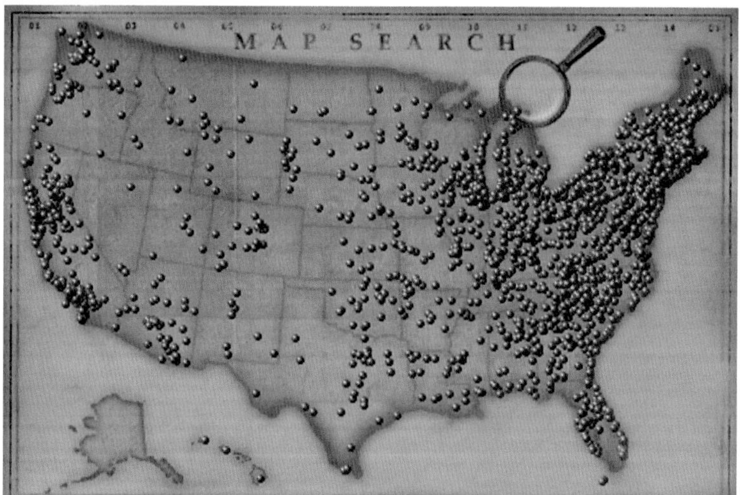
MAP SEARCH